NAKED
RACIAL
PREFERENCE

NAKED RACIAL PREFERENCE

CARL COHEN

MADISON BOOKS

Lanham • New York • London

Published by Madison Books
4720 Boston Way
Lanham, Maryland 20706

3 Henrietta Street
London WC2E 8LU, England

Distributed by National Book Network

Chapter 1, "Race and the Constitution," is reprinted from The Nation 220, no. 5 (February
8, 1975) with permission. Chapter 2, "Who Are Equals?" is reprinted from National Forum:
The Phi Kappa Phi Journal 58, no. 1 (Winter 1978) by permission of the publishers;
copyright Carl Cohen. Chapter 3, "Equality, Diversity, and Good Faith," is reprinted with
permission of Wayne Law Review 26, no. 4 (July 1980). Chapter 4, "Why Racial
Preference Is Illegal and Immoral," is reprinted with permission from Commentary 67, no. 6
(June 1979). Chapter 5, "Justice Debased: The Weber Decision," is reprinted with
permission from Commentary 68, no. 3 (September 1979). Chapter 6, "Naked Racial
Preference," is reprinted with permission from Commentary 81, no. 3 (March 1986).

Library of Congress Cataloging-in-Publication Data

Naked racial preference / Carl Cohen.
p. cm.
Includes bibliographical references.
1. Race discrimination—United States. 2. Discrimination in
education—United States. 3. Affirmative action programs
—United States. 4. United States—Race relations. 5. Afro-
Americans—Civil rights—Government policy. I. Title.
E185.615C637 1995 305.8'00973—dc20 95–7426 CIP

ISBN 1–56833–053–7 (cloth : alk. paper)

⊖™ The paper used in this publication meets the minimum requirements of
American National Standard for Information Sciences—Permanence of
Paper for Printed Library Materials, ANSI Z39.48–1964.
Manufactured in the United States of America.

Contents

Principal Cases

Prologue

What Is Affirmative Action?

In the middle decades of the twentieth century American society turned away from its history of racial and ethnic discrimination. That turn was not sharp, and is still far from complete. It began in earnest with the civil rights movement in the years following World War II; the first great triumph came with the Supreme Court decision in *Brown v. Board of Education* (1954) ordering an end to public school segregation. There followed a series of cases in which the deliberately preferential treatment of whites in public institutions was held unconstitutional. With the passage of the Civil Rights Act of 1964 a moral watershed was reached. Discrimination on the basis of race, nationality, or other like categories was forbidden for both public and private institutions, in most settings. Preference (in employment, in public accommodations, in college admissions, and so on) given *to anyone* simply "because of such individual's race, color, religion, sex, or national origin" became then and remains still, in our country, a violation of federal law.

Compliance did not come quickly. Defiant discriminatory treatment forced blacks and others to seek redress in federal courts. Recalcitrant parties were repeatedly ordered to cease to engage in discriminatory conduct. Federal agencies through their regulations, and the president by Executive Order, condemned every form of racial discrimination. Still it persisted.

Angered and exasperated, the courts were obliged to intervene more deeply. Striking down deliberate discrimination was not enough. They came eventually to order the deliberate eradication of practices that, although apparently innocuous, sustained entrenched patterns of racial preference. Admissions practices in colleges and universities that were superficially neutral but had historically discouraged the enrollment of racial minorities; recruitment practices in industry that had the effect of racial discrimination in hiring even though on the surface they made no mention of race; methods of voter registration that were superficially fair but had been designed to discourage the registration of minorities; membership practices in trade unions and promotion practices in police and fire departments that effectively excluded blacks and others — all these were to *stop*. The habits and devices, subtle and unsubtle, maintained by thoughtless oversight or by insidious design that had arisen to sustain preference for one race over another were at last to be rooted out. These steps, required to bring preference to an end, were given the generic name "affirmative action."

Affirmative action so conceived was a right and honorable response to deeply embedded problems. Putting an end to discrimination would involve more than ceasing to do deliberately evil things; *action* must be taken, *affirmative* action, to change the institutional environment in which racial discrimination had flourished. And that is precisely the spirit in which that phrase was used when it was introduced in the Civil Rights Act. When a court has found some practice to be unlawful discrimination, that court (the law said) may enjoin it, and may also "order such affirmative action as may be appropriate." The original object of affirmative action was the elimination of all preference by race.

But this original aim was soon diametrically transformed. The goods of society were plainly not being enjoyed proportionately by racial and ethnic groups; the lack of racial balance, it was argued, must everywhere be due to some residual, covert discrimination. If affirmative action in the original sense did not solve the problem, stronger medicine was needed. To overcome the deep-seated evil (it was argued) only the redistribution of the goods themselves — jobs, promotions, admissions, and the like — would do the trick. Treating applicants equally, applying a single standard to all in judging promise or performance, did not achieve the outcomes hoped for. Therefore, to make racially proportional distributions a reality, new preferences, deliberate racial preferences this time favoring the minorities formerly oppressed, were widely introduced.

These new preferential devices were also called "affirmative action" with an irony that was not intended. Programs that specified the ways in which opportunities for persons of different races were not to be equal were defended under the banner of equal opportunity. "Goals" were established for the number of blacks, Hispanics, American Indians, and so on, to be enrolled, hired, or promoted. Administrative failures to meet the established goals were heavily penalized by censure, or by superiors fearing censure, as they are still. Prudent administrators (who themselves had little to lose from the racial favoritism given) made certain that ethnic goals were met, or nearly met, and to this end they did whatever was needed. The demand for fairness in the process of hiring, or admission, was replaced by the demand for results in the form of numbers proving racial proportionality. Racial "quotas" were everywhere denied, while everywhere in practice "goals" functioned exactly like quotas, openly or surreptitiously. Accounts of minority hiring and admissions came to be pervaded by dishonesty; decent people with decent motives lied to themselves, and told themselves that the lie was justified by the results sought. Justice having been defined as a proportional outcome antecedently determined, affirmative action was transformed into machinery designed to yield that outcome. And that is what it is still.

The phrase "affirmative action" has lost the flavor of fairness that was its birthright. It no longer signifies fair treatment, and the application of a single standard to all, but the reverse of these. Affirmative action has come to *mean* the programs and devices used to insure certain results, results specified by the counting of minority members. The phrase is now a widely accepted euphemism for institutionalized favoritism.

Affirmative action has thus been turned completely on its head. What was once the name for the active pursuit of equal treatment regardless of race has become the name for instruments designed to give deliberate preference on the basis of race.

Racial preference breeds resentment, anger, and eventually (in this country) litigation. The Civil Rights Act forbidding racial preference was invoked by those disadvantaged, but defenders of preference contested the meaning of its words. The Constitutional guarantee of equality under the law was also invoked with anguish, but often, in the lower courts, without success. Losing parties appealed their cases; some appeals eventually reached the U.S. Supreme Court.

The most important of these Supreme Court battles over racial preference gave rise to the essays in this book. The first great test of racial preference (*DeFunis*, 1974) is examined in part A; the decision governing racial preference in college admissions (*Bakke*, 1978) is examined in part B; the tortured arguments pertaining to racial preference in employment (*Weber*, 1979) are examined in part C; racial preference in the public schools, leading to a landmark formulation of the standard for judgment (*Wygant*, 1986) is examined in part D. In part E the most recent major cases are reviewed, analyzing the continuing controversy through 1994.

The preferential programs at issue in these cases, or programs very much like them, remain largely in place today — in law and medical schools, in undergraduate colleges, in private industry, and in government policy. Indeed, the number of institutions in which racially preferential affirmative action is practiced has multiplied. Details and numbers change — but the schemes for preference described in these essays may be readily replaced with schemes currently in force and equally preferential. Administrators have become more adroit in obscuring what they do, advocates more subtle in describing double standards so as to make them palatable. But the preferential spirit of affirmative action has been retained, even reinforced. Every observant citizen of this country knows well that preference flatly based upon race, nationality, and sex is now widespread.

The object of the essays in this book was and is to marshal the arguments against racial preference, to explain in detail why racial preference is both *wrong* and *bad*. Put shortly, preference is wrong because it is a violation of fundamental moral principles, a violation of the U. S. Constitution, and a violation of the civil rights laws of the United States. It is bad because it does serious injury to all concerned. It corrupts the colleges and the companies that employ it, and it fosters the resentments and hostilities that now tear our society apart. Perhaps worst of all, racial preference does direct and serious harm to the very minorities it was designed to assist. However honorable the character of those who support it, preference by race is morally indefensible and socially counterproductive.

Race relations in our country continue to deteriorate. The practices examined in these essays, because they contribute directly to that deterioration, must concern us now more painfully than ever. The issues argued here will continue to confront us so long as race — any race — is used as the ground for advantage in employment or competitive admission, or in distributing public goods. We must thoughtfully reconsider the wisdom of our present widespread practice of naked racial discrimination.

A

Racial Preference in Law School Admissions

DeFunis v. Odegaard

The first great battle over preferential affirmative action ended in a draw. The law school at the University of Washington had set aside 16 percent of the places in its entering classes exclusively for members of racial or ethnic minorities: Philippine-Americans, Chicano-Americans, black Americans, and American Indians. All applicants were screened and categorized by race. Minority applicants were then admitted to the law school using standards much lower than the admission standards applied to whites.

While this affirmative action program was in force, a white applicant with a fine record, Marco DeFunis, was rejected by the law school in two successive years. Convinced that he (or some other white applicants in very similar circumstances) would surely have been admitted had his skin been of a different color, he sued the university for admission, claiming that he had been deprived of his constitutional right to the equal protection of the laws.

DeFunis won in the lower court; the university was ordered to admit him, and did so. But they appealed, and he lost in the highest Washington court; this order was stayed, however, while DeFunis appealed his case to the Supreme Court of the United States. When argument was finally heard before that court the university agreed that DeFunis, by this time nearing the end of his third year in law school, would be permitted to graduate whatever the legal outcome. Finding no remaining issue between the parties, the Supreme Court held the case moot*

Justice William Douglas, the leading liberal justice on the Court at that time, wrote a strong dissent. He argued at length that the issues were not moot, and that the Court ought to have addressed straightforwardly the constitutional questions presented by deliberate racial preference. As a committed civil libertarian, Douglas was plainly angered by the race-based inequality of treatment given by the university. "The equal protection clause commands the elimination of racial barriers," he wrote in that dissent, "not their creation in order to satisfy our theory as to how society ought to be organized." Had the *DeFunis* case been dealt with on its merits then, and had Douglas's views prevailed, the subsequent history of affirmative action in America might have been very different.

The case in support of racially preferential admissions was made, as forcefully and as sympathetically as has ever been done, by the Washington Supreme Court in upholding this law school's preferential devices. The intellectual and legal foundations of that argument, its thoughtfulness and its good spirit, are illuminated in the essay below in order to confront that argument squarely and to show why, even with the best of intentions, it *cannot* succeed under our Constitution. A detailed restatement of the position shared by the law school and the Washington Supreme Court is therefore given first. The attack follows.

---

* End notes will be found at the conclusion of each part. References to court cases usually contain three elements: the name of the series of reports in which a given decision appears, preceded by the number of the volume in that series, and followed by the page number in that volume. The date may follow in parentheses. Decisions of the U. S. Supreme Court are published in United States Reports, abbreviated as U.S. Thus the reference to *DeFunis v. Odegaard* appears as: 416 U.S. 312 (1974). When a particular passage is cited, the page number of that passage will also appear in the note.

Although the U.S. Supreme Court held this case moot, it did then issue what amounted to an invitation to others to return with like grievances that were not moot. By the time such cases came before them once again, however, Justice Douglas had left the Court, and racially preferential admissions had become widely ensconced in professional schools. The particulars of the admissions system devised at the University of Washington have been changed over the years, of course. But its most fundamental feature — giving preference in admission by race — remains in force in law schools across the country. Some of the predictions made by Justice Douglas and others in the discussion of *DeFunis*, regarding the consequences of such preference, have been all too painfully realized. Some of the arguments presented briefly in this essay are pursued at greater length in connection with other cases, in essays appearing later in this book.

1

Race and the Constitution*

All persons, without regard to race or religion or national origin, are equal before the law. The equal protection of the laws, expressly guaranteed by the U.S. Constitution, seems the plainest and most comprehensive requirement of justice. No sophistication is needed to appreciate its force; the common conviction that categories like race have no bearing upon the just application of law is dramatized by the blindfold that the Goddess of Justice wears while balancing her scales.

That conviction was made concretely applicable by the Supreme Court in 1954, in *Brown v. Board of Education*, condemning the "separate but equal" treatment of the races. It reached its apogee in the Civil Rights Act of 1964, condemning discrimination "because of race, color, religion, sex, or national origin" in virtually every public sphere. Splendid. Or is it? The answer given sometimes appears to depend upon whose ox is gored.

*This chapter was first published in *The Nation*, vol. 220, no. 5 (February 8, 1975). It appears here, slightly abbreviated, with the kind permission of the publishers of *The Nation* magazine. I acknowledge a special debt to the late Carey McWilliams, editor of *The Nation* at that time, who strongly encouraged the writing of this essay.

The ideal of blindfolded equal treatment, as applied to racial groups, encounters competing principles of compensatory justice. It is all very well to laud equality before the law; but when generations, or centuries, of discrimination and outright oppression based on race or ethnic origins have left minority groups in conditions of distressingly marked disadvantage, even-handed treatment cannot yield equal results. Affirmative action in pursuit of just outcomes, deliberate efforts to compensate for past wrongs, must be undertaken.

Affirmative action has many species. The arguments for and against one or another of these species are many and tangled. My aim in what follows is to explore a single slice of these controversies: the preferential admission of members of minority groups to programs in higher education. The issues raised in it are delicate and important; they will certainly recur.

Using the case of *DeFunis v. Odegaard*,[2] I propose to examine the central arguments upon which resolution of these issues will probably depend. That eventual resolution will come through judicial interpretation of constitutional principle. In giving concrete meaning to venerable principles, the courts — ultimately the Supreme Court — decide not simply what our Constitution requires but what it ought to be understood to require. In many matters, courts give clear moral guidance; judicial reasoning functions as moral reasoning.

In March 1973, the Supreme Court of Washington decided in favor of the University of Washington (Charles Odegaard then president) against Marco DeFunis, a white, male applicant to the university's Law School, who claimed that the system of admissions applied by that school, incorporating deliberate preference for members of minority groups, and resulting in his rejection, had denied him the equal protection of the laws. A lower court that had supported DeFunis was reversed; but its order obliging the university to admit him had remained in effect during the three years of ensuing litigation. It was DeFunis's impending graduation from that law school in the spring of 1974 that gave grounds for the ultimate holding by the U.S. Supreme Court that the case was moot.

DeFunis's central contention was that the admitting procedures of the University of Washington Law School (hereafter, the Law School) applied a double standard — one measure for minority group members, another for the rest — in such a way as to violate that clause of the Fourteenth Amendment of the U.S. Constitution which guarantees to all persons "the equal protection of the laws." It was reasonable, he argued, for the Law School to make admissions judgments among competing applicants based upon evidence of many different sorts — academic and nonacademic, numerical and nonnumerical — so long as that evidence was relevant to the program of study to which admission was sought. It was not reasonable or lawful, he claimed, for the measures used, whatever they were, to be applied in a systematically differential way to certain sets of persons for no other reason than that such persons were (or were not) members of racial or ethnic minority groups. The University of Washington did not dispute the fact that it gave preferential treatment to such groups in the fierce competition for the relatively few law school slots available each year. But such preference, based on race or national origin, DeFunis contended, is precisely what the equal protection of the laws precludes absolutely.

DeFunis lost, in a decision of the Supreme Court of Washington that stands as the most cogent and persuasive defense of preferential admissions extant. I propose to reconstruct the argument of that decision, to construct the most solid and plausible counterarguments, and to explain why one side of the argument fails.

The facts about DeFunis's application and rejection were not in dispute, and may be summarized briefly. A Washington resident, his academic performance as an undergraduate was very good (junior-senior grade-point average of 3.71 of a possible 4.0), and his performance on the Law School Admission Test (LSAT) placed him in the top 7 percent nationally. His overall credentials, academic and personal, were outstanding. He was nevertheless denied admission to the Washington Law School in 1970 and in 1971.

During those years the Law School used an affirmative action admissions system under which minority applicants were considered separately from all others. The university aimed at a "proportionate representation" of minority students, and therefore affirmative action applicants needed to compete only against each other for the 16 percent of the seats that had been set aside for them. The standard for the admission of minority applicants was admittedly much lower than that for DeFunis and other regular applicants. Among the minority admissions (one judge later reported): "were some whose college grades and aptitude scores were so low that, had they not been minority students, their applications would have been summarily denied."[3]

Had there been no system of preferential admission it is probable, but not certain, that DeFunis, high on the waiting list, would have been admitted. It is certain that, had there been no such system, *some* of the white applicants with fine records who were rejected would have been admitted. DeFunis was a young man with superior abilities and an excellent record. Some of the minority admissions were, all agree, of uncertain ability and mediocre record. There lies the nub of the complaint. Because of the preference given to some on the basis of race or ethnicity, others (in circumstances like those of DeFunis) were denied admission on the basis of their race or ethnicity.[4]

The complaint is plausible but problematic. This was obviously not a case of racial discrimination in the historical exploitative mold. If there was racial discrimination here, its evident and honorable objective was not to maintain inequality but to overcome an inequality that had become deeply rooted. The Law School had devised a deliberately compensatory instrument, honestly aimed at justice over the long run. Of course, long-term justice was sought with equal fervor by DeFunis and his defenders, who did not deny the historical facts of racial oppression or contest the need for some compensatory action. The two sides concurred in calling for affirmative action, positive steps aimed at uprooting a long-ensconced pattern of racial injustice.

In pursuit of this objective, what instruments are constitutionally permissible? That is the key question here. The controversy is not between good guys and bad guys, but between sophisticated parties who differ about what, in the effort to achieve a pressing and difficult end, we may rightly use as means.

The Supreme Court of Washington (hereafter, the court) dealt sensitively with this question. Its argument went to the heart of the matter and developed, in three steps, a powerful defense of the Law School. These steps take the form of answers to the following three questions:

1. Are classifications on the basis of race, for purposes of school admission and the like, *per se,* unconstitutional? Does "the equal protection of the laws" require that an admissions committee be "colorblind"? If the answer were yes, the matter would be settled. But if race can, under some circumstances, be considered as one factor in an admissions policy, there are further questions to resolve.

2. Suppose that consideration of race is under some circumstances permissible. What standard must then be applied to determine whether, in a particular instance, the racial classification used is constitutional?

3. Suppose that consideration of race is under some circumstances permissible, and that the standard of its constitutional application is known. Has the Law School in the *DeFunis* case met that standard in its policy and practice?

To the first of these questions the court's answer, carefully argued, was no. Consideration of race is not, always and in itself, unconstitutional. The equal protection clause of the Fourteenth Amendment plainly prohibits the operation of racially segregated public schools. Racial segregation, the Supreme Court held in *Brown v. Board of Education,*[5] stigmatizes the minority group and injures its members in ways not easily (if ever) undone. It is not constitutionally permissible. But, said the Washington court in 1973, the *Brown* decision does not warrant the conclusion that all racial classifications are, *per se*, unconstitutional. The leading principle in *Brown* was that racial classifications are unconstitutional when they are invidious, when they stigmatize a racial group with a stamp of inferiority. But a preferential admissions policy like that of the Washington Law School does not stigmatize the minority and is not invidious because its aim is not to separate the races but to bring them together.

The *Brown* case does not settle the matter. Even if, by that decision, only invidious racial classifications are ruled out, it remains to ask whether there are any contexts in which noninvidious racial classifications are ruled in. There are, said the court. The U.S. Supreme Court has held that there are circumstances in which doing justice demands not that we ignore race, but that we carefully attend to it. When, for example, a school board, charged with the responsibility of designing and implementing policy, proposes to eliminate a long-standing pattern of racial discrimination with a "freedom-of-choice" enrollment plan that does not work, that board will be compelled to come forward with a better scheme that does take steps adequate to abolish its past racially segregated system. "The burden on a school board today is to come forward with a plan that promises realistically to work, and promises realistically to work *now*."[6]

To fulfill such responsibilities, said the Supreme Court in a subsequent case, school authorities need not be "colorblind" when the consideration of race is essential to produce an appropriately mixed student body. "Awareness of the racial composition of the whole school system is likely to be a useful starting point in shaping a remedy to correct past constitutional violations.... Just as the race of students must be considered in determining whether a constitutional violation has occurred, so also must race be considered in formulating a remedy."[7]

Such decisions led the Washington court to conclude, in *DeFunis*, that the preferential admissions policy of the Law School, aimed at insuring a "reasonable representation" of minority persons in the student body, was not invidious. The Constitution, said the court, "is color conscious to prevent the perpetuation of discrimination and to undo the effects of past segregation."[8] The first question was thus answered: in some cases, the court concluded, racial classification is constitutionally permissible.

The second question concerns the standard to be applied to identify such cases. Racial classifications are manifestly suspect. What is the test for their proper use, where it is alleged that they have a proper use? The normal test of a questionable classification is whether that classification "is reasonably related to a legitimate public purpose." But where *race* is the basis of the classification the court concluded that a much heavier burden of justification must be imposed. The U.S. Supreme Court has been very firm on this point: "at the very least, the Equal Protection Clause demands that racial classifications … be subjected to 'the most rigid scrutiny.'"[9] The Washington court, seeking to obey that injunction with care, set this standard for the constitutionality of racial classifications: "The burden is upon the Law School to show that its consideration of race in admitting students is necessary to the accomplishment of a compelling state interest."

The third question is whether the Law School's preferential admission system had met this standard. This, in turn, raised two subordinate questions:

1. Are the interests of the state here compelling? The court's answer: Yes. The underrepresentation of minorities in law schools, and hence in the legal profession, is gross. Considering this imbalance — and in view of the tax support of this Law School by all, including minority groups, on an equal basis — the court held that the elimination of racial imbalance in public legal education is indeed compelling.

One possible objection to this conclusion is the claim that the need could be compelling only where the pattern of discrimination was *de jure*, the deliberate result of institutional practice — but that in the instant case the pattern was no more than *de facto*, the product of historical circumstances. This objection is ruled out by the court, reasoning that, whatever the cause of past racial discrimination in this sphere, the state has an "overriding interest" in eradicating its continuing effects. That interest is not reduced an iota because, in the past, a particular institution may have been neutral in the matter. We look to the remedy of social evil, said the court in effect, not to the apportionment of blame. Had the admissions policy in question been ordered by some court, the past behavior of the institution would be relevant in determining what plan of desegregation is justifiably enforced. But the Washington plan was not the outcome of such an order; it was developed voluntarily by the Law School as part of its autonomous effort to correct a historic injustice. At issue here, the court emphasized, is not whether the preferential admissions policy under examination is required, but only whether it is permissible.

The court concludes that "the shortage of minority attorneys — and, consequently, of minority prosecutors, judges and public officials — does constitute an undeniably compelling state interest."

2. Is the consideration of race, in admitting students, necessary for the accomplishment of this end? The court's answer: Yes. The evil to be corrected is the racial imbalance in the Law School student body. That imbalance can be put right only, the court affirms, by actually providing legal education to the minority groups previously denied it.

It is commonly argued that the proper way to do this is to improve elementary and secondary education for minority students to the point that equal representation of minorities in professional schools may be secured through direct competition with nonminority students, on the basis of the same criteria. But, at least to date, this simply has not worked. It is 1974, two decades since the *Brown* decision; the time for racial balance is now. Since the court concludes that the preferential admissions policy is the only one that "promises realistically to work *now*," no policy that is less restrictive will adequately serve the compelling governmental interest at stake.

The argument of the Washington Supreme Court is thus complete: "We conclude that defendants have shown the necessity of the racial classification herein to the accomplishment of an overriding state interest, and have thus sustained the heavy burden imposed upon them under the equal protection provision of the Fourteenth Amendment."

That decision could have gone the other way. A minority of the Washington Supreme Court, led by its chief justice, expressed dissenting judgment firmly. Justice William Douglas of the U.S. Supreme Court (concurring with Justices Brennan, Marshall, and White that the case was not moot) separately attacked the Law School's efforts to effect proportional representation based on race or ethnicity. But a full response to the Washington court, developed with careful attention to the logic of its argument, has not been given. I try now to supply that want.

Each of the three steps of that argument must be questioned. Preferential treatment for some racial or ethnic groups is what the words of the U.S. Constitution, given their plainest meaning, seem to prohibit. A great burden clearly falls upon those who defend such preference. If the chain constructed by the court to carry that burden breaks at any link, the case falls. In fact, upon careful scrutiny — and in spite of the most laudable aims of the Law School and the court — not one, but all three of the links in their argument crumble.

First. Are classifications on the basis of race, for purposes of law school admission and the like, *per se,* unconstitutional? The correct answer is yes. Indeed, the Fourteenth Amendment was deliberately formulated to prohibit precisely such classifications. The Constitution is and always must be, in that sense, colorblind. It cannot be, from time to time and at the discretion of certain agencies or administrators, color conscious in order to become colorblind at some future date. The principle that a person's race is simply not relevant in the application of the laws is a treasured one. If we are prepared to sacrifice that principle now and then, in an attempt to achieve some very pressing and very honorable objective, we will have given up its force as constitutional principle. No doubt intentions here are of the best, but so also are the intentions of those who would from time to time sacrifice other constitutional principles for the attainment of other very worthy ends. The enforcement of justice, the redistribution of wealth, the very protection of the nation, might all be more conveniently, more efficiently, even more effectively accomplished if, from time to time, we winked at the Constitution and did what, as we will be told with honest fervor, is of absolutely overriding importance. In this way is the congressional authority to declare war conveniently ignored; in this way is the constitutional protection of our persons, houses, papers, and effects from unreasonable search and seizure effectively (of course only "temporarily") bypassed. In this way, in sum, constitutional government, fragile network of principles that it is, comes apart.

But, some will reply, those other objectives — national security, protection against crime, etc. — are only claimed to be compelling;

racial justice, so long deliberately denied, really is so. Of course. And every person and every group has, at some time, objectives that are, to its complete and profound conviction, so utterly compelling that nothing must be allowed to stand in the way of their accomplishment.[10] But every such party must yield in turn to the restrictions of constitutional government; if those in authority do not enforce these restrictions, the Constitution is but paper. A constitution, ideally, is not an expression of particular social ends; rather, it identifies very general common purposes and lays down principles according to which the many specific ends of the body politic may be decided upon and pursued. Its most critical provisions will be those which absolutely preclude certain means. Thus, to say that a protection afforded citizens is "constitutional" is at least to affirm that it will be respected, come what may. The specific constitutional provision that each citizen is entitled to equal protection of the laws is assurance that, no matter how vital the government alleges its interest to be, or how laudable the objective of those who would temporarily suspend that principle, it will stand. The highest obligation to respect the guarantee of equal protection is owed by public institutions and government agencies.[11]

Preferential admission systems present instances of this sometimes agonizing tension between important ends and impermissible means. Hence the persuasiveness of the argument on both sides. In facing dilemmas of this kind, long experience has taught the supremacy of the procedural principle. With societies, as with individuals, the use of means in themselves corrupt tends to corrupt the user, and to infect the result. So it is with wiretapping, with censorship, with torture. So it is with discriminatory preference by racial grouping for racial balance.

But this is racial classification, the court insisted, not racial discrimination. The latter is indeed ruled out, said they, but the former is not; *Brown* and other powerful precedents forbid invidious racial classification, not all racial classification. This misses the central point — the sharpest bite of *Brown* and like cases — that in the distribution of benefits under the laws *all* racial classifications are necessarily invidious. Invidious distinctions are those tending to excite ill will, or envy, those likely to be viewed as unfair — and that is what racial classifications are likely to do and be when used as instrument for the apportionment of goods or opportunities.

Perhaps the court would respond: "Some such invidiousness is difficult to deny, but our main point is that the racial classifications condemned by *Brown* and succeeding cases are those that stigmatize one of the groups distinguished, stamping it with inferiority." The change of phrase provides no rescue. To stigmatize is to brand, or label, generally with disgrace — and that is exactly what is done by racial classification in this context. Indeed, put to the service of preferential admissions such classification is doubly stigmatizing. It marks one racial group as formally to be handicapped, its members burdened specifically by virtue of race; for the majority applicant (as formerly for the minority) earned personal qualifications will not be enough. Persons in the other racial category are to be officially treated as though unable to compete for the good in question on an equal basis; by physical characteristic the minority applicant is marked as in need of special help. On both sides morale is subverted, accomplishments clouded. On the one side all carry the handicap, regardless of their past deeds or capacity to bear it; on the other, all are received with the supposition of inferiority, regardless of their personal attainments or hatred of condescension. For all, the stigmata are visually prominent and permanent.[12]

I conclude that the first and fundamental step of the court's argument in defense of preferential admissions cannot be justly taken. Racial classifications, in the application of the laws, or in the distribution of benefits under the laws, are always invidious, always stigmatizing. That is why they are, *per se*, unconstitutional.

How account, then, for the great school desegregation cases, *Green* and *Swann*, in which the U.S. Supreme Court recognized the need to attend to race for the sake of justice? That the Washington court was most uncomfortable with its first premise, and troubled by the self-imposed obligation to defend it, is evident in its discussion of these cases. Badly needing some illustration of the reasonable use of race, but having only these as possible analogies, the court made much of them, while carefully avoiding all mention of the fundamental difference between the remedies approved in them, and the policy at issue in *DeFunis*. It is true that in these school cases the courts attend to race and racial mix. But it is not true that such attention involves, or permits, the classification by race to determine the apportionment of benefits, which is what preferential admission entails. The very reverse, in fact: the desegregation cases have as their main thrust absolute equality of treatment, equality of benefit under the law. Clearly, if that equality has been systematically denied by a school board or other agency through the segregation of races, effective remedy must look to the desegregation of races, and that was done. But no racial classification for the application of laws is there even entertained. Indeed, it is just the use of such classification that, through such cases, we are having now to undo. To use the need of that sort of remedy as a justification for the introduction of another disorder of the very kind that remedy was designed to cure is reasoning both convoluted and dangerous.[13]

Those who say, with the first Justice Harlan, "Our Constitution is colorblind, and neither knows nor tolerates classes among citizens" do not suppose that the courts may not attend to the special character of past wrongs done. Rather, the principle they are emphasizing is cautionary: in all circumstances courts must scrupulously avoid and prohibit the use of a person's race as, in itself, a qualification (or a disqualification) for anything that persons of another race are, for that racial reason disqualified (or qualified) for. The critical distinction between attention to race in the enforcement of equal treatment, and the use of race in the fashioning of unequal treatment, was blurred by the Washington court, but only by straining.

Furthermore, even in the school desegregation cases in which a deliberate racial injustice is identified for which specific remedy is sought, the attention to racial mix in providing that remedy is very delicately supervised by the courts. There is all the difference in the world between a specific remedy thus controlled (as in *Swann*[14]) and a general license to professional schools, or universities, or other institutions to ignore the constitutional prohibition of racial discrimination, and to engage in "reasonable" discriminatory activity to correct the effects of past social injustice as they consider such measures needful or convenient. To permit such practice is to abandon constitutional principle entirely.

Preferential admission procedures certainly do result in the discriminatory apportionment of benefits on the basis of race or ethnicity. When any resource is in short supply, and some by virtue of their race are given more of it, others by virtue of their race get less. If that resource be seats in a law school, procedures that assure preference to certain racial groups in allotting those seats necessarily produce a correlative denial of access to those not in the preferred categories. This plain consequence must not be overlooked. Whether the numbers be fixed or flexible; whether "quotas" be established and called "benign," whether they be measured by percentages or absolute quantities; whether the objective be "reasonable proportionality" or "appropriate representation" — the setting of benefit floors for some groups in this context inescapably entails benefit ceilings for other groups.

By fuzzing the numbers and softening the names, some manage to hide this conclusion from themselves. The majority of the Washington court, to its credit, did not do that. Although eager to minimize the discriminatory character of the instrument, it recognized candidly the inevitable result. It wrote: *"The minority admissions policy is certainly not benign with respect to non-minority students who are displaced by it."*[15] Preference by race is malign; its malignity has no clearer or more fitting name than racism. Widespread in American universities, this well-meant racism will indeed be found, upon reflection, to deny the equal protection of the laws.

Second. Suppose (what I do not grant) that the court was correct in its first step; suppose that racial classifications are in some cases constitutional, and that the school desegregation cases are illustrations of the exceptional cases. Still, to determine whether any specific uses of racial classification are constitutional, some standard for judgment is required. Recognizing that racial categories are always suspect, the Washington court concluded that any user of a racial classification in admissions is under an obligation to show "that its consideration of race in admitting students is necessary to the accomplishment of a compelling state interest."

Would this be the correct test? My answer is no. Although rightly higher than the normal standard (that of being reasonably related to a legitimate public purpose), the court's standard is not high enough. In addition to the need for the classification, and the compelling character of the interests served by it, "the individual interests *affected* by the classification" (in the words of the U.S. Supreme Court) must be considered. Where the basis for the classification is known to be "inherently suspect," and the individual interest affected is a fundamental constitutional right, the standard for review must be, said the highest Court, "exacting."[16]

To pass an exacting test a racial classification must not have the consequence of penalizing any person simply by virtue of his race. The importance of this restriction cannot be overemphasized. If it be argued that racial categories are in some contexts relevant to the application of the laws; if the school desegregation cases discussed above are viewed (incorrectly, I submit) as examples in which the just distribution of benefit relies upon racial classification, it is at least certain that such classification is not used in those cases to the prejudice of anyone. No person, under those decisions, gets less than another because of his or her race. That, we rightly sense, is a critical factor in any consideration of a racial classification. Whenever individuals are penalized solely because they manifest some adventitious characteristic wholly out of their control — their skin color, their national origin, or the like — the unfairness arouses strong indignation. Our viscera do not mislead us in this; such uses of race must be forbidden.

If racial classifications are ever to be used, I conclude, they must pass a more protective test than that invoked by the court. The user of any racial classification must show that consideration of race is necessary to the accomplishment of a compelling state interest, *and* that such consideration does not result in adverse consequence to any person simply because of that person's race or ethnic membership. Now it has been demonstrated that one result of preferential policies is to deny to some persons, simply because of their race, what they in every other respect deserve and would receive were they of the preferred skin color. It is therefore manifest that on this more protective standard no policy of preferential admission by race is acceptable.

Third. Suppose the first and second steps of the court's argument were correct: that racial classifications are sometimes permissible, and that when they are it need be shown only that they are necessary for the accomplishment of a compelling state interest. Would a preferential admissions policy on the Washington Law School model pass that test? No, it would not.

What are the interests to be served by the policy, and which of them are compelling? Three separate interests were identified by the university; and they have differing values.

The first is a general interest in the integration of law schools and the legal profession. Unless and until minorities have a fair and genuinely equal opportunity to prepare for the bar, they cannot function properly in many critical roles — that of judge or prosecutor, as well as attorney — to which the law schools give the only entry. And it is obviously unjust for any racial group to be denied opportunity to serve in those roles. Moreover, as the court pointed out, in this society lawyers have a specially important role in policy making because of their relatively high level of service in legislatures and other public bodies. The public policy that is molded in these bodies needs the input of the minorities universally concerned — for the sake of minorities and majorities alike. The social role of attorneys is such that their understanding of the needs and views of all slices of society is an important general concern.

Racial integration is indeed a deep and powerful interest. It is not, however, an interest compelling in the sense that, to serve it, *any* steps are justified. Integration does not, as an objective, justify discrimination believed useful in its achievement. Lawyers, judges, and prosecutors of all colors and ethnic identities we do need; but we cannot afford to pay for improvement on that front by basing professional qualifications partly on skin color. A community is not justified in advancing its own general health by denying to some of its members constitutional protections that apply to all. Because the classification of persons by irrelevant physical properties is so generally odious, the courts are explicit in de-

manding that the interests served by such classification be literally compelling, *overriding*. Grave though the need for integration is, overriding
in the sense required by the judicial test proposed it is not.

A second general interest urged by the advocates of preferential admissions policies is the achievement of numerical proportionality
among the races in the legal (and other) professions. Much different
from integration, this is a conception of racial balance which measures
justice by counting numbers of minority group members in the professions or professional schools, and then finds any result unsatisfactory
that does not manifest "reasonable proportionality" or "appropriate
representation."

On two levels it is clear that racial proportionality is not a compelling need. Numerical proportionality of races in the professions is commonly defended on the ground that without it the interests of minority
groups cannot be properly served. Surely this belief is mistaken if it
incorporates the conviction that only black lawyers can serve black clients adequately, that Indians, when sick, are treated properly only by
Indian physicians, or that white defendants cannot be fairly tried before
black judges. The insistence that proper and conscientious fulfillment
of professional function is dependent upon sameness of race or heritage
between client and practitioner is not only destructive but incorrect.
The record of professional services completely transcending differences
of race, religion, and national origin is long and honorable.

"We agree [the rejoinder might begin] that much professional service crosses racial lines; but as a practical matter it cannot be denied that,
without racial balance in the professional corps, it has proved impossible for racial minorities to obtain professional services in the quantity
and quality needed." That answer is misleading. It is true that the legal
and health needs of minority groups have not been adequately met, but
it is far from clear that the remedy for that lies in racial proportionality.
Differences in professional services are most closely tied to economic
considerations, within as well as between races; proportionality does
not even speak to that fundamental problem. Moreover, to defend
forced proportionality on the basis of the professional needs of the minority is to assume, tacitly, that minority group lawyers will, in fact,

devote themselves to ethnically exclusive practice. This may be true for some, but to expect that black professionals will practice only in the black community, or Mexican-Americans only in the Mexican-American community, is mistaken and unfair. The parochialism implicit in that expectation exerts heavy and unfair pressure upon minority professionals.

"Well then, [the rejoinder might continue] is there not a residual need felt by minority group members for lawyers (and doctors, etc.) of the same race or cultural heritage who are sensitive to their special attitudes and circumstances, share their ethnic spirit, and who alone can make them comfortable?" See where this argument takes us. If comfort, in this sense, really is good ground for official preference on the basis of race, it would be entirely appropriate for firms with chiefly minority clientele to discriminate openly against applicants from the ethnic majority in their hiring practices. "Our clients cannot be comfortable with white attorneys," they may say, "and good professional service to our clients requires their psychological confidence. That confidence is possible only with community of heritage." Racism is a two-way street. Depend upon it, this argument, so long used to justify racial discrimination against minority professionals, will be accepted with satisfaction by bigots on all sides.

Arguments of this kind for racial proportionality — some advanced even by the Washington court — mistakenly suppose a unity and distinctness of interest shared by all and only the members of a racial category. They assume that the diversity among whites, or among blacks, or among Philippine-Americans, or whatever, is wholly submerged, outweighed by racial identification, and that therefore the professional needs of persons of a given race will be fully met only by one of the same race. With decent purpose we are urged to think with our blood.

More deeply, the call for proportionality is inspired by a strange vision of ideal society — one that is pervaded by ethnic identification. According to that ideal the numerical proportionality of races is a measure of distributive justice in virtually every sphere of social life. In schools, courts, professions, in business and in recreation, in all public and in much private activity attention to race is encouraged, even obliged. For some this ideal offers a promise of homogeneity that proves captivating; inferences now commonly drawn from it verge upon the absurd. It has been suggested, for example, that a legislature or a jury that does not manifest proportionality of race (or sex, or age) is without legitimate authority. Calls for appropriate numerical representation by various ethnic groups — Italian-Americans, Catholic Americans, even homo-sexual Americans — have already been heard. It is realistic to expect many more, because once this principle for the distribution of benefits appears operative each group is under some pressure to stake an early claim. The pressure is greater when it cannot be known on what principles the cake will be cut, so that restraint by any group may result in an apportionment on some continuum taking no account of that group whatever. There is no limit to the variety of categories (racial, national, sexual, etc.) from which such demands may arise. Nor is there limit to the variety of public contexts to which such demands may be applied. All this is no longer speculation.

How seriously are such claims to be taken? That depends upon how seriously the premise of ethnic proportionality as ideal is received.[17] Its universal applicability will hardly be allowed. Yet it will be difficult to accept the ideal in some contexts while denying it in others that are strictly analogous. It will be difficult to defend the ideal in support of the claims of some ethnic groups while rejecting the coordinate claims of other groups.

The ideal of thorough ethnic proportionality, although impractical and tortuous, may be honestly pursued by some. Others, however in-consistently, may invoke it for some groups or some spheres, but not for other groups or spheres. Still others will reject the ideal. It is at least certain, I conclude, that the realization of such an ideal is not a compel-ling social need.[18]

There is a third general interest that the advocates of racially prefer-ential policies aim to advance: *compensation*. That wrongful injuries done earlier be compensated for now, to the extent possible, is part of the demands of justice. The form of that compensation no general prin-ciples can determine. Much depends upon the nature and gravity of the injury, and upon the circumstances at the time compensation is undertaken. To say that compensation for a past injury is required now is to call for an immediate process of tangible redress, suitable in form and substance. But that cannot tell us what precisely is to be done. Compensation is not a particular, describable end, like integration; it is at once more pressing and less measurable, an aim of justice.

This compensatory interest *is* compelling, but no scheme of racial or ethnic preference can be necessary to serve it. Compensation being a form of redress, it is justifiable only as a response to specific wrongs done to specific persons. Preferential admissions policies, by giving favor to all members of certain racial or ethnic groups, cannot be appropriate remedies for the wrongs in question.

Specific past injuries may justify specific present efforts to make up for what was wrongly done. In that spirit it is fair that those who have suffered wrongful economic disadvantage, or wrongful denial of opportunity, now be assisted with affirmative action to help redress those wrongs. Thus in deciding upon admissions to professional schools it may be quite reasonable to take into consideration some past injuries — e.g., whether schooling appropriate to ability had been denied a particular applicant, whether the economic need to work while in school had resulted in another applicant's lessened performance there, etc. Concrete assistance to those so disadvantaged, special efforts to recruit such applicants for professional courses and to retain such students by supplying special needs having root in that earlier maltreatment, offend no reasonable sense of justice.

Response in this compensatory spirit, however, cannot be tied to race or ethnicity; a compensatory remedy must be devised with a view to the injuries suffered by particular applicants, whatever their surname or color. Of each individually it may be asked: Is there, in this case, a history of wrongfully imposed disadvantage so grave as to justify special treatment now?

Advocates of preferential systems are likely to contend, in response, that the injury suffered by many is inextricably bound up with race, and hence the remedy must be so as well. That point, powerful in some contexts, is misapplied here. In the public schools of North Carolina, where the task was that of desegregating large numbers of equally qualified students already enrolled in the system who *had* long been sorted by race, a racially attentive remedy was in order. There are no considerations of this kind that could justify a remedy that is, as in *De-Funis*, intrinsically prejudicial. However ugly past uses of race have been, constitutional rights are now enjoyed by citizens entirely without regard to race. Hence no deprivation of such individual rights, based on race alone, may be tolerated. The equal protection clause is a safeguard not for groups of persons but for every citizen singly.

On this point the language of the U.S. Supreme Court in an earlier case is definitive: "The rights created by the first section of the Fourteenth Amendment are, by its terms, guaranteed to the individual. The rights established are personal rights.... Equal protection of the laws is not achieved through indiscriminate imposition of inequalities."[19]

The tacit supposition that rights are possessed by racial groups has caused much unfortunate confusion. But the formulation of the Fourteenth Amendment, recognizing rights as pertaining only to individuals, is exact on this matter. No state shall "deny to any person within its jurisdiction the equal protection of the laws." Any single individual, denied some benefit to which he or she is otherwise entitled, on the ground of some classification by race or ethnic origin, will have had rights under that clause infringed. The social interest in compensating other persons who are members of other groups which have, in general, been very cruelly treated in the past, gives no justification for deliberate discrimination against this individual now.[20]

Many among our ethnic minorities have suffered grievous disadvantage simply because they were black or brown or yellow. But the degree of disadvantage suffered, and even the fact of it, varies from case to case. Some have suffered no more than many nonminority persons who have unjustly experienced severe economic hardship or family catastrophe. Since every early adversity cannot be weighed in the school admissions process, it is usually thought right to consider the great majority of applicants on an equal footing, without analysis of past disadvantage, when reviewing admission qualifications.

Some past injuries may be thought so cruel and damaging as to justify special consideration for professional school admission. But whether a particular person has been so injured is a question of fact, to be answered in each case separately. If special consideration is in order for those whose early lives were cramped by extreme poverty, the penurious Appalachian white, the oppressed Asian-American from a Western state, the impoverished Finn from upper Michigan — these and all others similarly oppressed are equally entitled to that consideration.

This becomes complicated. If the complications grow excessive we may think it well to avoid the artificial inequities likely to flow from inadequate data, or flaws in the compensatory calculations, by refraining altogether from those calculations and again treating all applicants on the same footing. That would oblige reliance chiefly upon some roughly objective credential — past academic records, examinations, and the like — which we know, of course, yield results imperfect in other ways. Or we may think ourselves obliged, whatever the burden, to enter the thicket of compensatory calculations. But if we do so, it is clear that we must make these calculations for *all* applicants. What we weigh in the case of one we must weigh for all; whatever redress in the sphere of admissions is in order because of past injury is in order for every person who has suffered like injury, without regard to race or national origin.

What we may not do, constitutionally or morally, is announce: "You are black, you get plus points; you are yellow, you don't." An admissions committee must not classify by race or ethnicity and assume, for special consideration, cultural or economic deprivation for all of one category and for none of another. Nor may it do what amounts to the same thing — attend to the deprivations and injuries experienced by members of one ethnic group, but not to those experienced by members of others. Many small, foreign-language subgroups in our country have been humiliated, ostracized, oppressed; some religious groups have been scandalously treated; many in the white, Christian majority have suffered the terrible blight of family disorder and penury. Compensatory affirmative action, if undertaken at all, must be undertaken for every person who qualifies on some reasonably objective standard, a standard free of racial orientation.

Just here the system of the Washington Law School (and all others having essentially that pattern) fails badly. By grouping races separately, and applying different standards to the different racial groups, an admissions office not only *does what is not necessary* to meet the compensatory need but *fails to do what is necessary* to meet that need. The instrument is intolerably blunt. Preference based upon race necessarily fails to respect the principle that all persons are entitled equally to the benefits and protections of the laws.

Distinct from questions concerning compensation for past injury are questions about applicants which bear upon their ability or promise to fulfill the larger social duties of the profession they seek to enter. If participation in community affairs be one of these, an admissions committee may reasonably look to the applicant's record in school or community on that front; if leadership, or industry, or self-discipline be qualities essential in that profession, the applicant may be examined, quite apart from her or his numerical scores, on those matters; if social service be a critical factor, the applicant's past concern for other citizens, manifested in volunteer work of different sorts, might be weighed. All these and like factors may be considered by an admissions committee, and many of these commonly are considered, both as guides in the interpretation of numerical records, and as qualities which serve as predictors of success in the school and the profession.

Here again, however, the weighing of such matters cannot rightly depend upon the race of the applicant. Whatever is pertinent in considering applicants of one race is pertinent in considering applicants of all races, and should be given its due weight. Racial classifications by themselves are, as the Supreme Court said in another context, "obviously irrelevant and invidious."[21]

The third step of the Washington court's argument, I conclude, collapses upon scrutiny. The test proposed by the court itself — that the racial classification employed be necessary for the accomplishment of a compelling state purpose — though not stiff enough in fact, is too stiff to be met by the Law School's system of preferential admissions. Some of the interests served by that preferential system are not compelling in the required sense, some are not compelling in any sense, and of the one that is compelling it cannot be said that the system proposed is necessary for its accomplishment.

Of those who would defend preferential admissions by race, the Washington Supreme Court has been the most cogent. Yet the argument of that court, I submit, proves unsuccessful at every critical point.

Two final notes on the counterproductivity of racial preference:

1. The demand for racial proportionality in the professions, advanced through the consideration of race in professional school admissions, even where intellectual and other pertinent considerations are counterindicative, exacts a high price. It must result in the tendency, at least statistical, to yield minority group professionals less well qualified, less respected, less trusted than their counterparts in the majority. That is a great disservice to minority groups, stigmatizing their members in a most unfortunate way. "I wouldn't hit a dog with some of the minority students I've seen," says Dr. Charles DeLeon, a black psychiatrist at Case Western Reserve University Hospital, "and I have an idea that you honkies are taking in these dummies so that eight years from now you'll be able to turn around and say, 'Look how bad they all turned out.'"[22]

Results on bar examinations have been painful. In Michigan, for example, in the summer of 1971, results showed a passing rate of 71 percent for white candidates, 17 percent for black candidates. Some contend that such discrepancies, also encountered elsewhere, are due to the hidden racial bias of the bar exams. The measures may indeed be faulty; but it is unlikely that their flaws fully explain so large a discrepancy. Bar exams are given after three years of law school, the examination papers identified and graded by number, not name. It is probable that poorly prepared minority students, admitted preferentially to law schools, receive a sympathetic consideration in classes that is not possible in the grading of bar examination papers. The general suitability of bar examinations is now much discussed. Justice Douglas joined the National Bar Association (composed of black lawyers) in proposing their abolition. Whatever is necessary to evaluate candidates for the bar in a racially neutral way must be done, of course. But if, on such reasonable measures of

performance as there are, preferential admission has distinctly invidious results, it is likely to do much damage to the minority it aims to
assist.

2. One consequence of preferential admissions programs is cer-
    tain: fully qualified minority group professionals come to be
    viewed by many, of all races, as having gained their professional
    positions through favor by virtue of their race. No matter their
    excellence; it will be suspected that their credentials were re-
    ceived on a double, lower standard. When, in the minds of
    everyone, black and white, a physician's dark skin is subcon-
    sciously linked to inferiority, who among members of minority
    groups is served? Racial preference clouds the accomplish-
    ments and undermines the reputations of those superbly
    qualified minority-group professionals who neither need nor
    get special favor. It is a cruel result.

The cruelty comes clear in this statement by Prof. Thomas Sowell,
educated in Harlem, later professor of economics at UCLA:

> The actual harm done by quotas is far greater than having a few
> incompetent people here and there — and the harm that will
> actually be done will be harm primarily to the *black* population.
> What all the arguments and campaigns for quotas are really
> saying, loud and clear, is that *black people just don't have it*, and
> that they will have to be given something in order to have something.
> The devastating impact of this message on black people — particularly
> black young people — will outweigh any few extra jobs that may result
> from this strategy. Those black people who are already competent, and
> who could be instrumental in producing more competence among
> the rising generation, will be completely undermined, as black be-
> comes synonymous — in the minds of black and white alike — with
> incompetence, and black achievement becomes synonymous with
> charity or payoffs.[23]

The counterproductivity of racial preference should not be sur-
prising. The health of the body politic depends upon a widely shared
confidence by its members that public process will be governed by a

few very basic principles — among them, that the laws, however imperfect, will apply to all persons equally. Any device that seeks to remedy a sickness in that body by tinkering with its basal metabolism may be expected to do damage that far outweighs its good effects.

NOTES

1. *DeFunis v. Odegaard,* 416 U.S. 312 (1974).

2. Ibid.

3. 507 P. 2d 1191.

4. Similar systems of preferential admission had by then become, and remain still, widespread. For example: at the Stanford University Law School an admissions policy was then in force that, according to its dean at the time, was "strongly preferential in favor of minority applicants, since it will lead to admission of many minority students whose formal academic credentials are below those of hundreds, even thousands, of nonminority applicants to Stanford who will be rejected."

5. 347 U.S. 483 (1954).

6. *Green v. County School Board,* 391 U.S. 437 (1968).

7. *Swann v. Charlotte-Mecklenburg Board of Education,* 402 U.S. 45 (1971).

8. 507 P. 2d 1180.

9. *Loving v. Virginia,* 388 U.S. 10 (1967).

10. Justice Douglas, in his dissenting opinion in *DeFunis,* writes: "The argument is that a 'compelling' state interest can justify the racial discrimination that is practiced here.... If discrimination based on race is constitutionally permissible when those who hold the reins can come up with 'compelling' reasons to justify it, then constitutional guarantees acquire an accordion-like quality" (416 U.S. 343).

11. The only previous suspension of this constitutional protection was a national moral disaster. To meet the alleged danger of sabotage and espionage during the Second World War, American citizens of Japanese descent were peremptorily rounded up, moved, and excluded from large sections of our West Coast. The Supreme Court was pained,

but found this roundup and detention justified by "pressing public necessity" [*Korematsu v. United States*, 323 U.S. 216 (1944)]. Never before or since has the use of race in applying constitutional protection been expressly approved by our highest court.

12. Justice Douglas writes in his dissenting opinion: "A segregated admission process creates suggestions of stigma and caste no less than a segregated classroom, and in the end it may produce that result despite its contrary intentions.... [T]hat Blacks or Browns cannot make it on their individual merit ... is a stamp of inferiority that a state is not permitted to place on any lawyer" (416 U.S. 343).

13. Congress, especially through Title VII of the Civil Rights Act of 1964, has also sought to undo some of the results of racial categorizing. When discriminatory preference for minority races was attempted and tested in court, a unanimous Supreme Court interpreting this statute laid down the principle that job qualification standards must be performance-related, and that that may cut against certain types of irrelevant testing, just as it cuts against certain types of irrelevant grouping. "Discriminatory preference for any group, minority or majority, is precisely and only what Congress has proscribed. What is required by Congress is the removal of artificial, arbitrary, unnecessary barriers to employment when the barriers operate invidiously to discriminate on the basis of racial or other impermissible classification" [*Griggs v. Duke Power Co.*, 401 U.S. 430 (1971)].

14. 401 U.S. 1.

15. 507 P. 2d 1180. Emphasis added.

16. *Dunn v. Blumstein,* 405 U.S. 338 (1972).

17. Preliminary judgment on the premise of proportionality has been passed by the U.S. Supreme Court. It decided that the State of California has the right to ban picketing whose purpose — to compel the hiring of blacks in proportion to black customers — was unlawful. "To deny to California the right to ban picketing in the circumstances of this case would mean that there could be no prohibition of the pressure of picketing to secure proportional employment on ancestral grounds of Hungarians in Cleveland, of Poles in Buffalo, of Germans in Milwaukee, of Portuguese in New Bedford, of Mexicans in San An-

tonio, of the numerous minority groups in New York, and so on through the whole gamut of racial and religious concentrations in various cities" [*Hughes v. Superior Court of California* 339 U.S. 464 (1950)].

18. Justice Douglas writes in his dissent: "The state, however, may not proceed by racial classification to force strict population equivalences for every group in every occupation, overriding individual preferences. The Equal Protection Clause commands the elimination of racial barriers, not their creation in order to satisfy our theory as to how society ought to be organized. The purpose of the University of Washington cannot be to produce black lawyers for blacks, Polish lawyers for Poles, Jewish lawyers for Jews, Irish lawyers for the Irish. It should be to produce good lawyers for Americans" (416 U.S. 342).

19. *Shelly v. Kraemer*, 344 U.S. 22.

20. Justice Douglas, in his *DeFunis* dissent, is forceful on this point: "There is no constitutional right for any race to be preferred.... A DeFunis who is white is entitled to no advantage by reason of the fact; nor is he subject to any disability, no matter his race or color. Whatever his race, he had a constitutional right to have his application considered on its individual merits in a racially neutral manner"(416 U.S. 337).

21. *Gross v. Board of Education,* 373 U.S. 687 (1963).

22. *The New York Times,* April 7, 1974.

23. This passage (its emphases in the original) is from *Black Education: Myths and Tragedies,* published in 1972. Thomas Sowell is now Senior Fellow at the Hoover Institution in Stanford, California. His recent book, *Preferential Policies: An International Perspective* (Morrow, 1990), presents a detailed account of the devastating effects preferential policies have had, for the minorities preferred, in countries around the world. All those who, with good intentions, support racial preference in our country owe it to themselves to consider this painful report.

B

Racial Preference in Medical School Admissions

Regents of the University of California v. Bakke

The first landmark decision dealing with racially preferential affirmative action was issued by the U.S. Supreme Court in the *Bakke* case, in June of 1978.[1] Allan Bakke also was a white applicant with a fine record who sought admission to a public professional school — in this case the medical school of the University of California at Davis. Like DeFunis, Bakke was twice rejected, in 1974 and in 1975. Like DeFunis, Bakke was convinced that he (or some others in very similar circumstances) would certainly have been admitted had there not been in force at that medical school an admissions system designed to give preference to applicants from certain minority ethnic groups. Like DeFunis, Bakke contended that this racial preference had the effect of denying him the equal protection of the laws guaranteed by the U.S. Constitution.

A powerful argument that DeFunis did not put forward did apply in this case: Racially preferential affirmative action (Bakke contended) was also a clear violation of the Civil Rights Act of 1964, of which Title VI reads in part: "No person in the United States shall, on the grounds of race, color, or national origin, be excluded from participation in, be denied the benefits of, or be subjected to discrimination under any pro-

gram or activity receiving federal financial assistance."[2] The Davis
medical school did receive federal financial assistance, and Allan Bakke
was indubitably subjected to discrimination under the racially preferential admission program in force there.

The arguments commonly heard in support of racial preference
emerged forcefully in the *Bakke* case, and are examined closely in the
two essays that follow. On the one hand racial preference is often defended as *compensatory,* as reparation to minorities for injuries earlier
done to them. On the other hand, racial preference is widely defended
as *instrumental,* as a device required for the achievement of racial integration and racial balance. Both kinds of claims — quite different, yet
often confused — fail to justify racial favoritism of the kind practiced at
the University of California, as I argue in the first essay below.

It was no surprise, therefore, when Bakke's case reached the California Supreme Court (perhaps the most liberal in the country at that time),
that his arguments prevailed in largest part. The Davis affirmative action
program was struck down. But, unlike DeFunis, Bakke did not win a
court order that he be admitted because (said that court) it was not sure
that, had there been no preferential program in force, he (and not some
other white applicant in his place) would have been admitted. His case
was therefore certainly not moot. Tenaciously he sought admission; tenaciously the university sought to recover its authority to give preference by
race. Some advocates of affirmative action urged the university not to appeal the case further, fearing that a U.S. Supreme Court loss was likely,
and that the loss might be formulated in such a way as to preclude all
racial preference nationwide. Better, thought they, to live with the loss
already suffered in California. But in the end both parties cross-appealed
to the Supreme Court of the United States.

The *Bakke* case became a national sensation. More briefs were submitted by third party "friends of the court" — universities, ethnic societies, public interest groups, and so on — in this than in any previous
case in the entire history of the nation. The 1978 decision is truly a
landmark; its principles remain part of the law of the land.

But the *Bakke* decision proved to be less definitive than had been widely hoped. For the litigants themselves the outcome was perfectly clear: Bakke won. He was ordered admitted to the medical school at Davis (from which he was graduated three years later) and the racially preferential admission system at that medical school was found unlawful and struck down.

Because of the multiplicity of opinions (six judges wrote separately) and their complexity, the resolution of the larger issues in *Bakke* was not perfectly unambiguous. One major cause of the complexity was a disagreement, within the Court, over whether this case necessarily involved a constitutional issue, or was one that could (and therefore should) be resolved entirely by reference to the Civil Rights Act, cited just above. Four of the justices (Stevens, Stewart, Burger, and Rehnquist) emphasized what they thought to be the sufficiency of the Civil Rights Act of 1964; its unambiguous words make it evident, said they, that the medical school's affirmative action program was, on its face, a violation of federal law. Constitutional questions they did not address because, they argued, it simply was not necessary to do so. Four other justices (Brennan, Marshall, Blackmun, and White), resorting to constitutional interpretation, concluded that the affirmative action program at Davis was permissible. Everything therefore depended upon the opinion of the ninth and deciding justice, Lewis Powell.

Powell's pivotal decision — long, thoughtful, intricate — is the subject of the second essay below, published originally in the *Wayne Law Review*. His opinion has been much abused over the years; persons hostile to its thrust have portrayed it in ways that have engendered widespread misunderstanding. It is thoroughly reported and analyzed here because it is the controlling opinion in the *Bakke* case.

Powell rejected the racially preferential system at the Davis Medical School categorically. He fully agreed that Bakke was done an injustice, and he joined the Stevens group in striking down the affirmative action program that had done the injury. Powell did not agree, however, that the Civil Rights Act of 1964 was by itself sufficient to decide the matter.

That legislation was enacted to give effect to the equal protection clause of the U.S. Constitution; therefore, he argued, to apply the law in this controversial context we cannot escape the need to interpret that constitutional guarantee. Only in the light of what the Constitution means can the Civil Rights Act be correctly understood.

The constitutional guarantee of equal protection, Powell concludes, *does* prohibit preference based flatly on race, even if the intentions of those who discriminate are good. Therefore the Civil Rights Act does also prohibit such preference. The Davis affirmative action program is, therefore, a violation of *both* the Constitution and the federal law. His opinion is eloquent and forceful, his argument very carefully reasoned.

Justice Powell does not say, in this opinion, that a person's race may *never* be considered in deciding upon professional school admissions. Under special circumstances — when the First Amendment interests of intellectual diversity are essentially advanced by such consideration — admissions officers of a university may consider race as one factor among many in determining the makeup of an entering class. But race may enter the admissions process, said Powell, *only* when First Amendment considerations genuinely counterbalance equal protection concerns, and then *only* as one among many factors in such cases, *never* as compensatory redress, *and never as a form of social engineering*. The critical passages in Powell's opinion will be found verbatim in the second essay below. Phrases from this opinion taken out of context have been used by some advocates of racial preference to defend the retention of discriminatory practices that Powell — and the Supreme Court as a whole — specifically condemned. Some readers will be pained, perhaps infuriated, when they observe that what is presently done by some institutions in the name of ethnic "diversity" flies directly in the face of the restrictions upon the use of diversity as a factor in admissions that Powell very explicitly laid down.

All nine justices of the Supreme Court were in accord regarding one feature of this remarkable case: innocent persons like Allan

Bakke, deprived by a racially preferential system of what otherwise would have been theirs, have been injured. Some may think the injury justifiable, but no member of the Court denied the reality of the burden such preference imposes. Justice Blackmun, who did not support Bakke, was characteristically pained by the way in which Bakke had been, in his words, "disadvantaged." Blackmun wrote, almost apologetically, that he looked forward to the time when "persons will be regarded as persons, and discrimination of the type we address today will be an ugly feature of history."[3] So may we all.

2

Who Are Equals?*

Equals ought to have equality. But there still remains a question: equality or inequality of what?

— Aristotle, *Politics*

The Fourteenth Amendment to the U.S. Constitution reads in part: "No State shall ... deny to any person within its jurisdiction the equal protection of the laws." What is the point of this passage? What would a law be like that did not apply equally to those to whom it did apply? Imagine the law: "All citizens eighteen years of age and over shall have the right to vote." Under it, the seventeen-year-old and the nineteen-year-old are treated very differently; all nineteen-year-old citizens are treated in one way (if the law is obeyed) and all seventeen-year-old citizens in another; neither group is denied the equal protection of the law. Suppose, when I went to register to vote, the county clerk responded to my request with an embarrassed smile, saying: "Ah yes, Mr. Cohen, but you see, you're Jewish, so I'm afraid we can't register you." Well! We'd make short work of him.

*This chapter was first published in *National Forum: The Phi Kappa Phi Journal*, vol. 58, no. 1 (Winter 1978). It is here reprinted by permission of the publishers.

Now suppose the law were different. Suppose it read: "All citizens eighteen years of age and over *except Jews* shall have the right to vote." The clerk will not smile when he is handed my application in this case. "I'm sorry, Mr. Cohen," one can hear the mechanical voice of that bureaucrat, "but the law prescribes that Jews may not vote." I am stunned as I read the printed statute he puts before me, but there it is: non-Jews (over eighteen) vote, Jews don't. Suppose the clerk is efficient and incorruptible — all Jews are treated alike with utmost scrupulosity. Then it would appear that all were treated justly under that law, receiving its equal protection.

Surely we never supposed that the equal protection of the law entails identical treatment for everyone. We know that would be absurd. Employers have legal obligations that employees have not. Students have legal rights (and duties) that teachers have not. Rich people must pay taxes that poor people need not. Our legal codes are replete with distinctions — hundreds and thousands of distinctions determining the applicability of the laws. I may be angered by a distinction drawn — yet I will reluctantly agree that if that is the law, and if I am in a specific category, it is fair for me to be obliged under that law, as others are who are in the same class.

We argue about these distinctions — but in three very different ways. We may argue (lawyers are constantly arguing) about who are and who are not in the same class. When you defend a contested deduction on your income tax against the IRS, or I insist that as a college professor I am not a "public official" in the sense that would require public disclosure of my finances, we are disputing over the application of the legal categories drawn, not over the categories themselves. We may argue — as students of political science, or as legislators — that it is wise (or unwise) to introduce certain categorial distinctions. For example, should the law distinguish between large and small businesses in the application of industrial safety regulations? Should minimum wage requirements not apply to employees in certain age groups? And so on.

We may also argue about whether categories of a particular kind should be permitted in the law at all. Some legislation duly enacted, or administrative regulations duly authorized, may distinguish categories of persons we think ought not be distinguished. Some discriminations are worse than unwise; they are unjust.

Return now to the Fourteenth Amendment and its equal protection clause. The prohibition in that clause bears chiefly on arguments of the third sort. It does not bar legislatures from categorizing, but is interpreted so as to require categories used in laws to have a rational foundation. Some categorial distinctions will by that clause be prohibited altogether. Under Hitler's Nuremberg Laws all Jews were treated alike, but justice in America does not permit that sort of equal protection. The central thrust of the Fourteenth Amendment was, and is, to forbid the use — in law, or by administrators under color of law — of categories intrinsically unfair.

But which categories are unfair? The amendment itself was clearly designed to insure that blacks, former slaves, were to be as free as whites. The laws were to protect all races equally. Now, more than a century later, seeking to give redress for long-standing racial injustice, we encounter the problem of fairness from the other side. May we, in the honest effort to achieve real equality among the races, distinguish between black and white (and yellow and brown, etc.) giving preference to some over others? Does our commitment to the equal protection of the laws permit it?

When the courts, and especially the United States Supreme Court, speak to such questions, they decide not simply what the U.S. Constitution requires, but what (in their view) justice requires. High courts must frame principles for the resolution of disputes between real parties, in the case before them and in future cases. Judicial reasoning is often profoundly moral reasoning. Actual cases, faced and decided, are the grist that the mill of American justice grinds. We do well to philosophize with the courts, and as they do, in living contexts. The context now forcing a deeper understanding of "the equal protection of the laws" is that of racially preferential admissions to law schools and medical schools. Some call the problem that of "reverse discrimination," others "benign quotas." Let the name not prejudice the issues. None of the participants in this dispute question the need to give redress for racial injustice and to prevent its reoccurence. At issue is *what* we may justly do to advance these objectives — what categories we may (or must not) use, how we may (or must not) apply them.

The case of *The Regents of the University of California v. Allan Bakke*,[4] now (in 1977) before the Supreme Court of the United States, puts this problem in sharp focus. Allan Bakke was twice rejected (in 1973 and 1974) by the medical school of the University of California at Davis. His undergraduate performance was fine, his test scores excellent, his character and interview performance admirable; he ranked very high among the more than three thousand applicants for one hundred seats. But sixteen of those seats were reserved for minority-group applicants who faced admission standards deliberately and markedly lower than did majority group students like Bakke. The University of California (like many of its sister universities) was determined to enroll a representative proportion of blacks and members of other minority groups in its medical school — however distasteful the double standard believed necessary to accomplish that end.

The Davis medical school established a special committee to fill the reserved slots; this committee evaluated only the minority-group candidates, who competed only against one another. Officially, any disadvantaged person could seek admission under the special program; in fact, all persons admitted under that program, from its inception in 1969, were minority-group members. Officially, that committee reported to the admissions committee; in fact, the applicants chosen by the special committee were invariably admitted. In each of the years Bakke was rejected some minority-group admittees had grade-point averages so low (2.11 in 1973, 2.21 in 1974) that, if they had been white, they would have been summarily rejected. The University of California does not deny that the overall ranking of many of the minority-group applicants who were accepted — after interviews, and with character, interests, test scores, and averages all considered — was substantially below that of many majority applicants who were rejected. Bakke contends that had his skin been of a darker color he would certainly have been admitted. He argues that, refused admission solely because of his race, he was denied "the equal protection of the laws" guaranteed him by the Fourteenth Amendment to the U.S. Constitution.

All sides in this litigation agree that professional schools may properly use, in screening for admission, a host of factors other than test scores and grade-point averages: dedication or dexterity, compassion or professional aims. All sides agree that persons unfairly injured are entitled to full, appropriate, and timely redress. What remains at issue in this case is one thing only: *preference by race.*

The advocates of racially preferential systems reason as follows: Equal protection of the laws requires different treatment for people in different circumstances. Minority-group members are in very special circumstances. Preference by race is here a reasonable instrument to achieve, for members of minority groups, objectives both just and compelling.

Such preference (not denied by the medical school) is thus defended by two central arguments. The first is grounded in alleged demands of justice: Only by deliberately preferring minority applicants can we give adequate compensation for generations of oppressive maltreatment. The second is grounded in the alleged needs of society: If we do not continue to give deliberate racial preference, our medical and law schools will again become what they long were — white enclaves. *Compensation* is the heart of the first argument, *integration* of the second. Both arguments are profoundly mistaken.

Redress is rightly given for injury — not for being black or brown. Members of minority groups have been cruelly damaged, but whatever damage is rightly compensated for (cultural or economic deprivation, inferior schooling, or other), *any* applicant so unfairly damaged is fully entitled to the same special consideration, regardless of his or her race or ethnic group. The prohibition of special favor by race — any race — is the central thrust of a constitutional guarantee that all will receive the protection of the laws equally. Classification by race for the distribution of goods or opportunities is intrinsically odious, always invidious, and morally impermissible, no matter how laudable the goals in view.

What of the school-desegregation cases in which the U.S. Supreme Court has approved the use of racial categories to insure racial integration? Don't these show that racial preference is permissible if the aim is good? Certainly not. In these cases attention to race was allowed in order to ascertain whether school boards that had been discriminating wrongfully by race had really ceased to do so. Racial identification was there permitted — but only to insure that all students, of whatever race, received absolutely equal treatment. The distinction between that use of racial counting, and the use of racial categories to reintroduce special preference, is sharp and profound.

Can the University of California be defended on the ground that its system of racial preference is not injurious but benign? No. Results, not intentions, determine benignity. All racial quotas have injurious results and therefore cannot be benign. When the goods being distributed are in short supply, and some get more of those goods because of their race, then others get less because of their race. There is no escaping that cold logic. Bakke and others like him are seriously penalized for no other reason than their race. Such a system, as even the Washington State Supreme Court in the *DeFunis* case agreed, "is certainly not benign with respect to non-minority students who are displaced by it."[5]

All this says not an iota against compensation. If redress is due, let us give it, and give it fully. If compensation is to be offered through special favor in professional-school admissions — a questionable mode of payment but a possible one — then let us be certain we look in every case to the injury for which we give redress, and not to the race of the applicant.

If the requirements of justice cannot support racial preference, perhaps the society's interest in integration can. The Supreme Court of California, while upholding Bakke's claim, allowed, *arguendo*, that integration is a compelling interest. "Integration" has different meanings, of course. That ambiguity invites the university's most appealing complaint. "You have told us to integrate," the university has said, in effect, "and when we devise admissions systems designed to do just that, you tell us we may not use racial preference. But the problem is a racial one. We cannot achieve racial balance unless we give special preference to racial minorities. Do not ask the impossible of us. And do not ask us to do in indirect ways what you will not permit us to do directly."

That argument by the University of California is not sound. The reply is fourfold.

First, some of the ends in view are important, some are questionable. That the entire package is "compelling" is very doubtful.

1. Better medical and legal services for minorities is a pressing need, but it is far from obvious that minority professionals reared in city slums will return to practice there. And it is patently unfair to burden them with this restrictive expectation. If the intention to give service to particular segments of the community is to be a consideration in admission to professional school, let that be known, and let all persons, of whatever race, make their case for establishing such intentions, if they claim them.

2. Some defend preferential admission on the ground that many persons seeking professional help will be "more comfortable" with a lawyer or a doctor of their own race or religion. Possibly true. But the argument based upon this interest, now to serve as a justification of institutionalized racial preference, has long been used to exclude blacks from white hospitals and Jews from Christian law firms. It is an argument in which bigots of every color will take satisfaction.

3. Diversity of cultural background in the professional schools, and in the professions themselves, will increase the richness of education and of service, and will provide role models for youngsters from cultural groups long oppressed. These are genuine and worthy interests, but are they compelling? What *is* compelling is integration in the classical sense: the removal of every obstruction to genuinely equal opportunity, the elimination of every racial qualification. Integration in the now fashionable sense — entailing some *de facto* mix of races approaching proportionality — may be desirable in many contexts, but is in any case certainly not compelling.

Second, the Supreme Court of California emphasized that no party has shown that preference by race in admissions (which all agree is objectionable) is necessary to achieve appropriate social goals. Even if arbitrary numerical ratios are established as the only acceptable standard of success, that cannot be shown. But from whence comes that numerical standard? The entire history of our nation has been one of ethnic layering, in which different interests and activities tend to be pursued by different cultural and ethnic groups. That is not unwholesome. The effort to homogenize society in spite of this natural tendency is already proving to be divisive, frustrating, and unworkable. Substantial increases of diversity in some professions are reasonably sought. With non-preferential forms of affirmative action pursued vigorously, and admissions criteria enlarged and enriched and applied evenhandedly to all applicants, diversity and *de facto* integration may be much advanced. Still more might be accomplished if various compensatory schemes were introduced, but they must be applied in a racially neutral way. Some majority applicants who deserve compensatory preference will also benefit under such programs, but this is entirely fitting.

There is nothing crafty about this reply. The claim that these are but devious ways to reach the same ends is simply false, and betrays an inclination to introduce racial preference somehow, "through the back door" if necessary. That would be ugly. There is no reason to fear or to be ashamed of an honest admissions program, or of an honest compensatory program, honestly applied. The racial count that results may not be the same as that when racial preference is used, but perhaps it ought not be. Even if the count were the same, the individuals (admitted using morally relevant principles, not race) would be different, and that makes all the difference. It is certain that substantial progress in diversifying and integrating professional school classes can be achieved without racial preference.

Third, we must see that granting favor on the basis of race alone is a nasty business, however honorable the goal. The moral issue comes in classic form: Terribly pressing objectives (integrated professions, adequate legal and medical service for members of minority groups) appear to require impermissible means. Might we not wink at the Constitution, this once, in view of the importance and decency of our objectives?

Such winking is precisely the hope of every party having aims that are, to that party's profound conviction, of absolutely overriding importance. Constitutional short cuts have been and will be urged for the sake of national security (e.g., the internment of Japanese-Americans during

World War II), for the enforcement of criminal laws (e.g., admission of illegally seized evidence), and in other spheres. But wink we must not. Each party in its turn must abide the restrictions of constitutional process. The single most important feature of a constitution, if it is more than paper, is its preclusion of unjust means. Hence the preciousness and power of the guarantee of equality before the law. When good process and laudable objectives conflict, long experience teaches the priority of process. Means that are corrupt will infect the result and (with societies as with individuals) will corrupt the user in the end. So it is with wiretapping, with censorship, and with every shortcut taken knowingly at the expense of the rights of individuals. So it is also with racial preference, even when well-intended.

The *fourth* response to the integration argument adds bitter irony. Hating the taste of racial preference in admissions, the advocates of these programs swallow them only because of a conviction that they are so good for us. Bitter but (they think) medicinal. In this, too, they are mistaken. Racial preference is good for nobody, black or white, majority or minority. However much the advocates of such systems may hope for ultimate integration (though some do not share that ideal) the consequence of preferential systems is ever greater attention to race, agitation and tension about race. All comment about race, even scholarship with constructive intent, comes to be viewed as invidious. Rewards and penalties based on race are widely thought to be unfair, undeserved. Unfairness breeds resentment; resentment grows to anger. Racial preference does not integrate the races but *dis*integrates them, exciting envy, fostering ill-will and even hatred.

Racial preference is dynamite. Many who play with such preference are now blinded by honest zeal and hide from themselves the explosions likely in the sequel. Justice John Marshall Harlan, dissenting in 1896 from the Supreme Court ruling that established the "separate but equal" doctrine, insisted that the U.S. Constitution was and must be colorblind. Some would have the law be color-conscious now so that it may become colorblind in the future. That cannot be. One is reminded of political leaders who "suspend" constitutions to "build a firmer base for democracy." Once established as constitutionally acceptable grounds for discriminatory distribution, racial categories will wax, not wane, in importance. No prescription for racial disharmony could be surer of success.

Official favoritism by race or national origin is poison in society. In American society, built of manifold racial and ethnic layers, it is deadly poison. How gravely mistaken it will be to take new doses of the same stuff, while still suffering the pains of recovery from the old.

3

Equality, Diversity, and Good Faith*

The *Bakke* decision[6] has been both inappropriately praised and wrongly criticized. The opinion of Justice Powell especially has been commonly misrepresented, its force and ramifications widely misapprehended. I seek now to bring some clarity to the analysis of *Bakke* by doing the following things:

    I. Review briefly some common misconceptions of that Supreme Court decision

    II. Explicate the role of Justice Powell's opinion in *Bakke*

    III. Argue that Powell's opinion is not only pivotal but controlling

    IV. Identify the principles that undergird Powell's opinion

    V. Respond to the objection that Powell's principles are not feasible

    VI. Refute the objection that Powell's principles are fundamentally incoherent

    VII. Expose a serious and widespread mistake in the interpretation of *Bakke*

*This chapter was first published in the *Wayne Law Review* (Wayne State University, Detroit), vol. 26, no. 4 (July 1980). It is reprinted here with the kind permission of that journal.

VIII. Exhibit two important consequences of the *Bakke* decision that have gone largely unrecognized

  IX. Specify one troubling aspect of the *Bakke* decision that deserves more attention than it has received

I turn to each of these in the order given.

I

The *Bakke* decision has been praised as a masterful compromise, slicing the affirmative action baby with "Solomonic" wisdom. In fact the decision is not a compromise at all, not a resolution agreed upon as the result of the conflicting parties giving and getting. Justice Powell's opinion, which occupies the central ground, may reasonably be thought controlling, but its dominance results from the configuration of the several opinions, not from his or anyone else's efforts to straddle the fence. One who reads the several opinions must quickly realize that no one of the nine justices was compromising.   Strong convictions pervade each of the six opinions, and some, particularly those of Justices Marshall and Powell, are written with fervor. We should not wish it otherwise. The job of the Court is not to find a middle way that is politically palatable, but to determine, with intelligence and integrity, what the laws and the Constitution forbid and what they demand. That was done in *Bakke*. It is inappropriate to praise the Court for devising a political compromise that was neither its proper goal nor its actual product.

The decision has been criticized for being indecisive, inconclusive, and confused. It is certainly not indecisive; Allan Bakke won. He was admitted to the University of California Medical School at Davis, which was the central object of his efforts. The special admissions program which, he argued, had denied him the equal protection of the laws, has been eliminated by court order. The decision is not inconclusive with respect to the sphere of university admissions. Principles have been laid down by which college administrators and admissions officers may be firmly guided respecting the permissible uses of race and ethnicity in selecting among applicants for admission. Principles governing the uses of race in other spheres of American life — employment, or housing, for example — are of course not provided by the *Bakke* decision, the setting and scope of which is specifically academic. We should not want the Court to pontificate upon matters not germane to the issues essentially before it, and it would be wrong to criticize the justices for not doing, in this case, what they should not have done. Much more litigation over the uses of race in the public distribution of benefits and opportunities is inevitable; everyone understands that.[7]

Nor is the *Bakke* decision confused. It is complicated, yes; but its complexity may be taken as a mark both of deep division in the nation, and of sophistication within the Court. A decision that did not in any way reflect the agonizing conflicts created by the well-intentioned use of racial preference would be insensitive as well as simplistic. Some on both sides of the case hoped for a clarion call. Wise judges, however, resolve complicated matters with opinions refined enough to deal fairly with those complications, blowing clarions only when they must. We take pride in the Court's restrained effort to do justice rationally.

What is not confused may yet be confusing. The complications of the *Bakke* decision arise not only from the density of the issues, but also from the fact that the disagreements among the nine justices were of different kinds, resulting in the emergence of three groups, opposed yet overlapping in judgment. The central disagreement was on the question of the permissibility of the minority admissions program at the Davis Medical School. A majority found it not permissible. On this issue Bakke plainly won.

There was also sharp division among the justices on the question of whether the uses of race in the Davis admissions system were forbidden by federal statute or by the Constitution.[8] On these issues there was no definitive outcome. Four of the five justices supporting Bakke's admission (Stevens, Stewart, Burger and Rehnquist) relied exclusively on the statute. They deliberately refrained from addressing any constitutional issues because, they argued, it would be out of order to do so when the program in question was so plainly a violation of federal law. The fifth justice supporting Bakke, Powell, did so on constitutional grounds. The four justices holding against Bakke (Brennan, Marshall, Blackmun, and White) also grounded their opinions on the Constitution. The legal bases of the result are therefore mixed, but the central result itself is not.

II

In effect the opinion of Justice Powell decides the case. His opinion is but one of nine, and in itself has no more weight than that of any other member of the Court. Without his opinion, however, the Court is evenly divided: four justices (the Stevens group) support Bakke, condemn the Davis program, and find the Civil Rights Act dispositive; four (the Brennan group) support the regents, approve the Davis program, and find the Civil Rights Act not dispositive. Powell joins each of the two groups on different matters. On the substance of the central issue he agrees with the Stevens group; the Davis program is intolerable and Bakke must be admitted. But he does not agree that this result can be drawn from the Civil Rights Act by itself; on this issue he holds, with the Brennan group, that the case does raise constitutional questions demanding answers. Answering them, he finds the Davis program not merely unlawful, but also a violation of the equal protection clause.

III

Justice Powell's opinion is manifestly *pivotal*. Is it also *controlling?* Do the principles he formulates now govern the conduct of university admissions? I argue that they do, for three reasons.

First, the logic of decision making compels that result. Without Powell's opinion the remaining eight justices are in perfect deadlock, agreeing neither upon the result nor the legal ground. With his opinion the case at hand is resolved. It is no accident that in addition to his own opinion, Justice Powell was chosen to announce the formal judgment of the Court: that the racially preferential admissions program at Davis be struck down.

Each one of the five decisive votes counts equally, of course, and in that sense none is more entitled to control than any other. But the five votes of the majority differ in the following respect. Four strike down the Davis special admissions plan. They formulate no constitutional principles because for them the racial preference at issue was so patently a violation of federal law that no question of constitutional principle was raised by it. The fifth vote, Powell's, is carefully grounded on the Constitution. Powell also does not think the Davis plan lawful. But why it is unlawful or what the scope of the Civil Rights Act may be can only be determined, he contended, by referring to the equal protection clause.

Powell does not conclude that the Constitution requires admissions committees to be absolutely colorblind. He joins the Brennan four in reversing that portion of the California Supreme Court decision which held that race may never be considered in the college admissions process. But Powell also concludes that, to justify any such consideration of race, some constitutional value that can countervail the principle of equal protection of the laws must be adduced. He finds such a value in the First Amendment — guaranteeing freedom of speech and expression — which is greatly served by diversity in college and professional school classes. Powell's opinion restricts the uses of race in college admissions programs very tightly, yet is distinctly more permissive than the opinion of the Stevens four with whom he is allied in substance. To treat the Powell opinion as controlling, therefore — as prudent admissions officers will — is to read the majority view in its most liberal form, specifying most carefully what the Constitution permits.

Second, good authority strongly supports the conclusion that Powell's opinion is controlling. In choosing among competing interpretations of a complicated decision even the most objective scholars will have a natural inclination to select that interpretation most fully suiting their own larger theories or objectives. If, however, those least in sympathy with Powell, those whose larger purposes and general perspectives are sharply opposed to Powell's principles, nevertheless treat his opinion as controlling, or nearly so, one may be reasonably confident that that reading of the whole decision is fair. Such persons and institutions do so treat the Powell opinion.

The American Council on Education (ACE) and the Association of American Law Schools (AALS) are two large and influential institutions that bridle with evident pain against the restrictions upon the uses of race in the Powell opinion. Both submitted briefs, as interested third parties, in vigorous support of the Davis admissions system. Subsequent to the decision they prepared a lengthy joint report which, while struggling to give an accurate and balanced interpretation, is in large part devoted to the consideration of variant admissions systems that might be sustained within the frame of Powell's opinion, while incorporating as much racial preference as possible.[9] Doggedly they searched for a path that would do what the Davis program did, yet would also satisfy Justice Powell's demands that only diversity be the aim of race-consciousness, and that no individual applicant be deprived, by race, of equal opportunity. Their efforts to achieve this reconciliation clearly show that in their judgment the Powell opinion is controlling.

Justice Powell's most thoughtful and most outspoken critic is Prof. Ronald Dworkin of Oxford University; he has attacked the opinion as incoherent and wrongheaded. He has argued at length not only that the Davis program should have been approved, but that Bakke "had no case."[10]

Yet Dworkin comes at last to admit, with no pleasure, that if no one of the justices of the Stevens group takes a less restrictive position regarding the use of race, "Powell's line will become the Supreme Court's line."[11]

Scholarly authority should be viewed with skepticism — but when scholars emerge with an interpretation unfavorable to their own aims their authority is the more trustworthy. That is the present case.

Finally, Powell's opinion does permit certain very narrow uses of race in college admissions. Beyond that, it is widely agreed, we may not now go. But why? A majority of the Supreme Court has not supported his precise restrictions. Indeed, four justices have come down on one side of him and another four, apparently, on the other side. What then obliges us, in now adjusting college admissions practices, to adhere closely to the restrictive side of a decision so nearly balanced?

The answer is rooted in the history of Supreme Court decisions pertaining to race and the equal protection of the laws. The case of Allan Bakke, after all, is but one of a long chain of cases in which the Court has grappled with the uses — evil and honorable — of racial classifications. Some classifications have been permitted under carefully specified circumstances. Most racial and other ethnic classifications used in the distribution of public benefits have been forbidden on the premise that, save in very special circumstances, classification by race is a nasty business, often malicious in intent and usually malignant in result. Our federal courts have therefore repeatedly insisted that certain classifications of persons, by race above all, are *suspect*. Such classifications, to be approved in any public context, must pass the test of *strict scrutiny:* they must be shown *necessary* to achieve a public purpose of *compelling* importance.

Whether the racially preferential admissions system at Davis met that test was the core of the argument in *Bakke*. Powell had no doubt that it did not. The California Supreme Court, deciding earlier for Bakke on all counts (by a six to one majority) on constitutional grounds, also had no doubt that racial preference in university admissions fails that test.[12] The Washington Supreme Court, upholding (in a split decision) a racially preferential admissions system at the University of Washington Law School, did so because it believed that such uses of race did meet the appropriate standard of strict scrutiny.[13] That standard, and the need to apply it wherever programs are proposed that distribute goods by race, is the foundation of Justice Powell's opinion. He writes in a context in which all understand clearly that public bodies must act on the premise that racial classification is permissible only where its object has been proved *compelling*, and the racial instrument proved *necessary* to achieve it. Absent those proofs, racial classification may not be used.

This explains why those who had hoped *Bakke* would give approval to race-conscious admissions are pained by the Powell opinion, yet know themselves governed by it. Institutions do not have the same freedom of action on the two sides of the line Powell has drawn. Toward greater restrictiveness in the use of race there is room for choice; race may be considered in accordance with his restrictions, or we may elect not to consider it at all. Toward greater permissiveness we may not go. The state and its institutions may use race only when the strict scrutiny test has been passed. Race-conscious admissions systems (except to achieve diversity in the student body or to give remedy for injury unlawfully imposed by that school) do not pass that test; Powell makes that very clear.

Powell's opinion governs in this sphere, therefore, because it established constitutional limits. A university administrator may reasonably ask: If we think it wise to use race or national origin in choosing from among those who apply for admission, may we do so? Under what restrictions do we lie in doing so? Powell answered these questions clearly and firmly. He draws the line up to which the use of race in admissions is permitted. In that sense Justice Powell's opinion is controlling.

Speculation about the future path of the Supreme Court in this sphere is intriguing, but has no bearing on the present duties of university admissions officers. It is unsound to argue, as some do, that because the decision in *Bakke* is "fragile," university officials are justified in evading its demands for a while. When the Warren Court (by five to four majority) established the *Miranda* rules, requiring that the rights of an accused be carefully explained to him before interrogation, some contended that the "fragility" of that decision might justify its temporary evasion by police officers. That fragility argument was unacceptable then, and is no less so now. The possibility of future changes in the interpretation of the equal protection clause by the Supreme Court is no excuse for present noncompliance with its present interpretation.

We know, without speculation, what the rules are now, and we have the obligation to comply with the principles of Justice Powell's pivotal opinion. He is, for the present, the gatekeeper for the uses of race in college admissions; no admissions program is permissible if it fails to meet the conditions he laid down.

IV

What conditions are these? They are specific prohibitions respecting both the *aims* of any uses of race in admission, and the *means* with which those aims are pursued.

One narrow purpose only, for Powell, justifies the use of race in college admissions — student diversity. Three other goals often advanced to justify such programs he explicitly rejected.[14]

1. He firmly rejects a university's use of race "to assure within its student body some specified percentage of a particular group merely because of its race or ethnic origin."[15] That is plain racial discrimination, he explains, and on its face is forbidden by the Constitution.

2. A university might conceivably use race in admissions to improve the professional services delivered to communities presently underserved, but only if it could prove that such use of race was necessary for that end — and that, Powell concludes, has not been shown at all.[16] Classification by race for preference in admission presently appears to have no significant effect upon health care delivery; until proved to have such an effect that justification of racial preference must also be rejected.

3. Most importantly, universities may *not* consider race in admissions for the purpose of helping certain groups perceived as victims of societal discrimination. The end in that case may be honorable but, Powell insists, it "does not justify a classification that imposes disadvantages upon persons like respondent [Bakke], who bear no responsibility for whatever harm the beneficiaries of the special admissions program are thought to have suffered."[17] A college has no business, Powell tells us, giving advantages to members of one race at the expense of disadvantaging members of another race, to compensate for damages that the college believes were done by society at large. Powell specifies that racial preference, as a remedy for injustice, may be given only where an institution has been found, by an appropriate authority, to have violated the laws or the Constitution to the harm of identifiable persons. Without that finding, publicly supported institutions have no adequate justification for inflicting the harm on those such as Bakke that racially preferential admissions programs do.[18] Universities do not have the authority to grant, at their pleasure, social remedies for some at the cost of injury to blameless third parties. College admissions committees are neither legislatures nor courts.

The one goal that may justify the use of race in admissions (but does not oblige that use) is "the attainment of a diverse student body,"[19] a First Amendment interest fitting for a university in view of its special functions. Colleges, Powell writes, have "the right to select those students who will contribute the most to 'the robust exchange of ideas',"[20] and they may consider ethnicity in admissions to advance that end — but only that end. It follows that attention to race is permissible only where a broad array of differing characteristics are, in fact, seriously and competitively weighed, "of which racial or ethnic origin is but a single though important element."[21] If the only diversity sought is among ethnic groups, that will not by itself satisfy the First Amendment value which alone may justify a consideration of race normally forbidden. Powell is specific. A college practice sensitive to the race of applicants must be concretely devised to achieve diversity on *many* dimensions. Nor may administrators say that since diversity has long been *one* of our objectives, business may go on as usual. Powell is emphatic. We are permitted attention to race for no reasons *other* than diversity; and our service to diversity, if race is involved, must be more than with our lips.

So much for the one *goal* that may justify the use of race in admissions. The *means* to achieve that goal are also narrowly restricted in the Powell opinion. Whatever system a university employs, it must guarantee that what applies to persons of one race applies equally to persons of every other race. Powell is unequivocal on this point. "The guarantee of equal protection cannot mean one thing when applied to one individual and something else when applied to a person of another color. If both are not accorded the same protection, then it is not equal."[22] Any program, therefore, that utilizes a double standard openly or covertly, or that excludes from the competition for any set of seats or benefits any persons because of their ethnic features fails this constitutional test. It is not saved by the good intentions of its authors. Any "system of allocating benefits and privileges on the basis of skin color and ethnic origin," manifests "inherent unfairness."[23] Applicants for admission must be treated as individuals; any special program dealing with applicants by race exhibits a "fatal flaw."[24] The bearing of these principles on present practice is much greater than has been generally realized. Virtually all special admissions programs have been, in Powell's sense, fatally flawed. Most have maintained double lists and double standards, have categorized by color and ethnic origin to set screening levels and procedures. Many still do exclude whites, or white males, from competition for certain places or other benefits. Most special admissions programs were deliberately devised to deal with people by race. Their objectives, moreover, have commonly been the very ones Powell rejects as impermissible. Most were frankly designed to "assure ... some specified percentage of a particular group merely because of its race or ethnic origin."[25] Whether by "goal" or "quota" (a distinction Justice Powell dismisses as superficial) their targets have been racial or ethnic proportions, an aim Powell finds unconstitutional. Or they have been designed to compensate minorities for societal injury. Or they have been put forward as plans to compensate disadvantaged students, where "disadvantaged" commonly serves as euphemism for black or brown in institutions embarrassed by plain racial discrimination. If Justice Powell's opinion is controlling, special admissions programs may no longer be defended on those grounds. If those are the grounds on which they rest, explicitly or tacitly, such programs, at least in state-supported institutions, are not in compliance with the law of the land.[26]

V

Objections to the Powell opinion are of two kinds. One concerns its merits — whether, after considering the many complexities of racially preferential admission systems, he would have been wiser to adopt some other interpretation of the equal protection clause. Some would wish the governing interpretation more restrictive, precluding all uses of race. Some would wish it less restrictive, permitting more uses of race. But as a matter of rule that issue (until it comes before the Supreme Court, if ever, in another admissions case) is for the present closed.

A second set of objections deal not with the substantive merit of the opinion, but with its suitability as a set of governing principles for college admissions. Here the objections are of two subtypes, the first directed at the *feasibility* of the Powell principles, the second at their *coherence*. I deal with each of these in turn. Feasibility is a proper concern, even for those who do not quarrel with the authority of the principles outlined above. Can professional schools, in view of the enormous number of applicants for very few places, seriously hope to treat each applicant as an individual and not as a member of a group? Is the demand that ethnicity be no more than one of many dimensions on which all applicants are evaluated singly a realistic one? If not, the Powell principles, however right in theory, will be abandoned in practice, not out of defiance but out of practical necessity.

One who has experienced the complexity and burden of the admissions process at a fine college will appreciate the sincerity of this complaint. But it is entirely answerable. In the first place, most colleges and universities are troubled now not by excess of applicants, but by declining applications. Many institutions have faculties and residence halls larger than their present enrollments can justify. The decline is likely to continue. A number of private colleges are closing; some state colleges may follow suit. The problem of feasibility for the Powell principles seems greater than it is because of the general tendency to focus on a few premier colleges and professional schools where, indeed, applications outnumber places by twenty or thirty or more to one.

Even in these premier institutions the Powell principles can be applied by conscientious admissions officers. Objectives other than diversity for the use of race must be eliminated; there is no difficulty in that. But how can administrators achieve diversity without bundling applications in groups: rural and urban, out-of-state and in-state, male and female, over thirty and under thirty, black and brown and white, and so on? The identification of such characteristics will be entailed by a quest for diversity, but the process need not (and now must not) *center* upon the division of applicants into ethnic piles, and it must not be a process whose result is fashioned to reach certain numerical results with respect to those piles. Rather, the primary sorting will be by intellectual attainment or promise (or other characteristics reasonably linked to successful performance in the program in question) with subsidiary sortings by other characteristics that may reasonably be supposed to advance the aims of student diversity. Ethnicity may be one of these. The task is complicated. But the admissions process in such premier institutions must be complicated to be fair. There is nothing in the restrictions Powell lays down that cannot be readily incorporated in a just and rational admissions process.

Would that not impose a terrible burden of inconvenience and cost upon the college? No. Eliminating the double-standard system now commonly in use will effect substantial savings of time and energy. It will reduce the need to hide what is really going on. And treating ethnicity as but one of an array of subsidiary characteristics, most of which are already considered, will introduce no great additional complexity, and can be fitted readily into most race-neutral systems.

But the ultimate answer to the complaint that Powell's principles are burdensome is that, whatever the burden, it must be borne if ethnicity is to be weighed. The Supreme Court has laid down the ways in which race may be used in admissions *if it is to be used at all*. No college is obliged to consider race in admissions; a college may be well advised not to do so. But should it determine that diversity is essential, and that ethnic diversity is vital, the administrative costs in pursuing these goals lawfully may not serve to justify allegedly more convenient "two-class" systems that violate the equal protection guarantee of the Fourteenth Amendment. This judgment was explicitly confirmed by the Federal Court in *Hopwood v. Texas* in 1994:"*Bakke* gives no indication that the burden to a school in implementing a constitutionally valid program should be considered as a reason to diminish the need for individual comparison."

A related objection touches upon the genesis of Powell's principles, and his alleged misapplication of them. The critic contends that Justice Powell mistakenly supposes that admissions criteria arising in an undergraduate context and applicable chiefly to schools of liberal arts must be applied equally to professional schools. So he provides as a model for the consideration of race in a competitive medical school the admissions document from Harvard. Diversity may be an important consideration in undergraduate selection, but for the selection of future doctors or lawyers it has (says this critic) much reduced significance, perhaps none. To permit diversity as the only ground for the use of race in such professional contexts appears to exhibit a naive confusion.

But Powell is neither naive nor confused on this point. Those who register this criticism would do well to study this portion of his opinion more carefully.[27] Powell is fully aware that the need for diversity may vary with context. As former president of the American Bar Association, he may be supposed to have some understanding of the needs of the professional schools; he believes that diversity of students in the class is a desideratum as important in medical and legal education as in the liberal arts. Reasonable persons may differ on this question. Powell's point, however, is that *if* race is to be a factor in professional school admissions it may be a factor for no *other* reasons. Where diversity is believed a dimension of little import to medical or legal education, admissions officers are at liberty to ignore it. Powell, unlike some of his critics, is not searching for a handle with which racial preference can be saved. He is identifying a ground, the only one, upon which the consideration of race is permissible. Student diversity is that ground; ethnicity may enter the admissions process for no other reason.

VI

That Powell's principles do not make sense, that they cannot coherently achieve their aim, is a second subtype of complaint against them. Here also the thrust is practical, the spirit sometimes derisive. Everyone knows that under the language of the Harvard admissions program (appended by Powell to his opinion as an example of an admission system in which race enters only for the achievement of diversity), a college can do precisely what the Davis Medical School did through open racial preference. "The cynical," wrote Justice Blackmun in his dissenting opinion, "may say that under a program such as Harvard's one may accomplish covertly what Davis concedes it does openly."[28] Justice Brennan wrote similarly:

> That the Harvard approach does not also make public the extent of the [racial] preference and the precise workings of the system, while the Davis program employs a specific, openly stated number, does not condemn the latter plan.... It may be that the Harvard plan is more acceptable to the public than is

the Davis "quota." ... But there is no basis for preferring a particular preference program simply because in achieving the same goals that the Davis Medical School is pursuing it proceeds in a manner that is not immediately apparent to the public.[29]

This objection to the Powell principle is profoundly mistaken. Certainly some may cheat. Surely some may, under the cover of a set of approved words, engage in a pattern of action whose hidden principle, if exposed, would be found impermissible. Some say that Harvard itself is guilty of such duplicity. But the example Powell has given is not what Harvard *does*, but what Harvard *says* it does, which is, precisely, to consider race for the attainment of student diversity, and for that purpose only. If in truth a school considers race in admissions for reasons other than diversity it does wrong. We are all expected not to act so as to deceive the courts.

Between the Davis program and the Harvard program, Powell points out, there is this crucial difference: the former exhibits on its face an intent to discriminate by race, the latter does not. It is of course possible to adopt and present to the world language that reveals no discriminatory intent, and then, knowingly but covertly, to act with precisely the intention that is forbidden. The possibility of such subterfuge, although real, proves nothing. Frequent allusion to it suggests — unfairly in my view — that admissions officers are a breed specially prone to employ unlawful chicanery to achieve their ends.

If one college uses the Harvard language honestly, and another college uses the same language to cheat, there is between the two a most important distinction: the *intent* of their administrators. One can picture Justice Powell deliberately looking at us and saying emphatically, as he writes near the conclusion of his long and thoughtful opinion: "And a Court would not assume that a university, professing to employ a non-discriminatory admissions policy would operate it as a cover for the functional equivalent of a quota system. In short, good faith would be presumed."[30] All university officers must hear themselves addressed by these words.[31]

An objection to the Powell principles closely related to this one is presented by Ronald Dworkin, who reasons as follows: to reserve certain places in a medical school entering class for minority applicants only, while opening the remainder to all applicants through competition, is indeed to handicap the white, majority applicant in some degree.[32] But to weigh the blackness or brownness of a minority applicant's skin as a plus factor in a quest for diversity is also to handicap the white, majority applicant to some degree. It cannot matter to the white applicants which way they are handicapped. What is important to them is the degree of the handicap. It may prove more to their advantage to be excluded from the competition for a few seats reserved for minorities than to have a crack at every seat yet be substantially handicapped by the "diversity" factor. Justice Powell thus draws a distinction without a real difference. He thinks that reserving places for minority applicants is unfair, while giving "plus points" for minority group membership is fair. But these are only two ways of doing the same thing. It is the size of the handicap imposed, the critic argues, not the mode of its imposition, that really counts. Dworkin writes:

> Whether an applicant competes for all or only part of the places, the privilege of calling attention to other qualifications does not in any degree lessen the burden of his handicap, or the unfairness of that handicap, if it is unfair at all. If the handicap does not violate his rights in a flexible plan [i.e., one pursuing only diversity], a partial exclusion does not violate his rights under a quota. The handicap and the partial exclusion are only different means of enforcing the same fundamental classifications. In principle, they affect a white applicant in the same way — by reducing his overall chances — and neither is, in any important sense, more "individualized" than the other. The point is not (as Powell once suggested it is) that faculty administering a flexible system may covertly transform it into a quota plan. The point is rather that there is no difference, from the standpoint of individual rights, between the two systems at all.[33]

This complaint appears shrewd, but it rests upon a fundamental misunderstanding of Powell's distinction between the consideration of

race as one factor in a quest for diversity (on the one hand) and plain
racial preference (on the other). *If* our object were simply to favor non-
white applicants by imposing a "handicap" on white applicants, there
are many ways this could be accomplished. It can, of course, be accomplished by giving enough "plus points" for blackness or brownness to
achieve the results desired. Any racial proportions antecedently chosen
can be obtained by the manipulation of the diversity factor as well as by
reserving places. But that use of diversity is fraudulent. To use diversity
in that way is to do, under the cover of nondiscriminatory language, just
what has been forbidden. Once we decide to *handicap* one racial group,
the instrument is of no great consequence, save that some instruments
are more detectable than others. But imposing a handicap on any ethnic
group is precisely what is *not* permitted. Dworkin's reasoning reveals
what *his* objective is: to save racial preference. But the intention to do
that, *either* by reserving places or by manipulating the diversity factor,
has been precluded by the Powell principles. Seeking diversity honestly
is one thing; scheming under the name of diversity is another. Again,
intent makes all the difference.

The critic may try to avoid this moral response by arguing that a
handicap is simply a handicap — taken descriptively it involves no intent whatever. If minorities are advantaged in the quest for diversity
because they are fewer, the majority is that far handicapped. That
handicap (he may say) is intrinsically no different from one imposed
deliberately by reserving places, irrespective of intent. If the degree of
overall disadvantage is the same, intent makes no difference. The critic
maintains that Powell is simply confused in believing that one system
hurts the white majority unfairly while the other does not. Either both
systems are unfair or neither is.

This version of the complaint is obtuse. An applicant is not treated
unfairly when the characteristics that she or he does or does not in fact
possess are weighed, along with those of all other applicants, in a system
reasonably designed to choose the best entering class. If, in a medical
school, diversity really is one consideration in the overall selection of the
entering class, being in certain categories (having a rural background or
indigent parents, being an experienced engineer or a Hawaiian, etc.)

might reasonably be considered in one's favor, in small degree, after more fundamental intellectual characteristics had left some difficult choices before the admitting committee. When the unusual are favored, at the margins, the usual are disfavored that far. Everyone understands that, and the good reasons for it. No one, in that circumstance, is done injustice. But when the applicants are first categorized by race, and all members of one race are favored simply because of their race, while the members of other races or ethnic groups are disfavored by the same device, the matter is wholly different — as our courts have made very plain. That *is* unjust and is not to be tolerated.

In an honest quest for diversity one's race may be considered in one's favor as an applicant. But so also might one's family background be considered, or one's artistic accomplishments, or economic circumstances — or any other characteristics one possesses that may contribute to the larger goals that diversity itself serves. Each applicant is just what he or she is — exhibiting just his or her own degree of poise or poverty or whatever. There is all the difference in the world between disadvantage arising out of ordinariness, a marginal handicap every white male has the opportunity to overcome by exhibiting other features that enable him to contribute richly to the class, and disfavor flatly imposed because of one's race. Even if the degree of disadvantage were to prove the same (a most improbable outcome unless the diversity factor were being manipulated), the ground of the disadvantage matters a very great deal: racial preference is unfair in a way that advantage from unusualness is not.

Nor may it be argued that, although honestly seeking diversity, a scheme may be devised to consider only race because the other elements of diversity — sex, age, geographical origins, etc. — are incorporated without special attention. Diversity, this argument supposes, simply boils down to *racial* diversity. This objection will not do because, if diversity really is the honest aim of an individualized process, every applicant must have at least the equal opportunity to strengthen the case for his or her admission on the basis of diversity manifested in other ways. To provide that opportunity a deliberate and conscious, not incidental, attention must be paid to at least a substantial range of applicant differences. The precise boundaries of the range may vary, but without explicit attention to manifold factors of which race is but one, diversity will not have been employed in such a way as to meet the demand of the Fourteenth Amendment — that no person, viewed as an individual, may be denied the equal protection of the laws.

Powell's principles are distinguished at bottom from attempted obfuscation or evasion by *intent*. He expects universities to act *in good faith;* this expectation cannot be emphasized too strongly. When explicit Supreme Court rules permit the use of race in admission only for certain purposes, and only in certain ways, institutions of higher learning have a powerful obligation to comply with the spirit of those rules. What we *intend* is part of the *act* governed by those principles.

In universities, of all places, intellectual integrity and civic responsibility must be sensitively and concretely honored. Devious schemes through which a college may satisfy the letter while evading the substance of its obligations are clearly not tolerable. Nor may a university respond to the law with procedures designed to obscure or mislead. Compliance must be unambiguous and forthright; for a university nothing less will be compliance in "good faith."

Universities that do not live up to this expectation will fail in their duty. They will also be acting imprudently. College officers who hide impermissible ends with hypocritical language may be obliged to answer for it. Admissions systems cannot be permanently shrouded in secrecy. Duplicity will not prove very hard to expose. Institutions that connive to avoid the law will bring upon themselves the policing of their intra-institutional processes by government in ways more painful than any our universities have yet experienced, to the serious detriment of their larger purposes.[34]

VII

A serious mistake about the *Bakke* decision has been very widely promoted by careless reporting — the belief that the *Bakke* decision, while striking down "rigid quotas," permits most university programs, giving minority preferences without quotas, to go on as usual. That, as we have seen in reviewing Powell's principles, is simply not the case.

State-supported racially preferential admissions systems, whether incorporating quotas, or goals, or using any other language, have been found impermissable. What was condemned by a majority of the Court in this case is not merely the use of quotas, but the system of favoritism by race of which it was the tool. Any tool having the same object is subject to the same condemnation.[35]

What explains this and other common distortions? Partly, perceptions are being colored by desire. When those doing the interpreting have themselves been long engaged in the practice now outlawed, they are tempted to construe critical court decisions very leniently. But the authority of persons who interpret a rule proscribing conduct in which they have been engaged is highly suspect. We should as well have court rulings protecting the rights of criminal defendants given their definitive interpretation by police chiefs and associations of prosecuting attorneys.

Is the *Bakke* decision, then, a serious blow to affirmative action in this sphere? That depends upon what one means by "affirmative action." If one means by it, as many now do, racial preference for minorities as such, the answer is yes. Everyone, minorities most of all, should give thanks for that. Institutionalized preference by race is not only unjust, but seriously damaging to those whom it purports to aid.

If by "affirmative action" we mean, however, what the phrase was originally intended to convey — the taking of positive steps to insure that earlier discriminatory practices would be uprooted — the *Bakke* decision will advance, not deter, such action. To recruit from all sources fairly; to test fairly and without racial bias; to weigh merits (intellectual or other) on an individual basis, with all handicap flowing from race scrupulously eliminated — these affirmative steps the *Bakke* decision supports without dissent. It was not affirmative action in this wholesome, impartial sense that was at issue in this case. Favor by race was the issue; it was here condemned.

VIII

The long-term ramifications of the *Bakke* decision have been underestimated. Two themes embodied in it will reverberate for many years to come, contributing substantially to our constitutional history.

The first of these bears chiefly upon colleges and universities. They are forbidden, by *Bakke,* from using admission standards to achieve societal objectives that are not properly in their sphere. Justice Powell writes:

> We have never approved a classification that aids persons perceived as members of relatively victimized groups at the expense of other innocent individuals in the absence of judicial, legislative or administrative findings of constitutional or statutory violations.... Without such findings of constitutional or statutory violations it cannot be said that the government has any greater interest in helping one individual than in refraining from harming another.

> Petitioner [the University of California] does not purport to have made, and is in no position to make, such findings. Its broad mission is education, not the formulation of any legislative policy or the adjudication of particular claims of illegality.[36]

By this firm restriction we — I speak for the academic world of which I am a member — are done a great service. Universities have repeatedly and rightly argued that legislatures should not seek to use us, deform us, to achieve political objectives foreign to our essential purposes. It is incumbent upon us to restrain ourselves from that same perversion. Restorative justice — taking from some and giving to others to right social wrong — is an enterprise universities and their admissions committees are not likely to be very good at. But even if our admissions officers were as well trained as judges, that is not our proper role. We are neither judges nor legislators. It is simply wrong for us to exercise our powers as though we were, conducting admissions policies not merely as a college function but as a device to correct social wrongs that we decide deserve remedy, at whatever costs to other parties we deem reasonable.

If we make it our business to set things right in the world, what may we expect from legislatures when we decline to serve as their political instrument in some other context they deem pressing? Shall we tell them then that ours is an educative mission, and that we ought not be made tools of social policy? Can we then expect to be taken seriously? Once the principle is accepted — indeed urged by us! — that we, the universities, are a proper court in equity, to take from X and give to Y to remedy historical social wrongs, we will face a host of moral and political claims, many entirely reasonable, to which we shall be obliged to respond. What a dreadful service that will be, both to education and to justice. Justice Powell, in forbidding this course to us, saves us from our overzealous selves. He takes the nonpolitical nature of higher education seriously, as we ought always do. His protection of the universities from self-assignment into political or juridical service is likely to prove, in the years ahead, a feature of the *Bakke* decision for which all will be grateful.

A second neglected aspect of *Bakke* is the understanding implicit in it throughout that persons like Allan Bakke, when displaced or disadvantaged by a racially preferential system, are *injured*. They are done *constitutional* injury in being deprived of what they ordinarily would not have been deprived of under the Constitution.

All nine Supreme Court justices are in accord on this, not just the four justices of the Stevens group, not just they and Powell. The Brennan group, although approving the Davis plan, agrees throughout that Bakke was substantially hurt, and that his hurt was serious enough to require very solid justification. Justice Blackmun, one of the anti-Bakke four, writes in his separate opinion that he looks forward to the time when "persons will be regarded as persons and discrimination of the type we address today [i.e., against Bakke] will be an ugly feature of history ... that is behind us."[37]

Reverse discrimination, in sum, is real and bad. In *Bakke*, for the first time, the Supreme Court recognized that reality explicitly, and made very clear to all that such discrimination, however well-intended, is not to be taken lightly. Until *Bakke* there were many who assumed that, so long as intentions were good, universities could act pretty much as they thought just, giving and taking as they pleased. Not so. There are those who believe that some reverse discrimination can be justified. But the lasting impact of the *Bakke* decision, practical and symbolic, is this: the advocates of racial discrimination face a mighty burden of proof. When, as in most contexts, that burden cannot be met in court, colleges and universities are well advised to avoid scrupulously all preference by race.

IX

Finally, there is one troubling aspect of the *Bakke* decision that flows directly from the Powell principles. It may be taken to proffer an invitation that could lead to most unhappy practices. We are told that the Constitution permits the consideration of race in admissions for the sake of diversity to further the First Amendment interest in free expression. That being so, it would appear that other suspect classifications — by political affiliation or by religion — may also be used for the sake of diversity. This is a disquieting result. Should the fact that one is a Republican or a Socialist, Catholic or Jew, be allowed to count in the distribution of opportunities? Even if by invoking such considerations we could increase diversity in some contexts, they surely ought never be factors in the apportionment of any public goods. History gives us strong reasons to conclude that the uses of such classifications, even for putatively honorable goals, invite disaster. We forswear them. For the same reasons, even if *Bakke* permits us to promote diversity in a student body, it will be the part of wisdom to forswear the use of race as well.

NOTES

1. *Regents of The University of California v. Bakke*, 438 U.S. 265 (1978).

2. Section 601, Civil Rights Act of 1964, 78 Stat. 252, 42 U.S.C. Sec. 2000(d).

3. *Regents v. Bakke,* 438 U.S. 265, 403 (1978).

4. 438 U.S. 265 (1978). This essay was written in 1977, before this reference could have been inserted, of course.

5. 507 P. 2d 1180.

6. *Regents of the University of California v. Bakke*, 438 U.S. 265 (1978).

7. A precise formulation of the standard by which the uses of racial classifications are to be judged in general was later provided by the Supreme Court in *Wygant v. Jackson Board of Education*, 476 U.S. 267 (1986). That standard is discussed in detail below, pages 179-82.

8. Title VI of the Civil Rights Act of 1964 § 601, 42 U.S.C. § 200d (1970) provides that: "No person in the United States shall, on the grounds of race, color, or national origin, be excluded from participation in, be denied the benefits of, or be subjected to discrimination under any program or activity receiving Federal financial assistance." The U.S. Constitution, Amendment XIV, provides in part: "No State shall ... deny to any person within its jurisdiction the equal protection of the laws."

9. American Council on Education and Association of American Law Schools, "The Bakke Decision: Implication for Higher Education Admissions "(1978).

10. Dworkin, "Why Bakke Has No Case," *New York Review of Books*, Nov 10, 1977, p. 11.

11. Dworkin, "The Bakke Decision: Did it Decide Anything?" *New York Review of Books*, Aug. 17, 1978, p. 20.

12. *Bakke v. Regents of the Univ. of Cal.*, 553 P. 2d 1152 (1976).

13. *DeFunis v. Odegaard*, 507 P. 2d 1169 (1973).

14. 438 U.S. at 305-11.

15. Ibid., p. 307.

16. Ibid., pp. 310-11.

17. Ibid., p. 310.

18. Ibid., pp. 307-09.

19. Ibid., p. 311.

20. Ibid., p. 313.

21. Ibid., p. 315.

22. Ibid., pp. 289-90.

23. Ibid., p. 294 n. 34.

24. Ibid., p. 320.

25. Ibid., p. 307.

26. *Bakke* still governs. In 1994 a federal court struck down a racially preferential admissions program at the law school of the University of Texas, under which minority and nonminority applicants were evaluated separately, minority applicants competing only against other minority applicants, very much as had been done at the Davis Medical School twenty years before. The Court wrote: "Two wrongs do not make a right; nor does blatant discrimination cure the ills of past discrimination. Indeed, affirmative action that ignores the importance of individual rights may further widen the gap between the races ... and create racial hostility. The only proper means of assuring that all important societal interests are met, whether in the context of creating diversity or redressing the ill effects of past wrongs, is to provide a procedure or method by which the qualifications of each individual are evaluated and compared to those of all other individuals in the pool, whether minority or nonminority" *(Cheryl Hopwood, et al. v. State of Texas*, U.S. District Court, Western District of Texas; Memorandum Opinion, p. 64, 13 August 1994).

27. 438 U.S. 265, at 311-19.

28. Ibid., p. 406.

29. Ibid., p. 379.

30. Ibid., pp. 318-19.

31. This passage has been grossly misinterpreted by some as an invitation to colleges to go underground, through an indirect assurance that the courts will not inspect their processes. The central holding of *Bakke* is *not* (as one anonymous attorney suggested) that schools are supposed to lie about what they are doing with respect to minority admissions. Many do lie. But nothing could be further from the spirit of Justice Powell's opinion than that. One who reads deviousness into a passage designed to warn against deviousness reveals the nature of his or her own intentions.

32., Dworkin, "The Bakke Decision," pp. 22-23.

33. Ibid., p. 23.

34. The accountability to which college administrators would be subject was greatly overestimated at the time this was written. In fact, duplicity and secrecy have pervaded affirmative action programs in the years since *Bakke*. Powell's principles, clearly formulated as part of the law of the land, have been defied, or knowingly ignored, by admissions officers and their superiors contending with immediate political pressures. College officers ought to have been held accountable for widespread deception and occasional dishonesty, but generally that has not happened. At least, it has not happened yet..

35. Some accounts of the outcome in *Bakke* are dumbfounding. Here is one example from the work of a prominent Harvard professor of law, Lawrence Tribe, an ardent supporter of racial preference in admissions. Of the *Bakke* decision, he wrote, "The Court thus approved the kind of affirmative action used by most American colleges and universities, while striking down only the unusually mechanical approach taken by the Medical School of the University of California at Davis" [L. Tribe, *American Constitutional Law* 88 (Supp. 1979)].

36. 438 U.S. at 307-9.

37. Ibid., p. 403.

C

Racial Preference in Employment

Steelworkers v. Weber

Differential treatment on the basis of race and ethnicity remains exceedingly common. Many Americans feel its impact every day in their workplaces. Such preference would certainly be held discriminatory and unlawful if blacks or other minorities were disadvantaged by it. What accounts for the fact that the preference is thought acceptable when it is those in the majority who are disadvantaged? One cause of this apparent acceptability is the 1979 Supreme Court decision in a battle between a workman, Brian Weber, and the combined power of the giant firm that employed him and the giant union of which he was a member. The two essays that follow, both many times reprinted, explore the issues of the *Weber* case, and the reasoning of the remarkable decision to which it led.[1]

Brian Weber came to court for reasons much like those of Allan Bakke and Marco DeFunis. He was white, as they were; he was denied an opportunity to which he was clearly entitled, as they were. In Weber's case, however, what he was deprived of would *indubitably* have been his had he been black — or almost any color other than white. A plainer and more indisputable case of reverse discrimination by race would be difficult to imagine.

What he was deprived of was the chance to advance from menial employment to a craft employment — an opportunity Weber had been five years working for. There was, however, little empathy for him among many sophisticated folks who had complained strenuously about racially preferential affirmative action when its unfairness was evident in medical school and law school admissions. Ultimately Weber lost, and with him vast numbers of working-class Americans lost as well. The *Weber* decision has probably done more than any other in this century to set back the cause of racial justice in America.

The facts are recounted in the first essay below. The nub of the case was this: two separate lists, one of whites and one of minorities, were maintained (by the company and the union) for the allocation of advancement opportunities in a steel plant in Grammercy, Louisiana — and preference was expressly given to those on the minority list. Passed over only because he was white, Weber brought his complaint to the Federal District Court in New Orleans where he won his suit, hands down. Racial discrimination on the job is prohibited by the Civil Rights Act of 1964 unambiguously and explicitly. Racial discrimination was openly practiced by the employer (Kaiser Aluminum) and by the union (United Steelworkers) in this plant; they did not deny that Weber had been denied an employment opportunity only because of his racial classification under that "affirmative action" program. So he had to win. The decision of the court was straightforward and forceful.

His employer and union appealed to the federal circuit court. The affirmative action scheme at issue — its undisputed details were set forth in the contract between them — were (they believed) good for business and good for the country. Of course they lost again. They *had* to lose; it did not require great depth or learning to see how ineluctably the words of the law applied to the facts of Weber's complaint.

A great deal was at stake in this case. Major corporations and unions, like Kaiser and the Steelworkers, long complicit in schemes designed to give racial preference, feared for the future of preferential affirmative action. Describing themselves in modern doublethink as "equal opportunity employers," firms like the Kaiser Aluminum Corporation were in fact (and commonly are still) *un*equal opportunity employers. Convinced that their ends justified their deliberate discriminatory practices, the union and Kaiser jointly appealed again to the United States Supreme Court. The first essay below, "Why Racial Preference Is Illegal and Immoral," was published in *Commentary* while the case was still under deliberation.

To give the Supreme Court a handle with which preferential affirmative action in the workplace might be saved, third party "friends of the court" — employers, unions, even the ACLU — concocted every conceivable defense. But no legal twist or turn, no maneuver however devious, could evade the plain words of the Civil Rights Act, its inescapable applicability to the case at hand, or the plain truth of the racial discrimination to which Weber had been subjected. All the arguments supporting the preference that are even remotely plausible are examined in this essay; every one is found wanting.

Yet Weber did lose. The Supreme Court reversed the decision of the lower courts. It approved the affirmative action scheme implemented by Kaiser and the union in what is surely one of the most unsupportable and poorly reasoned decisions in its history. Justice Powell would almost certainly have resisted this result, but he had been too ill to participate; Justice Stevens would likely have condemned the result, but an earlier personal association with one of the law firms involved had obliged him to recuse himself. The five to two reversal of the courts below was authored by Justice Brennan. Scornful dissenting opinions were registered by both Justice Rehnquist and Chief Justice Burger.

Injustice was done by this decision to Brian Weber; uncountable injustices to uncountable factory and office workers in like circumstances were ratified and encouraged by it. The majority of the Court at that time had clearly decided to do whatever was necessary to avoid striking down an affirmative action plan giving preference to minorities in industrial employment.[2] They were determined to sustain that preference and did so, although doing so required them to defend an interpretation of the Civil Rights Act that strains credulity beyond its limit.

Here follow the plain words of Title VII:

It shall be an unlawful employment practice for an employer —

(1) to fail or refuse to hire or discharge any individual, or otherwise to discriminate against any individual with respect to his compensation, terms, conditions, or privileges of employment, because of such individual's race, color, religion, sex, or national origin; or

(2) to limit, segregate, or classify his employees or applicants for employment in any way which would deprive any individual of employment opportunities or otherwise adversely affect his status as an employee, because of such individual's race, color, religion, sex, or national origin.[3]

Did the Congress, when it made these words law in June of 1964, intend to *permit* some kinds of racial preference for some minority groups? The answer is no, categorically and indisputably no — as the reader of the second essay below, "Justice Debased," is likely to agree.

The issues presented in this case will sooner or later confront the Supreme Court once again; *Weber* will probably be overturned one day. But that day may come later rather than sooner; until then the abuse of justice in the *Weber* case will continue to exact a heavy price from working men and women in America.

4

Why Racial Preference Is
Illegal and Immoral*

The role of race in assuring social justice is again squarely before the Supreme Court in a case whose full and revealing name is: *Kaiser Aluminum & Chemical Corporation and United Steelworkers of America, AFL-CIO, v. Brian F. Weber, individually and on behalf of all other persons similarly situated.*

Weber, a white unskilled steelworker, is Bakke's analogue. The Steelworkers Union and Kaiser Aluminum are not the only forces against him. The United Auto Workers and the United Mine Workers, the National Education Association, the Coalition of Black Trade Unionists, and assorted other unions are against him. The American Civil Liberties Union is against him. Even the United States government is formally aligned against him. On Weber's side is the Anti-Defamation League of B'nai B'rith (with some associated non-Jewish ethnic groups) and, according to repeated surveys, an overwhelming majority of the American population, including a majority of the black population.

---

* This chapter was first published in *Commentary*, vol. 67, no. 6 (June 1979). It is reprinted here with the kind permission of the editors.

But the issues at stake here, touching the most fundamental rights of individual persons, are not to be decided by counting noses. The chief things going for Weber are the Fourteenth Amendment of the U.S. Constitution, the Civil Rights Act of 1964 as amended, and sound moral principles. Thrice armed is he who hath his quarrel just.

Weber has thus far been victorious, both in the Federal District Court, and in the Federal Court of Appeals (5th Circuit, New Orleans). His formidable opponents find it difficult to overcome the plain words of the law applied straightforwardly to the undisputed facts of his case. The law (Title VII of the Civil Rights Act, Sec. 703) forbids flatly all discrimination in employment because of race.[4]

Beyond any possible doubt (as we shall see) Weber was discriminated against by his employer, was classified by race, and had his status as an employee adversely affected because of his race. That the employment practice through which this was done is a violation of this federal law is an ineluctable conclusion of any rational mind.

Is it not remarkable, then, that unions, industry, and government should now join in the effort to persuade the Supreme Court to evade this conclusion? Weber's opponents are neither foolish nor evil. They seek to surmount the legal barriers to racially discriminatory treatment in order to achieve objectives they think good. Reflection upon this case will oblige the Supreme Court — and all citizens who would reach thoughtful judgment on these issues — to reconsider the merit of those objectives, and to appraise the means by which they have been pursued.

The *Bakke* case, and the *DeFunis* case before it, dealt with racially discriminatory practices in professional-school admissions — a matter for which the middle classes have, rightly, a tender concern. *Weber* deals with racial discrimination in blue-collar employment. The injury done Brian Weber was at least as great as that done Allan Bakke, and the class Weber formally represents is very much larger, if less articulate, than that directly affected by racially preferential school admissions. It is disturbing, therefore, that the voices raised in behalf of Weber's rights, and the rights of literally millions of individual citizens in like circumstances, were so painfully few. Silence now from quarters that were outspoken in opposition to racial preference in higher education may lead some to infer that self-interest, more than justice, was what motivated that earlier concern.

In both spheres, school admissions and industrial employment, the same issues arise: in the allocation of scarce goods, may one's race count in one's favor? If ever, when? In *Bakke* a racially preferential admission system at the University of California Medical School at Davis was struck down, but attention to race in the admissions process was held permissible within very narrow limits: to advance the diversity of an entering class, or to remedy the condition of specific persons who had been discriminated against by the school using the racial instrument. *Weber* is different in several important respects. Here the factor of diversity does not enter; here matters pertaining to intellectual qualifications are replaced by matters pertaining to seniority. Here the stakes are greater and the underlying moral issues are presented more cleanly.

I

This is what happened. Kaiser (Kaiser Aluminum & Chemical Corporation) and the union (United Steelworkers of America, AFL- CIO) sought to increase the number of minority workers in the skilled crafts at Kaiser's Grammercy, Louisiana, plant. To this end, in a 1974 collective-bargaining agreement, they changed the system selecting employees for on-the-job training. Entrance ratios, by race, were established for acceptance in the job-training program. For each white worker admitted one minority worker would be admitted, until the percentage of minority craft workers in the Grammercy plant roughly approximated the percentage of the minority population in the surrounding area, then about 39 percent. Dual seniority lists were established, one black and one white; each two vacancies were filled with the persons at the top of the two racially distinct lists.

It was an inevitable result of this system that some employees would be favored because of their race, and some would be injured because of theirs. Brian Weber was refused admission to the job-training program although his seniority was higher than that of some employees from the other racial list who were admitted. Weber sued on his own behalf and on behalf of all nonminority employees who applied for on-the-job training at the Grammercy plant after that labor agreement was signed.

A racially preferential scheme for allocating on-the-job training opportunities, he argued, is a clear violation of the Federal Civil Rights Act.

One portion of Title VII deals explicitly with on-the-job training programs. That portion (subsection (d) of Sec. 703) reads as follows:

> It shall be an unlawful employment practice for any employer, labor organization, or joint labor-management committee controlling apprenticeship or other training or retraining, *including on-the-job training programs,* to discriminate against any individual because of his race, color, religion, sex, or national origin in admission to, or employment in, any program established to provide apprenticeship or other training.[5]

Was it prescience that caused the Congress to formulate this ban with language so precisely covering the case at hand? Not at all. Title VII had as its purpose the elimination of all ethnic favoritism in employment; there had been, at the time of its adoption, plenty of experience of the ways in which racial prejudice can be given effect, one of the commonest being in job-training programs. In that form as in all forms, said the Congress in effect, racial discrimination in employment is no longer permissible.

How can Kaiser and the union (and the U.S. Department of Justice) reasonably contend that their scheme was nevertheless lawful or fair? They argue that the law, properly interpreted, does not forbid this variety of racial preference, which they think justified by our history of discrimination. They argue that if the pursuit of pressing social objectives now imposes incidental costs on individuals, Weber and his like are the right persons to bear those costs. They argue that they were ordered, by the U.S. government, to introduce racial preference of precisely this kind. And they argue that Weber wasn't really injured by this program at all. I examine these arguments in turn.

II

Kaiser and the union [the first argument begins] reached an agreement that was fully in accord with the spirit of Title VII. Theirs was a voluntary effort to bring a greater number of minority workers into the skilled crafts. Congress never intended to forbid such voluntary efforts.

If now the product of such agreements, reached through collective bargaining, is struck down, the cause of racial justice will have been dealt a devastating blow.

We must [this argument continues] permit management and labor to join, as in this case, to correct a racially unbalanced situation flowing from the historical and social realities of American life. Blacks have been discriminated against, cruelly and consistently, by industry and by unions. Now an effort is being made to give redress. It is an ironic inversion of the Civil Rights Act to use that Act to forbid the only instruments that may effectively achieve its own intended result.

It is true [the argument proceeds] that Title VII specifies that preferential treatment of racial minorities is not required [Section 703(j)]. But that is not to say it is forbidden. When its aim is precisely that of the Act itself, it must not be forbidden. Weber relies upon the narrowest construction of the words and misses, inadvertently or deliberately, the remedial spirit of the law and of the Kaiser program here in question.

The argument of Weber's opponents boils down to this: If the Court agrees that racial quotas such as this one are discriminatory, we will be kept from doing what many of us think it is necessary to do, and do quickly, in the interest of long-term justice. Let it be understood, therefore [the argument concludes], that this quota, although it does of course distinguish by race, and does, admittedly, give favor by race, does not 'discriminate' by race in the bad sense that the law condemns. When we come to realize that some plans for racial balance, while they may have adverse effects upon some white workers, are nevertheless justified by pressing societal needs, we will also see what interpretation of the law is required by justice.

To put the argument plainly is to see both its earnestness and its frailty. The requirements of the Civil Rights Act, which were intended to give concrete meaning to the constitutional demand that no citizen be denied the equal protection of the laws, were aimed at bringing to a final halt all formal discrimination on the basis of race — and color, religion, sex, and national origin. It certainly was not intended, and it obviously was not formulated, to forbid only such racial discrimination as employers and unions thought objectionable, while permitting any racially discriminatory schemes that employers and unions might by agreement find worthy or convenient. What the employer and the union happen to prefer, whether their motives be honorable or crass, has absolutely no weight, says the law in effect, against the *right* of each individual citizen to be dealt with, in matters pertaining to employment, without regard to race, religion, or national origin.

III

But that cannot be the correct interpretation of the law, answer Kaiser and the union in chorus, because the Supreme Court has several times, in the years since, recognized the lawfulness and wisdom of racially preferential employment schemes. Indeed, our federal courts have *ordered* the imposition of such racial preference in some cases! So it is clearly false that *all* racial preference has been forbidden. If that is so, then it is not obviously true that this scheme for racial preference has been forbidden.

This rejoinder brings us to the core, legal and moral, of the controversy in *Weber*. What kind of attention to race does the Civil Rights Act (and, indirectly, the Constitution) permit? And what should it permit? In the *Bakke* case, this question was complicated by the entry of First Amendment considerations pertaining to the robust exchange of ideas in the classroom; the holding in *Bakke* was tangled by the fact that Justice Powell's pivotal opinion, although condemning racial favoritism, permits attention to race to advance diversity among an entering school class. Here, in *Weber*, such First Amendment considerations are totally absent. What, if anything, remains to justify race-conscience employment practices?

There is a clear and honorable answer to this question, given forcefully by federal courts at every level. Title VII of the Civil Rights Act forbids all deliberate discrimination by race, save only in cases where racial classification is absolutely essential to give redress to *identifiable persons* injured by racial discrimination *and where the injury done them was done by the same party upon whom the numerical program is imposed.* One purpose only may justify numerical schemes using racial categories: the *making whole* of those to whom redress for racial injury is specifically owed, by those who owe it.

For example: the known victims of racial discrimination by a trucking company have been held entitled, as a remedy, to a place in the seniority lists of that company that would have been theirs if they had not been so victimized. To put them now in as good a place as they would have been in but for the discriminatory employment practice from which they can be shown to have suffered, it may be necessary to attend to race. Only in that way can the victims be made whole; they would otherwise remain subordinate to persons who, had it not been for racial discrimination in that company, would now be their subordinates.[6] In such cases, the racially oriented remedy cannot be refused on the ground that the effect on other employees is adverse because, although the employees who suffer from the imposition of the plan are very possibly innocent themselves, they have clearly benefited, in seniority, from the specific discriminatory practice for which remedy is being given. Race- conscious remedies for the victims of illegal discrimination are lawful, consistent with Title VII, only in such circumstances.

Weber and Kaiser Aluminum are in no such circumstances. Upon examining the facts, the federal district court found that Kaiser had not been guilty of any discriminatory hiring or promotion at its Grammercy plant. Kaiser's industrial-relations superintendent at that plant testified that, prior to 1974, Kaiser had vigorously sought trained black craftsmen from the general community. Advertising in periodicals and newspapers that were published primarily for black subscribers, Kaiser found it very difficult to attract black craftsmen. The evidence established two key facts:

1. Kaiser had a serious, operational, no-discrimination hiring policy at its Grammercy plant from the day of the plant's opening in 1958.

2. Not one of the black employees who were offered on-the-job training opportunities over more senior white employees (pursuant to the 1974 Labor Agreement) had been subject to any prior employment discrimination by Kaiser.

From these facts it is an inescapable conclusion that the quota system at Kaiser's Grammercy plant was not an instrument for the specific redress of persons injured by racial discrimination there; it was un-abashed racial preference aimed at numerical proportions having noth-ing to do with past conduct in that plant. Such preference Title VII outlaws. The distinction, between impermissible racial preference and permissible remedy for past discrimination, is put eloquently by the Fifth Circuit Court of Appeals in affirming Weber's rights:

> If employees who have been arbitrarily favored are deprived of benefits capriciously conferred on them in order that those who were arbitrarily deprived may receive what they should, in fair-ness, have had to begin with, no law is violated. This is so even if both the class whose rights are restored and the class required to "move over" are defined by race — if the original arbitrari-ness was defined in that manner. And the reason is that no one is being favored or disfavored, advantaged or injured, under these circumstances *because* of race; rather, those who have been unjustly deprived receive their due and those who have been arbitrarily favored surrender some of the largesse capriciously conferred on them. That these consequences end by race is a mere incident of the fact that they began that way.[7]

But those who were favored by race at Weber's expense were admit-tedly not the victims of such original arbitrariness. The Circuit Court's support of Weber is therefore categorical: "[U]nless a preference is en-acted to restore employees to their rightful places within a particular employment scheme it is strictly forbidden by Title VII."[8]

IV

Since it is clear that the beneficiaries of this racial program were not victims of Kaiser's previous discrimination, and equally clear that the use of dual seniority lists is an explicit effort to favor blacks over whites, the defenders of this program are compelled to resort to a different justification — past "societal discrimination."

We cannot deny [say the defenders in effect] that the two-list system deliberately favors one race over another. But we do deny that favoring this race at this time in this country is unfair. We contend that, in view of the historical discrimination against blacks (and other minorities), the racially preferential device now before us is entirely justifiable. It is justifiable not only because blacks have been so long oppressed, but also because as a corollary, whites have been unfairly *advantaged* by racial prejudice. The white employees of Kaiser who are passed over by this plan may indeed be innocent of any racial discrimination themselves, but they have been and are the beneficiaries of racial discrimination by others. This is the heart of our justification. Favor to blacks now is just because of the favor whites have enjoyed until now.

This is the principled argument by which many without selfish interests in these programs are persuaded that they are fair. One might have expected the American Civil Liberties Union, for example, to spring to the defense of the rights of an almost defenseless individual. Instead it joined the forces against Weber; the ACLU convinced itself that his rights had not really been infringed, even though he suffered deliberate disadvantage because of race. How can that be?

Racial preference in employment is justified [the argument proceeds] when it is a response to the morally legitimate demand that the *lingering effects* of past racial discrimination be remedied. The lingering effects of historical oppression include the continuing losses of decent employment, together with the money and status that it brings. But the same historical race prejudice that has systematically blocked minorities from access to decent jobs has conferred an involuntary benefit upon whites because, while the number of desirable jobs remains roughly constant, the elimination of competition by minority workers results in the availability of desirable jobs for whites in generous disproportion to their numbers. This benefit is conferred even upon those whites who may, in fact, deplore the prejudice from which they gain. Yet they did gain. Now, with racial quotas favoring blacks, they lose. Their present loss is morally justified by their earlier gain. The primary target of racially preferential programs should be those guilty of past unlawful discrimination, of course. But where those guilty parties simply cannot be identified or are no longer available to make restitution, a secondary but legitimate target is the unjust enrichment attributable to that racial discrimination. Quota plans, like the one devised by Kaiser and the union, seek to redistribute that unjust enrichment. Seen in this light, their fairness — the moral rightness of racial preference for societal rebalancing — cannot be denied. So reasoned the ACLU explicitly, and many other honest citizens implicitly, in giving pained approval to race quotas.

The argument fails utterly upon inspection. It relies upon a premise that is clearly and admittedly false in the *Weber* case and like cases. And were all its premises true, they could still not justify the racial preference here in question.

Consider the premises first. The adverse impact on Weber is held justifiable by his alleged unjust enrichment resulting from the bad conduct of others. But if Weber were in any way the beneficiary of past discrimination, he certainly was not unjustly enriched by employment discrimination in the Grammercy plant. In that plant, it is agreed by advocates of the quota and by the courts, there had been no refusal to hire or promote blacks or other minorities, no racial discrimination from which Weber benefited. Yet the injustice done to Weber is manifested in the loss of entitlements he earned by five years of work in that plant — not in the Kaiser Corporation or in the workforce at large. His entitlements in this matter cannot have been acquired as the result of the historical misconduct of others. Long before Weber came to work at that plant blacks and whites received equal employment treatment there, so the claim that simply by virtue of his having the seniority that he did in the Grammercy plant Weber was enjoying an unjust enrichment is simply false. That false premise cannot justify "redistribution." The circuit court put the matter crisply: "Whatever other effects societal discrimination may have, it has had — by the specific finding of the court below — *no effect* on the seniority of any party here. It is therefore inappropriate to meddle with any party's seniority or with any perquisites attendant upon it, since none has obtained any unfair seniority advantage at the expense of any other."[9]

But suppose *arguendo* (what is not true) that Weber had been unfairly enriched by past racial discrimination. What would follow? The enrichment thus identified might then be a target for redistribution. Among whom? To take from Weber and give to another because Weber got his seniority "unjustly" could conceivably be justified (if ever) *only* if those to whom the redistribution were made were the same persons from whom the spoils had been taken in the first instance. The appealing argument by which so many are persuaded makes the faulty supposition that, if X has gained fortuitously but undeservedly from some unidentifiable Y, we are morally justified in taking from him and giving to a wholly different Z who suffered no loss to X's benefit, but who happens to be of the same *race* as that injured but unidentifiable Y. Implicit in this reasoning process is the mistaken premise that the distribution of goods or opportunities is rightly made by racial categories. Z, the person now given preference over X because of race, has a right to get from him (this premise supposes) because Z is black, and blacks have been so long oppressed. But rights do not and cannot inhere in skin-color groups. Individuals have rights, not races. It is true, of course, that many persons have been cruelly deprived of rights simply because of their blackness. Whatever the remedy all such persons deserve, it is deserved by those injured and because of their injury; nothing is deserved because of the color of one's skin. This is the philosophical nub of the *Weber* case.

V

So long-lasting and self-perpetuating have been the damages done to many blacks and others by discrimination that some corrective steps must be undertaken. The moral anxiety created by this need for affirmative action accounts, in part, for the willingness of some to tolerate outright racial quotas. In the passion to make social restitution, sensitive and otherwise fair-minded people have gotten the moral claims of living persons badly confused. The head of the Office of Federal Contract Compliance (by whom, as we shall see, Kaiser was threatened) epitomizes this confusion: "Society is trying to correct an age-old problem, and Weber is a victim of that process. There is nothing I can say to him. This is something that has to happen. The question is whether you give priority to a group that's been systematically deprived of opportunity while Brian Weber's parents and grandparents were not discriminated against. If someone has to bear the sins of the fathers, surely it has to be their children.[10]

But deliberately visiting the sins of the fathers upon their innocent children and grandchildren, to the special advantage of persons not connected with the original sinning, is conduct neither lawful nor morally right. To suppose that both the beneficiaries of redress and those who are made to carry its burden are properly identified by race is, to be plain, racism. It is ethical racism because supposed with good will. It is simplistic because, on this view, race by itself — without consideration of the nature or degrees of past injuries, present advantages, or future pains — is sufficient to trigger the preferential device. The mistaken view in question is therefore properly called *simplistic ethical racism.*

Injuries are suffered in fact, claims made and burdens carried, by individual persons. Civil society is constituted to protect the rights of individuals; the sacrifice of fundamental individual rights cannot be justified by the desire to advance the well-being of any ethnic group. Precisely such justification is precluded by the Fourteenth Amendment of our Constitution, whose words — no state "shall deny to any person within its jurisdiction the equal protection of the laws" — express no mere legalism but a philosophical principle of the deepest importance. Explicating that clause, in a now famous passage, the Supreme Court wrote: "The rights created by the first section of the Fourteenth Amendment are, by its terms, guaranteed to the individual. The rights established are personal rights. ... Equal protection of the laws is not advanced through indiscriminate imposition of inequalities."[11]

The nature and degree of the injury done to many Americans because they were black or brown or yellow varies greatly from case to case. Some such injuries may justify compensatory advantage now to those injured. But the calculation of who is due what from whom is a sticky business; compensatory instruments are likely to compound injustice unless the individual circumstances of all involved — those who were originally hurt, those who benefit now, and those who will bear the cost — are carefully considered. Whatever compensatory advantage may be given, in employment or elsewhere, it must be given to all and only those who have suffered like injury, without regard to their race. What we may not do, constitutionally or morally, is announce in effect: "No matter that you, *X*, were innocent and gained no advantage; you are white and therefore lose points. No matter whether you, Z, were damaged or not; you are black and therefore gain points." If the moral ground for compensatory affirmative action is the redress of injury, the uninjured have no claim to it, and all those individuals of whatever ethnic group who have suffered the injury in question have an equal claim to it.

Racially based numerical instruments have this grave and unavoidable defect: they cannot make the morally crucial distinctions between the blameworthy and the blameless, between the deserving and the undeserving. As compensatory devices they are *underinclusive* in failing to remedy the same damage when it has been done to persons of the nonfavored races; they are *overinclusive* in benefiting some in the favored categories who are without claims, often at substantial cost to innocent persons. Except in those cases where the discriminatory policy of the employer is established, and the identity of injured applicants or employees determinable, racial preference in employment is intolerably blunt, incapable of respecting the rights of individuals.

VI

This unsuitability of the racial means to the compensatory end partly explains the slippery language with which the advocates of "numerical instruments" defend their schemes. Although they truly believe their aims are good, there is widespread shame among them that they resort to racial preference to advance them. Hence the use of euphemisms like "disadvantaged" in identifying the beneficiaries of racial programs, when what is really meant is "black" or "minority." Not all minorities are disadvantaged, and not all those disadvantaged are minorities, obviously. But it is tempting to hide the racial character of a program that, if exposed, would be legally and morally intolerable.[12]

"Affirmative action" is a phrase now commonly used in the same duplicitous way. Affirmative steps to eliminate racially discriminatory practices rightly win the assent of all. Affirmative efforts to recruit fairly (whether for on-the-job training programs or for professional schools), affirmative inquiry to determine whether testing is job-related and to insure that evaluation of performance is not racially infected — in such forms affirmative action is of unquestionable merit. But when, in the name of affirmative action for racial equality, the deliberately unequal treatment of the races is introduced, we suffer a national epidemic of doublespeak. Employment advertisements everywhere exhibit this duplicity with an almost ritualized motto: "An equal opportunity/affirmative action employer." The term "affirmative action" has lost its honor and has become, for most, a euphemism for racial preference.

The unsavory character of their means is recognized by the advocates of racial instruments; that recognition is revealed by covertness in conduct and equivocation in language. Unsavoriness is tolerated here, however, even by organizations whose normal pride it is to expose immoral expedience in the body politic. Nothing is more indicative of the true spirit of a community than the character of the instruments it permits, and of those it precludes, in advancing public policy. Police surveillance to root out spies, the suppression of speech (radical or conservative) to protect the peace — all such instruments are rejected in a decent society. Civil libertarians wisely insist that we forswear instruments that invade the rights of individuals, even when forswearing proves inconvenient.

The use of such instruments is forbidden not just to evil people but to all people. Preference by race is one of these forbidden instruments. The very high priority given to this principle, and its applicability to all including the state itself, marks it as *constitutional* in the most profound sense.

Efforts to cut constitutional corners, however well-intentioned, corrupt a civil society. The means we use penetrate the ends we achieve; when the instrument is unjust, the outcome will be infected by that injustice. This lesson even civil libertarians must always be relearning.

VII

The inconsistency between racially preferential means and the end of honestly equal treatment is exquisitely exhibited in one aspect of the *Weber* case upon which Kaiser and the union place emphasis. "We are caught [say they] in a monstrous double bind. What will you have us do? Desegregate, you say. Integrate your workforce; show us that you mean to undo, affirmatively, the wrongs earlier done. We do it, making serious efforts to increase the number of minorities in craft jobs through advertisement, recruitment, encouragement. We get some results, but they are not dramatic. Then you, the nation speaking through your regulatory agencies, tell us that what we have done is not enough. You threaten us! Of course we take action in response to your threat — and having done so, we are threatened at law on the other side! Such inconsistency is unbearable. You, the body politic, must speak with one tongue!"

What is that first threat of which Kaiser complains? It came from the Office of Federal Contract Compliance whose regulations mandate "affirmative action" by all government contractors. The withdrawal of all federal contracts was the price Kaiser might have had to pay if, to avoid being found in "noncompliance," racial preference for minorities had not been introduced. Whence did the OFCC get the authority to make such threats? From an order of the President of the United States, say they, Executive Order 11246. This Order requires federal contractors to take affirmative action to prevent low employment of women and minorities in their workforces, on the assumption that most disproportionately low employment is the result of discrimination. Since the racial instrument agreed upon was a direct response to federal authority exercised under that valid order, it is unreasonable now, say Kaiser and the union, to attack us for violation of the Civil Rights Act.

This response to official inconsistency cannot help but evoke some sympathy. But as a defense of racial quotas it is worthless. The argument fails on two levels. First, Executive Order 11246 does not require and cannot justify racial quotas in cases like this one, in which the conduct of the employer has not been unlawfully discriminatory. The order says nothing about numerical ratios. Indeed, its plain words *forbid* all racial preference. The relevant passage of the order reads: "The contractor will take affirmative action to insure that applicants are employed, and that employees are treated during employment, without regard to their race, color, religion, sex, or national origin."[13]

Some numerical plans to protect employment for minorities have been upheld by the courts as valid executive actions, but they have been so upheld as responses to specifically identified violations by those upon whom the remedy was imposed. The so-called Philadelphia Plan was held permissible under Title VII, but that holding was explicitly tied to prior exclusionary practices by the six trade unions controlling the workforce in the construction industry in Philadelphia. Whatever tools the Office of Federal Contract Compliance may think itself entitled to employ, it has no authority in law, and certainly none in morals, to press for a racial quota in cases where, as here, those getting preference under the scheme had not been injured by that employer, and those injured by the scheme had not benefited from any misconduct of that employer.

The argument fails at a second level as well. If Executive Order 11246 be interpreted so as to authorize the OFCC to require racial quotas in cases like this one, the Executive Order itself is plainly unlawful, an illegitimate exercise of administrative authority in conflict with federal statute. The Civil Rights Act specifically prohibits racial classification in admission to on-the-job training programs.[14] The quota plan devised by Kaiser and the union is, as we have seen, patently in violation of this section. When the law and an executive order clash, there can be no doubt of the outcome. Writes the circuit court: "If Executive Order 11246 mandates a racial quota for admission to on-the-job training by Kaiser, *in the absence of any prior hiring or promotion discrimination,* the executive order must fall before this direct congressional prohibition."[15]

Only by resolutely enforcing the rights of citizens can the insolence of office be restrained. Individual workers, without power or money, need to be protected against civil servants who take it upon themselves to threaten in order to be able to report numerical ratios they think desirable, claiming only to be following the orders of their superiors.

VIII

Defenses of racial preference — by efforts to reinterpret the law, by confused arguments based on "societal discrimination," by claim of executive order — all collapse. It is important to see why they *should* collapse. The defenders, conscious of their own righteous pursuit of racial justice, little doubt that the tools they wish to employ would have the good consequences they hope for. To question the merit of those tools is for them almost a betrayal of the oppressed in whose behalf they claim to battle. In their eyes the conflict is only over whether they are to be permitted to do a good deed — i.e., *give preference to racial minorities* — not whether it is a good deed, or whether its consequences will be good.

Decency of motivation, however, does not insure the goodness of the immediate object, or the goodness of its consequences. Racial justice is an aim that all share; it is distorted when transformed into formulas for ethnic proportionality in workforces and professions based (as in this case) upon ethnic populations in the surrounding area. What accounts for this transformation? Motives honorable in their general statement are blended with a vision of cultural homogeneity that is profoundly unhealthy. The objectives then sought in making that blend operational often prove inconsistent with the original aim. It is this inchoate vision of homogeneity — made concrete in numerical proportions — that lies behind racial instruments like the one at issue in *Weber*. Federal appellate courts have not been oblivious to the evils that ensue:

There are good reasons why the use of racial criteria should be strictly scrutinized and given legal sanction only where a compelling need for remedial action can be shown. …Government recognition and sanction of racial classifications may be inherently divisive, reinforcing prejudices, confirming perceived differences between the races, and weakening the government's educative role on behalf of equality and neutrality. It may also have unexpected results, such as the development of indicia for placing individuals into different racial categories. Once racial classifications are embedded in the law, their purpose may become perverted: a benign preference under certain conditions may shade into malignant preference at other times. Moreover, a racial preference for members of one minority might result in discrimination against another minority, a higher proportion of whose members had previously enjoyed access to a certain opportunity.[16]

In this spirit federal circuit courts have repeatedly refused to approve racial quotas in the absence of proved past discriminatory practice
dictating that specific remedy.

Racial classifications have insidious long-term results: anger and
envy flowing from rewards or penalties based on race; solidification of
racial barriers and the encouragement of racial separatism; inappropriate entry of race into unrelated intellectual or economic matters; the
indirect support of condescension and invidious judgments among ethnic groups — in sum, the promotion of all the conditions that produce
racial *dis*harmony and racial *dis*integration. What Kaiser and the union
defend is very far from an innocuous good deed. It is a plan having very
damaging consequences to very many people.

Some of the damage, direct and substantial, is done to those like
Weber and Bakke who bear the immediate burden. "Society" does not
pay; the "white majority" does not pay; individual citizens pay. The
penalty to them is great and undeserved. *Reverse discrimination* is not
an invention or a hypothesis yet to be confirmed; it is a sociological and
legal fact.

IX

The recognition of the hurts caused by racial instruments introduces
one of the most intriguing aspects of the *Weber* case. A dispute arose
between the district and the circuit court beneath which lies an important philosophical issue. Numerical remedies based on race do damage,
the two courts agree; they further agree that this is a case in which the
imposition of such a numerical remedy cannot be justified because
there has been, in fact, no previous unlawful discrimination by the
employer here. However, in those cases in which such remedy might
prove justifiable (previous discriminatory practice in that setting being
alleged), the following question arises: may that numerical instrument
of redress be devised and executed on the authority of the employer
and union acting jointly? Or is a racial quota permissible as remedy
only on the express authority of the judiciary? The district court found
the preferential remedy unjustifiable, but held in addition that such
onerous remedies would in no case be in the province of unions and
management to impose. The circuit court, agreeing on the first point,

did not agree on the second. Voluntary remedial action (said they) is preferable to court action; therefore, to insist upon judicial imposition of remedies would interfere unduly with reasonable private amelioration. The underlying issue here is the locus of authority in resolving questions of justice. Which court is the wiser?

In permitting numerical remedies to be imposed (if at all) only by the judiciary, the district court is deeply right. The reasons for this are several and complicated.

First, the question of whether the circumstances are such as to justify the imposition of a numerical remedy (a question that must be answered affirmatively if any such remedy is to be lawful) is precisely the kind of question that cannot be answered fairly by employers and unions acting in their joint interests. Individuals will bear the burden; if the case were of a kind to justify the imposition of that burden on Weber and his like, past discrimination by that employer in that context must be proved or admitted. No employer is likely to make that admission. To do so would invite a host of very expensive lawsuits on behalf of those injured. Employers will therefore enter such agreements only with the understanding that no past discrimination has been proved or admitted. That very understanding (however arguable it may be) on which an employer might be willing to enter an agreement with a union to give racial preference to minorities is precisely the understanding that, if reflecting the facts truly, shows that racial preference is unjustly injurious and unlawful.

This peculiar feature of "voluntary" racial instruments is admitted — even emphasized, ironically — by the United Auto Workers, the National Education Association, and other assorted unions. If (they argue) voluntary racial preference is permissible only when the employer's past conduct would be found in violation of Title VII, there will be no voluntary race-conscious action. For, as they agree: "[I]t is usually difficult to predict whether or not [previous] discrimination would be found."[17] Indeed! For this reason precisely it is a question of such a kind that no answer to it reached as part of a labor-management agreement could be trusted.

The associated unions continue: "Moreover, the employer would, by taking voluntary action, put itself in a no-win situation in a suit such as this. Either its past conduct will be determined to be unlawful, thereby inviting litigation by discriminatees, or the remedial action will be found unlawful, and liability to white employees will exist."[18] Just so! But the authors of this candid statement apparently do not see where their argument leads. They would like the courts to conclude that, since the present standard (that "voluntary" racial quotas suppose the same finding of unlawful discrimination which alone might justify court-imposed remedies) effectively precludes "voluntary" quotas altogether, we should permit the introduction of a new standard, one that would allow "voluntary" quotas under some factual circumstances that — as they admit — would not justify a court in imposing them! What could serve as such a standard? The lone dissenting judge of the circuit court, pursuing the same line, is driven to propose an astounding answer: A "voluntary" quota plan should be upheld, he suggests, if it is "a *reasonable remedy* for an *arguable violation* of Title VII."[19]

This standard is neither feasible in practice, nor morally acceptable if it were. As a practical matter, such notions as "reasonable remedy" and "arguable violation" have virtually no objective content. Only the courts could resolve, on a case-by-case basis, disputed claims about "arguable violations" and about the reasonableness of remedy. Endless litigation could not be avoided — but it is the elimination of time-consuming litigation that is alleged to be the great merit of "voluntary" racial instruments. The increase in court involvement that would result undercuts any proposed justification of "voluntary" quotas on grounds of efficiency.

More important than its inefficiency, however, is the fact that the proposed standard (that a voluntary quota plan should be upheld if it is "a reasonable remedy for an arguable violation of Title VII") is morally unacceptable. Just remedies presuppose some determinable wrongs for which they give redress and by which they are justified. It is confusion of mind to propose a *remedy* for an *arguable* violation; one cannot put right what might prove on more judicious examination to have been no wrong at all.

All "voluntary" quotas (i.e., those introduced without court imposition) presuppose reliance upon some standard that must encounter essentially the same problem. The philosophical dimensions of the dispute between the two courts here emerge. The circuit court's position exhibits irremediable moral defect: by permitting racially preferential programs without the backing of judicial authority, it permits the delegation of questions of justice to private hands that are neither equipped, nor disposed, nor authorized to resolve them fairly.

To resolve a matter of individual right the bargaining process between labor and management is almost the worst imaginable tool. The impartial determination of facts without regard to interest, and the honest application of principles without regard to advantage, are essential in adjudicating questions of right — but the elimination of regard for self-interest and advantage is impossible at the bargaining table.

Even if the needed impartiality were possible there, it would be inappropriate, uncommon, and surely could not be relied upon. Union and management bargainers are duty-bound to press for the advantage of the units they represent. The process is designed to deal with issues of pay and working conditions, not with the protection of individual rights. Justice entails giving to each his due, whether or not others can negotiate for it successfully.

Most important, the authority to resolve questions of justice cannot lie in a labor-management bargain. Individual rights *may not* — as a matter of law or morals — be bargained away. As a matter of constitutional principle, the Supreme Court has spoken definitively on this issue. A union, they agree, may waive some of it rights to *collective* activity, such as the right to strike, in a bargaining agreement made with the aim of economic advantage for its members. The Court continues:

> Title VII, on the other hand, stands on plainly different ground; *it concerns not majoritarian processes, but an individual's right to equal employment opportunities.* Title VII's strictures are absolute and represent a congressional command that *each* employee be free from discriminatory practices. Of necessity, *the rights conferred can form no part of the collective bargaining process* since waiver of these rights would defeat the paramount

congressional purpose behind Title VII. In these circumstances, an employee's rights under Title VII are not susceptible of prospective waiver.[20]

Contracts reached through collective bargaining may, of course, introduce different terms of employment for different groups of employees in the light of the relevant conditions of those groups. Race, however, is never relevant in that sense. Because racial discrimination invariably touches the nonbargaining rights of all individuals adversely affected, race itself has been identified as an inappropriate criterion for the classification of employees.[21]

In sum: the courts have repeatedly held that, in compromising with an employer, a union may not take race into account. Programs like the one at issue in *Weber* explicitly take race into account. The conclusion of this syllogism is inescapable.

The unions take another tack. "You fail to note [they rejoin in effect] that this is a *voluntary* program. Weber and his fellows may be said to have relinquished their rights in this matter because, when the plan was devised, they were adequately represented by their union. The union has a duty to represent all of its members; its bargainers are selected democratically; and since white workers constitute a majority of the bargaining unit, the union process may be relied upon to reach no agreement that will violate the rights of individual white members."

It is hard to take this argument seriously. Union process is often genuinely democratic; negotiators for unions generally do seek to represent the interests of all the members of the bargaining unit. But the most sympathetic review of union process could not rationally conclude that the fairness of unions to their members over the long term has been such as to justify the delegation, to bargainers, of matters of fundamental individual right. The current flow of complaints about reverse discrimination in employment contracts in itself provides substantial evidence that the bargaining process, notwithstanding its general fairness, cannot be depended upon in this sphere. "Voluntary" is an appealing word. But its use here suggests what is not true — that those who were injured by the racial instruments devised in the contract did themselves volunteer to carry the burden. Weber's sacrifice cannot plausibly be called "voluntary." This defense of "voluntary" racial instruments (even if unions were invariably sensitive to matters of individual right) avoids the key question of legitimate authority. At stake here are the rights of individuals to the most fundamental of democratic conditions — equal treatment under the law — and, moreover, their rights to that equal treatment as it bears upon the most suspect of all categorical distinctions, race. Even legislators, it may be argued, however powerful their assembly, honorable their election, and dutiful their conduct, may not take from individual citizens certain fundamental rights. With the noblest of intentions, it is not within their authority to pursue public policy at the cost of compromising the individual citizen's right not to be discriminated against because of race or religion. Philosophers will differ about the grounds of legislative authority, but few will seriously deny that upon such authority there must be some hard limits. Unequal treatment because of race is as clear an example as there is of the violation of those limits.

If the principle here expressed were somehow mistaken, if it were sometimes just, in the cause of racial redress, to sacrifice the rights of some blameless nonbeneficiaries to advantage others who had not been injured, even so it would at least be certain that no such decision could be properly made by any save the legislature of highest authority, subject to the review of the court of highest jurisdiction. The notion that, to encourage "voluntary affirmative action plans," we may bypass the body politic, investing unions and management with the authority to bargain with fundamental human rights, makes the prospect of Weber's loss very distressing. Not substantive entitlements alone are at issue here, but also the procedural rights of working people to have questions of justice decided by legislatures and courts.

X

Weber and *Bakke* are analogous in this procedural regard. Weber's right to equal treatment was infringed by a union-management agreement, Bakke's by a medical school admissions committee. Legitimate authority was exceeded in both cases. When it was asked, in *Bakke*, for what purposes a university might consider race in admissions, Justice Powell replied that it may be considered for the sake of First Amendment concerns, or, conceivably, as compensation to the specific victims of specific injustices. "Societal discrimination" as a ground for racial preference he explicitly considered and rejected. Powell wrote:

> We [i.e., the Supreme Court] have never approved a classification that aids persons perceived as members of relatively victimized groups at the expense of other innocent individuals, in the absence of judicial, legislative, or administrative findings of constitutional or statutory violations. After such findings have been made, the governmental interest in preferring members of the injured groups at the expense of others is substantial, since the legal rights of the victims must be vindicated. In such a case the extent of the injury and the consequent remedy will have been judicially, legislatively, or administratively defined. Also, the remedial action usually remains subject to continuing oversight to assure that it will work the least harm possible to other innocent persons competing for the benefit. Without such findings of constitutional or statutory violations it cannot be said that the government has any greater interest in helping one individual than in refraining from harming another. Thus the government has no compelling justification for inflicting such harm.[22]

But findings of constitutional or statutory violations it is not the business of private bodies — unions, or managements, or medical school committees — to make. Powell continued:

> Petitioner [the Regents of the University] does not purport to have made, *and is in no position to make*, such findings.... [Even] isolated segments of our vast governmental structures are not competent to make those decisions, at least in the absence of legislative mandates and legislatively determined criteria. Before relying upon these sorts of findings in establishing a racial classification, a governmental body must have the authority and capability to establish, in the record, that the classification is responsive to identified discrimination.[23]

Powell's point is that a medical school admissions committee (even though indirectly an agent of the state) is entirely without the requisite authority. Kaiser and the union have a far weaker claim to the needed authority than did they. An admissions committee is not competent to make the findings that might justify racial preference, granted. But if the admissions committee had sought to present such findings of identified discrimination at the Davis medical school (discrimination that, in fact, the university specifically denied), they might conceivably contend that as one agent of one arm of one element of the state, it was within their province to do so, and thus might conceivably seek to justify their racial program as remedy. That claim would surely fail, the mission of the medical school and all its subsidiary elements being educative, not judicial. The analogous claim made by Kaiser and the union — that they are authorized to make findings of "societal discrimination" that will justify inflicting harm on Weber and other blameless parties — is totally without warrant.

XI

In the absence of any showing or admission of previous illegal discrimination at the Grammercy plant, every defense of racially preferential remedy must prove unsatisfactory. Sensitive to this point, the American Civil Liberties Union argued at length that the factual circumstances of this case have been misunderstood, that Kaiser Aluminum *did* discriminate against minorities.[24] The pattern of employment by Kaiser at other plants in earlier years is reviewed, and much is made of the racially disproportionate impact, at the Grammercy plant, of a "purportedly neutral criterion." Using the percentage of the minority population in the surrounding parishes of Louisiana as benchmark, the argument concludes that Kaiser's workforce at the Grammercy plant in skilled-craft positions was "severely underrepresentative."[25] Putting aside the question of how "representativeness" might rationally be established, or, if it had been established, what bearing that would have upon the lawfulness of Kaiser's previous conduct, it is important to note that the entire thrust of this argument is misdirected. The *Weber* case presents an appeal to our highest court on a matter of fundamental principle. That principle must be argued on the basis of a factual record established at trial in a responsible federal district court. Appellate courts, and the Supreme Court, face the question of principle *given that record*. Even the district court could analyze only the facts brought before it by the parties. Kaiser testified to its nondiscriminatory practices at the Grammercy plant from its opening, and of its many efforts to recruit black craftsmen from the general community. They would not and could not report otherwise. If (as some now claim) the record should have shown hidden unlawful conduct by Kaiser, such findings could only have entered the record at the trial level. The issue of principle is, supposing the record complete and accurate, whether this racial quota is permissible *without* such previous violations established.

Had the facts been different, had the courts found, after examining all the evidence, that Kaiser had previously discriminated against minorities in its Grammercy plant, the issues to be decided in *Weber* would not even have arisen.[26]

XII

Brian Weber did not get the job-training opportunity he was entitled to. Most ordinary people, and most judges, have no difficulty in seeing that. So zealous are some advocates of racial preference, however, that they claim not to see it. Weber was never really hurt, say they. He has a legitimate complaint only if he was discriminated against unfairly. But he wasn't discriminated against at all! Hence he has no case.

Puzzling though this last-ditch claim appears, it is defended in two ways. It is argued first, that the loss to Weber was of minimal importance. It is argued second, that Weber suffered no genuine loss at all. I address these in turn.

First, *minimization*. Weber (it is claimed) lost nothing more than seniority entitlements. But seniority systems may be altered by labor-management agreement, and in any event, seniority rights are not vested in the individual employee but in the collective-bargaining unit. Therefore, when a voluntary quota plan results in Weber's getting less than he expected in view of his greater seniority, he loses nothing that belonged to him in the first place. The injury done to him (it is contended) is apparent, not real.

This argument is twice faulty. It underplays the importance of individual seniority entitlements in the industrial context; and it does not face up to the discriminatory nature of the seniority deprivation in this case.

In allocating scarce opportunities and goods in the industrial world, seniority is critically important. For very many workers their most critical concerns — job security, opportunities for advanced training, vacation and retirement benefits — depend chiefly upon the number of years of service they have given. Nothing remains to them after years of service but their seniority claims. To deny that harm is done to an unskilled worker on an hourly wage when he is deprived of entitlements flowing normally from five years seniority reveals ignorance or moral insensitivity. Seniority does not insure qualification for positions demanding special talents, of course; but where qualifications are roughly equal, or not distinguishable, seniority above all other considerations will be relied upon in the interests of fairness.

Seniority entitlements are tied to individuals, not just to the bargaining unit. In matters of job assignment, transfer, layoff and recall, and job training, opportunities must be distributed among competing employees. Competitive-status seniority is therefore of great moral as well as practical importance, and directly affects individuals more importantly than it does the bargaining collective. Noncompetitive benefits also — pensions, sick leave, paid vacations — are commonly determined in part by length of service and therefore must be tied to individuals. Seniority, the Supreme Court writes, "has become of overriding importance, and one of its major functions is to determine who gets or who keeps an available job."[27] The "who" in this passage refers to individual persons, not to groups.

Seniority systems are bargainable, true. It does not follow, however, that all seniority rights are bargainable. It is essential not to confuse the *system* of seniority with individual *entitlements* under a given system in force. Once a seniority system has become a reality in rule and in practice, a worker's rights and expectations under that system are his or hers and very precious. It is callous to minimize the injury done when such rights are not respected.

When the ground of that disrespect is race, the injury is particularly offensive. Entitlements in themselves minor (which an opportunity for on-the-job training is not) become matters of grave concern when manipulated for racial reasons. Where one must sit on a bus or go to the toilet understandably becomes a source of rage and an issue of constitutional proportions when the determination is made by race. Protests over segregated lunch counters had as their target not the culinary opportunities denied, but the immoral character of the ground of their denial. Even if Weber's seniority expectations be thought trivial, the racial ground of the unequal treatment he received is very far from trivial.

Some who understand clearly why Allan Bakke was injured when excluded from medical school in a racially discriminatory way fail to see that the injury done to Brian Weber is equally unjust. Applicants to a competitive program, they appreciate, have a right to evaluation on some set of relevant criteria — past performance, intellectual promise, character, or whatever — and if deserving on the basis of those criteria, ought not be deprived of place because of race. But if the performance qualifications of all applicants are roughly equal (as were those of Weber and the minority workers chosen in his place), where, they ask, is the injustice?

The injustice lies in the deprivation, on improper grounds, of what one is otherwise entitled to. The basis for the entitlement will be different in different contexts. Scarce places in medical or law schools are rightly allocated to persons best exhibiting the characteristics determined relevant to the studies to be pursued. Scarce on-the-job training opportunities are rightly allocated to those having certain seniority entitlements. The factual bases of Weber's and Bakke's claims to that of which they were deprived are very different, but the principle is the same: both were wrongly denied what they would have received if the scarce available goods had been distributed in accord with established criteria in a morally just way. Both were the plain victims of racial discrimination, losing out because of the color of their skin.

Persons concerned about such injustice when done in the academic world ought seriously to consider the wisdom of remaining silent when the same injustice (although with respect to different entitlements) is done in the industrial world. If preference by race is held to justify the deprivation of what is fairly earned by a laborer, the security of what is fairly earned by anyone in any sphere is similarly threatened.

XIII

If the damage to Weber cannot reasonably be minimized, can it be wholly *denied*? This is the second line of defense to which Kaiser and the union fall back in the effort to show that Weber was not really discriminated against. Weber's rights were not infringed, they say, because he never had any seniority rights to job training here. The argument goes like this: "Where admission to a training program is properly a function of seniority, and seniority like Weber's is untainted by the employer's previous discrimination, he would be damaged if race were allowed to supervene. But Weber errs in thinking that seniority gives him any claim under *this* quota program, which was initiated in 1974, by Kaiser and the union, specifically to increase minority representation in the craft employments. New rights were then created, Kaiser and the union agreeing to use seniority only for the distribution of available slots *within* the two racial lists, black and white. If, in the new plan, they had agreed to use the lottery method — two separate lotteries, one for whites and one for blacks — it would be obvious that seniority was not the real issue here. They could have done just that. Weber's claim that he was deprived of seniority rights is a red herring, because the mode of selecting from each racial pool is irrelevant. So the Kaiser plan, as the dissenting judge wrote, "stands or falls on its separation of workers into two racial pools for assignment to job training."[28]

This argument is a compound of perceptivity and blindness. Seniority was the system deliberately adopted by Kaiser and the union — but they did not make that choice at random. Years of past work in the very plant where those training opportunities were to arise was thought the fairest consideration in allocating scarce places to otherwise equally qualified workers. Seniority was adopted as a relevant and rational principle. To create two seniority lists, black and white, and then choose the top person from each list, even if that person has less seniority than the fourth or twentieth person on the other list, is to override the seniority principle with race. If the basis chosen for the fair distribution of scarce opportunities had not been seniority, but (say) a lottery, then the just application of the lottery principle would require that *it* not be overridden by race. It is therefore perceptive to note that the real issue here goes beyond seniority — that the plan fails simply because it separates the workers into two *racial* pools — every such separation being necessarily invidious. Any system used to distribute opportunities among the members of each racial pool, even if of itself fair, must be distorted by that antecedent racial classification. Whatever besides seniority might prove just as a ground for the distribution of goods, skin color isn't it.

Is it correct to say, then, that Weber had no seniority rights here at all? No. When it is agreed by union and employer that, for allocating these job-training opportunities, length of service is the appropriate basis, employees acquire entitlements on that basis. The injustice of racial favoritism manifests itself, in this case, in the deprivation of those entitlements. Were workers' entitlements based on some other feature of their circumstances — perhaps experience or performance on competitive examinations — then the injustice of racial favoritism might be manifested in the deprivation of entitlements flowing from those. Weber had a right to nondiscriminatory treatment. To contend that he never had any rights in this matter because the respect in which he was discriminated against isn't the only respect in which he might have been discriminated against is a last-ditch effort to obscure the wrong that was done him.

XIV

The villain of the piece — here, in *Bakke,* wherever it raises its head — is preference by race. The *Weber* case provides an opportunity to reaffirm the moral and constitutional commitment to govern ourselves without preference to any by reason of color, or religion, or national origin. If we undermine that commitment — even though it be in an honest effort to do good — we will reap the whirlwind.

5

Justice Debased:
The Weber Decision*

A racial quota in the allotment of on-the-job training opportunities among competing employees, instituted by management-union agreement, was held lawful by the Supreme Court in the recent case of *Steelworkers v. Weber.*[29] This was an important decision, and a very bad one. Its badness lies not only in the substantive result, upholding preference in employment by race, but also in the reasons given by the Court in defending that result, and in the abuse of judicial discretion manifested.

I

The precise question decided was this: does Title VII of the Civil Rights Act of 1964 forbid employers and unions in the private sector from adopting racially preferential employment programs like the one adopted by Kaiser Aluminum and the steelworkers union? The answer was no. The evaluation of that answer requires a brief description of the quota plan approved, and a brief review of the statute in question.

* This chapter was first published in *Commentary,* vol. 68, no. 3 (September 1979). It is reprinted here, slightly revised, with the kind permission of the editors.

The plan, adopted as part of a collective-bargaining agreement between Kaiser Aluminum & Chemical Corporation and the United Steelworkers of America, provides that, in filling apprentice and craft jobs, "at a minimum not less than one minority employee will enter for every non-minority employee entering" until the percentage of blacks in craft jobs equals the percentage of blacks in the local work force — about 39 percent at the Grammercy, Louisiana, plant where Brian Weber works. Seniority in the plant was the criterion on which employees competing for admission to on-the-job training vacancies were ranked. But two seniority lists were maintained pursuant to this agreement, one for whites and one for blacks; vacancies were filled alternately from the top of the two lists. Weber, a white employee with five years seniority in that plant at that time, was refused admission to three different training programs — although, because of the quota plan in force, some non-white employees having less seniority than Weber were admitted. Believing that he had been displaced only because he was white, Weber brought suit against Kaiser and the union, on behalf of himself and all white employees at that plant similarly situated. His target was the racial preference in that job-training scheme.

The words of the law in question, Title VII of the Civil Rights Act of 1964, are central to the dispute, and must be borne in mind:

It shall be an unlawful employment practice for an employer —

(1) to fail or refuse to hire or discharge any individual, or otherwise to discriminate against any individual with respect to his compensation, terms, conditions, or privileges of employment, because of such individual's race, color, religion, sex, or national origin; or

(2) to limit, segregate, or classify his employees or applicants for employment in any way which would deprive any individual of employment opportunities or otherwise adversely affect his status as an employee, because of such individual's race, color, religion, sex, or national origin.[30]

It seems hardly possible to deny that this statute does plainly prohibit racially preferential programs of the kind described above. Thus, as one would expect, Weber won his case in the federal district court and won again, on appeal, in the Fifth Circuit Court of Appeals.

That result was reversed by the Supreme Court. The opinion of the five-member majority, authored by Justice Brennan, is devoted almost entirely to an explanation of why, in their view, Title VII does not prohibit the plan in question. This explanation cries out for response. Response was given in two dissenting opinions, one crisp and condemnatory by Chief Justice Burger, and a second by Justice Rehnquist that is scathing and detailed. Justice Rehnquist's tightly woven treatise, to which I will be referring, demolishes the majority position. Its cogency is acknowledged by the majority itself.

II

On what grounds does the majority reach its result? The *intent* of Congress in enacting Title VII, says the majority, was not to forbid racial preference having the wholesome purpose this program did. The key to the problem, in the majority's view, is not the "literal" meaning of the statute, but its "spirit." If, by studying the history of the act, one can discover the purposes of Congress in its adoption, and if this plan advances those purposes, the plan will be (says the majority) if not "within the letter of the statute," yet still "within its spirit," "within the intentions of its makers."[31] Now the aims of Congress in passing this legislation can be readily discovered. In a nutshell, Congress aimed to counteract black unemployment, to protect and promote the opportunities of blacks to get decent jobs. In legislative debate Senators Humphrey, Clark, and others contended that, without such a bill, discrimination against blacks would become a source of social unrest and intolerable injustice. The majority's defense of their interpretation of Title VII rests principally upon the fact that the proponents of the bill repeatedly insisted upon the importance of jobs for minority groups. That having been the goal, they continue, it cannot have been the case that Congress intended to prohibit private parties "from taking effective steps to accomplish the goal the Congress designed Title VII to achieve."[32]

The argument of the majority, in effect, is this: We know the purpose of Congress; we know the purpose of this plan; they are fully consonant. It must be, therefore, that Congress did not intend to forbid this plan. If the literal language of Congress says otherwise, we must interpret that language to mean what it did not say, while saying what it did not mean.

III

What Congress really did intend with this statute is a matter about which I shall have much to say. Before turning to that historical question, however, I comment on the logic of the argument. The majority blunders seriously by confusing *purpose* with *intent*. That the purpose of Congress was to promote employment opportunities for blacks is beyond doubt. It certainly does not follow that any special scheme having that purpose was intended to be permitted. Different persons, or different pieces of legislation, may share the same aim yet differ greatly in what are believed the wise or the just steps properly taken to achieve that aim. This simple but important point is what underlies the common homily: "The end doesn't justify the means." The aphorism is imperfect, of course; ends do serve to justify means. But the moral point of the aphorism is sound: ends, even very good ones, don't justify *any* means that may be thought effective in achieving them. That ends are shared is no proof that there will be agreement on the justice or the desirability of particular instruments or programs for their attainment.

Consider this hypothetical example: Suppose funds were appropriated by Congress to explore alternative sources of energy, one of the major purposes of the appropriation being, in the minds of the legislators, to reduce dependence on foreign oil. By adopting some measures clearly having that objective, Congress would not warrant the inference that every measure having the same tendency had thereby been permitted. Suppose the expenditure of the funds appropriated for the exploration of alternative energy sources, although having the larger aim of energy independence, were also restricted by the explicit provision that these funds were not to be spent on the development of nuclear energy. It would not then be rational to conclude that a plan to spend the funds on the development of nuclear energy was "within the intentions" of the legislature because (as Justice Brennan says of the racial quota in

Weber) "the purposes of the plan mirror those of the statute."[33] To find out whether Congress intended to advance its larger purposes in that way we would have to read the enacted statute. If the statute said: "It shall be unlawful to expend any of these funds on the development of nuclear energy," we might or might not have thought that restriction wise. But it does not take great profundity to distinguish between Congress's *purpose* in legislating and its *intent* in that law — between what they hoped to accomplish and what they actually proposed to do.

In seeking to advance employment opportunities for blacks in 1964, Congress adopted legislation forbidding *all* racial discrimination in employment. To argue, as the majority does, that they cannot have intended to forbid all discrimination because some racial discrimination might also serve their larger purposes, does not do credit to a high appellate court.

IV

Under what circumstances is it appropriate for any court to inquire into the *intent* of a legislature in enacting the legislation being applied? When the applicability of the language of the statute is unclear, or its wording is ambiguous, that inquiry may be very much in order. Such circumstances do arise. In some cases, new conditions, unforeseen by the legislature at the time of a law's enactment, may present problems of interpretation that cannot be resolved by its language alone. A court may then be obliged to construe what the legislative intent might most reasonably have been in order to determine fairly the bearing of the statutory language upon the new conditions. In other cases, legislation may be formulated in deliberately ambiguous language for political reasons. Courts may later be obliged to apply that language to cases treated equivocally in the statute, then having to construe some reasonable legislative intent to guide them.

Nothing like either of these circumstances arises in the present case. The language of Title VII, as Chief Justice Burger observes, exhibits "no lack of clarity, no ambiguity."[34] The Kaiser quota plan, as all agree, discriminates against individual white employees seeking admission to on-the-job training programs simply because they are white. Under the very plain language of the statute that is "an unlawful employment practice."

Could it be, perhaps, that the real meaning of the language of the statute is unclear because it has been sometimes construed by the Court, in past instances, to prohibit discrimination against blacks, but not discrimination against whites? No, that was put out of the question by the Supreme Court in 1976, explicitly interpreting this title of this statute. White employees who were dismissed after being charged with misappropriating company property brought suit under Title VII because black employees, similarly charged, had not been dismissed. The Supreme Court then concluded, from the "uncontradicted legislative history," that "Title VII prohibits racial discrimination against the white petitioners in this case upon the same standards as would be applicable were they Negroes."[35]

So there is no doubt that the Civil Rights Act does — or did! — apply equally to all races. That is what the Supreme Court has repeatedly affirmed. Title VII, they earlier insisted, "prohibits *all* racial discrimination in employment, without exception for any group of particular employees."[36] A few years earlier, in a landmark interpretation of Title VII, the Supreme Court had agreed unanimously on a definitive account of the legislative intent of Title VII: "The objective of Congress in the enactment of Title VII is plain from the language of the statute. It was to achieve equality of employment opportunity. ... Discriminatory preference for any group, minority or majority, is precisely and only what Congress has proscribed."[37] And just one year before *Weber* the very same point was hammered home by the same Court in the context of employment ratios. "It is clear beyond cavil that the obligation imposed by Title VII is to provide an equal opportunity for *each* applicant regardless of race, without regard to whether members of the applicant's race are already proportionately represented in the work force."[38]

There is no trace of ambiguity, no vestige of unclarity, either in the language of the statute or in the interpretation repeatedly given to that language, respecting the question of whether Title VII protects whites as well as nonwhites. There is, therefore, no justification here for opening the question of legislative intent. Justice Rehnquist, understandably infuriated, called attention to the Court's oft-repeated principle applied in another case just decided: "[O]ur duty is to construe rather than re-write legislation."[39]

V

Having opened the question of congressional intent where it was not proper to do so, the majority gives to that legislative intent a reading that flouts the facts. It is not appropriate in this case even to ask whether Congress intended to permit some racial discrimination with Title VII, but once asked, the task of answering that factual, historical question is exceedingly easy. The lengthy debates in the House and the Senate are open to us in the *Congressional Record;* majority and minority committee reports of the House on the proposed bill are also open to us; a lengthy, scholarly study of the legislative history of precisely this title of this act is available to us.[40] One who has examined the legislative record can have no genuine doubt about the intent of the Congress in choosing the language they did choose. Democrats and Republicans *both,* conservatives and liberals *both,* insisted repeatedly and at great length, illustrating their explanations with detailed examples, that H.R. 7152 (which eventually became the Civil Rights Act of 1964) would forbid *all* racial preference for *any* race.

VI

In the House of Representatives the bill was amended by the Committee on the Judiciary to include Title VII because no compulsory provisions to deal with private discrimination in employment had been included in its original form. It was added, the committee noted, "to eliminate … discrimination in employment based on race, color, religion, or national origin."[41] That title was further amended on the floor of the House to include an added Section, 703(d), which specifically extended the prohibition against discrimination in general [formulated in 703(a) quoted above on p. 84] to on-the-job training! Section (d) of 703 reads as follows:

It shall be an unlawful employment practice for any employer, labor organization, or joint labor-management committee controlling apprenticeship or other training or retraining, *including on-the-job training programs,* to discriminate against any individual because of his race, color, religion, sex, or national origin in admission to, or employment in, any program established to provide apprenticeship or other training.[42]

Included with the Report of the Judiciary Committee were the lengthy "Additional Views on H.R. 7152" of a group of its advocates, which incorporated a passage referred to by Vaas as fairly stating the consensus of the proponents as they guided the bill toward adoption. This representative passage includes these sentences:

Internal affairs of employers and labor organizations must not be interfered with [under Title VII] except to the limited extent that correction is required in discrimination practices. Its [the Equal Opportunity Employment Commission's] primary task is to make certain that the channels of employment are open to persons regardless of their race and that jobs in companies or membership in unions are strictly filled on the basis of qualification.[43]

The major objection faced by Title VII in the House (and again later in the Senate) was the claim that under it racial proportionality in employment might subsequently be required by some federal agency, acting under color of that law. This fear was epitomized in the Minority Report, which suggested, as one serious concern, that an employer, under Title VII, *"may be forced to hire according to race,* to 'racially balance' those who work for him *in every job classification* or be in violation of Federal law."[44] That fear had to be allayed; proponents of the bill strenuously and repeatedly reassured their colleagues that *no such racial balancing was contemplated,* and that *none would be required or even permitted* under this title.

Representative Celler, one of the sponsors of the bill and chairman of the Committee on the Judiciary, opening the debate in the House, made the intent of the language of 703(a) unmistakable. The fear that it would require or permit hiring or promotion on the basis of race resulted, he said, from a description of the bill that was "entirely wrong." He continued:

> Even ... the court could not order that any preference be given to any particular race, religion or other group, but would be limited to ordering an end to discrimination. The statement that a Federal inspector could order the employment and promotion only of members of a specific racial or religious group is therefore patently erroneous....
>
> The Bill would do no more than prevent a union, as it would prevent employers, from discriminating against or in favor of workers because of their race, religion, or national origin. It is likewise not true that the Equal Employment Opportunity Commission [established by Title VII] would have power to rectify existing "racial or religious imbalance" in employment by requiring the hiring of certain people without regard to their qualifications simply because they are of a given race or religion. Only actual discrimination could be stopped.[45]

This theme was echoed repeatedly in the course of the debate in the House of Representatives. Representative Lindsay of New York, among others, took up the defense of Title VII:

> This legislation ... does not, as has been suggested heretofore both on and off the floor, force acceptance of people in schools, jobs, housing, or public accommodations because they are Negro. It does not impose quotas or any special privileges of seniority or acceptance. There is nothing whatever in the bill about racial balance.... What the bill does do is prohibit discrimination because of race.[46]

With that clear understanding the bill passed the House, 290 to 130, on February 10, 1964.

VII

In the Senate, the expression of legislative intent was voluminous and unequivocal. Again the fear of opponents was that some federal inspector might one day seek to impose racial balance under color of this law. Again — and again and again and again — the defenders of the bill replied with reassurance, insisting vehemently that such fears were totally unfounded. The key term, "discrimination," appearing in Sections 703(a) and 703(d) and elsewhere in the bill, was examined minutely on the Senate floor. Could it be taken to mean (the critics asked) only numerical imbalance? Answer: definitely not. Could it have been, for the framers of the legislation, a technical term, whose hidden meaning was "discrimination against blacks" but not "discrimination against whites?" No, definitely not. Senator Humphrey put that suggestion permanently to rest: "[T]he meaning of racial or religious discrimination is perfectly clear.... [I]t means a distinction in treatment given to different individuals because of their different race, religion, or national origin."[47] The only freedom of employers that the bill limits, he emphasized, is the freedom to take action based on race, religion, sex, or national origin.

When the Senate took up the substance of the act directly, after deciding not to submit it to committee, it again became essential for the bill's advocates to answer the complaint that the bill might lead to racial preference. Not so, they insisted. Senator Humphrey again:

> That bugaboo has been brought up a dozen times; but it is nonexistent. In fact, the very opposite is true. Title VII prohibits discrimination. In effect, it says that race, religion, and national origin are not to be used as the basis for hiring and firing. Title VII is designed to encourage hiring on the basis of ability and qualifications, not race or religion.[48]

In the same speech Senator Humphrey gives a series of examples that "makes clear what is implicit throughout the whole title; namely, that employers may hire and fire, promote and refuse to promote for any reason, good or bad, provided only that individuals may not be discriminated against because of race, religion, sex, or national origin." He repeats himself so that even the deaf may hear: "The truth is that this title forbids discriminating against anyone on account of race. This is the simple and complete truth about Title VII."[49] Humphrey was majority whip and the floor leader for the Civil Rights Act in the Senate. In his support rose senator after senator to give the same explanatory assurances about the intent of the legislation.

Senator Kuchel, the minority whip, emphasized that the seniority rights of workers already employed would not be affected by Title VII. He said:

> Employers and labor organizations could not discriminate in favor or against a person because of his race, his religion, or his national origin. In such matters, the Constitution, and the bill now before us drawn to conform to the Constitution, is color-blind.[50]

Senators Clark and Case were floor captains in the Senate for Title VII specifically. To them fell the task of explaining that title, what it meant and did not mean, what it permitted and what it prohibited. Their chief task was to refute the charge that Title VII would result in preference for racial minorities. In a memorandum prepared for the Senate they expressed the intent of Title VII unequivocally:

> [A]ny deliberate attempt to maintain a racial balance, whatever such a balance may be, would involve a violation of Title VII because maintaining such a balance would require an employer to hire or to refuse to hire on the basis of race. It must be emphasized that discrimination is prohibited as to any individual.[51]

A different memorandum, prepared by the U.S. Department of Justice at Senator Clark's request, also makes the point that there is no need to fear employers' being required to maintain racial balance:

> No employer is required to maintain any ratio of Negroes to whites, Jews to Gentiles, Italians to English, or women to men. The same is true of labor organizations. On the contrary, any deliberate attempt to maintain a given balance would almost certainly run afoul of Title VII because it would involve a failure or refusal to hire some individual because of his race, color, religion, sex, or national origin. What Title VII seeks to accom-

plish, what the civil rights bill seeks to accomplish is equal treatment for all.[52]

Senators Smathers and Sparkman, granting that the bill did not require the use of hiring quotas, put the attack against Title VII more subtly. Under it, they suggested, employers might be *coerced,* by federal agencies, into giving preference by race. Would that not be permitted under this law? The answer, this time from Senator Williams, was an emphatic negative. Opponents, he replies,

> persist in opposing a provision which is not only not contained in the bill, but is specifically excluded from it. Those opposed to H.R. 7152 should realize that to hire a Negro solely because he is a Negro is racial discrimination, just as much as a "white only" employment policy. Both forms of discrimination are prohibited by Title VII of this bill. The language of the title simply states that race is not a qualification for employment.... [A]ll men are to have an equal opportunity to be considered for a particular job. Some people charge that H.R. 7152 favors the Negro, at the expense of the white majority. But how can the language of equality favor one race or one religion over another? Equality can have only one meaning, and that meaning is self-evident to reasonable men. Those who say that equality means favoritism do violence to common sense.[53]

Still the fear that racially preferential hiring would somehow be encouraged or permitted under Title VII could not be allayed. Once again the floor leader, Humphrey, took up the battle:

> The title [Title VII] does not provide that any preferential treatment in employment shall be given to Negroes or to any other persons or groups. It does not provide that any quota systems may be established to maintain racial balance in employment. *In fact, the title would prohibit preferential treatment for any particular group,* and any person, whether or not a member of any minority group, would be permitted to file a complaint of discriminatory employment practices.[54]

VIII

How could the majority of the Supreme Court, in *Weber*, escape the force of this parade of unequivocal accounts marching across the printed record of the process of its adoption? Could they contend, perhaps, that although racial preference was indeed prohibited, that prohibition did not bear upon efforts to overcome the effects of *past* discrimination upon the seniority rights of employees? At one point, conceding that it was the intent of the Senate to forbid the maintenance of racial balance, the majority grasps at a straw: this Kaiser quota plan was not introduced to maintain racial balance, they contend, but to "eliminate a manifest racial imbalance."[55] Can the net of clear congressional intent be thus eluded, by making the distinction between "maintaining" racial balance and "eliminating" racial imbalance, holding that Title VII forbids the former but not the latter?

Not a chance. Explicating Title VII, its most thorough congressional students, Senators Clark and Case, wrote in their joint memorandum:

> Title VII would have no effect on established seniority rights. *Its effect is prospective and not retrospective.* Thus, for example, if a business has been discriminating in the past and as a result has an all white working force, when the title comes into effect the employer's obligation would be simply to fill future vacancies on a nondiscriminatory basis. He would not be obliged — or indeed, permitted — to fire whites in order to hire Negroes, or *to prefer Negroes for future vacancies, or... to give them special seniority rights at the expense of the white workers hired earlier.*[56]

The Justice Department had earlier drawn the same conclusion: Title VII could not be used to alter seniority entitlements because of discrimination in employment before its adoption:

> Title VII would have no effect on seniority rights existing at the time it takes effect....
>
> This would be true even in the case where owing to discrimination prior to the effective date of the title, white workers had more seniority than Negroes.... [A]ssuming that seniority

rights were built up over a period of time during which Negroes were not hired, these rights would not be set aside by the taking effect of Title VII. Employers and labor organizations would simply be under a duty not to discriminate against Negroes because of their race.[57]

The distinction between "maintaining" and "achieving" racial balance was, manifestly, never part of the understanding of the legislature that adopted Title VII.

That distinction, moreover, would have been and is specious from the point of view both of advocates and critics of racial preference. If, after the achievement of racial balance through racial preference, craft jobs again were to become predominantly white, the advocates of racial preference would certainly not be content. Convinced that such imbalance is in itself wrong, they would then insist that if racial preference be permitted for the achievement of racial balance, it must be permitted for its reachievement. It will be of little consequence to their disciples that the majority in *Weber* leaned on a tenuous distinction that they will later ignore. And the opponents of racial preference — including the 88th Congress of 1964 — may rightly insist that if preference by race is in principle wrong, it is no less wrong in the one case than in the other. Indeed, both the Justice Department and the floor captains for Title VII in the Senate very carefully pointed out that maintaining racial balance would be forbidden "*because* it would involve a failure or refusal to hire some individual because of his race. ..."[58] These arguments specifically refer to the actual words of Section 703(a) cited on page 84 above. Adverse effects upon an employee or applicant because of race would result whether the goal had been the maintenance of racial balance or the achieving of it.

The argument that Congress intended Title VII to permit racial preference in achieving racial balance, but forbade it for maintaining racial balance, and that therefore once proportionality is achieved all such preference will cease, is unworthy of the Supreme Court; it is a sop designed to placate critics with unreliable assurances that the instrument approved will be only "temporary." In fact ethnic preference, once solidly ensconced, will be nearly impossible to eradicate. To mitigate its unfairness, more and different ethnic preferences will be introduced, as already they are being introduced.

Opponents of racial favoritism condemn it whether aimed at achieving or at maintaining racial balance; proponents will not object to its use in either role. That distinction cannot serve to render plausible the majority's interpretation of congressional intent in enacting Title VII of the Civil Rights Act.

IX

As debate over the Civil Rights Act continued in the Senate it became evident that the bill would have to be amended to make absolutely clear the fact that it could not later serve as the justification, by any federal agency, of the imposition of racial preference. Only thus might the repeated objections of its most implacable opponents be successfully met. A bipartisan coalition, made up of Senators Dirksen, Mansfield, Humphrey, and Kuchel, cooperating with leaders in the House of Representatives, devised the "Dirksen-Mansfield" amendment, ultimately adopted. Among the changes thus introduced was a clarifying addition, Section 703(j), specifically addressing the critics' fears of imposed racial balancing. This section provides that nothing in the entire title shall be interpreted to require the giving of preferential treatment to any individual because of race. It reads:

> Nothing contained in this subchapter shall be interpreted to require any employer, employment agency, labor organization, or joint labor-management committee subject to this subchapter to grant preferential treatment to any individual or to any group because of the race, color, religion, sex, or national origin of such individual or group on account of an imbalance which may exist with respect to the total number or percentage of persons of any race, color, religion, sex, or national origin employed by any employer, referred or classified by any employment agency or labor organization, or admitted to, or employed in, any apprenticeship or other training program, in comparison with the total number of persons of such race, color, religion, sex, or national origin in any community, State, section, or other

area, or in the available work force in any community, State, section, or other area.[59]

In an ironic and extraordinary turn, the Supreme Court majority in *Weber* used the language of this section to infer (relying upon what Justice Burger calls a "negative pregnant") that since it bars the requirement of racial preference, but does not specifically prohibit racial preference, it must have been the intention of Congress not to prohibit it! The majority writes:

> The section does *not* state that "nothing in Title VII shall be interpreted to *permit*" voluntary affirmative efforts to correct racial imbalances. The natural inference is that Congress chose not to forbid all voluntary race-conscious affirmative action.[60]

This inference is either disingenuous or obtuse. This added section was designed specifically to meet the objection that racial preference might somehow be required. No one thought preference would or could be introduced voluntarily because "voluntary" racial preference had been explicitly forbidden by the plain language of the earlier key section, 703(a), cited above on page 84. Debate in the Senate went on for almost three full months. Never in that entire period was it argued, *by either side,* that employers could, of their own accord, give preference by race. Both proponents and opponents made perfectly clear their understanding that voluntary racial preference by employers, for blacks or for whites, was entirely precluded by the flat and unambiguous wording of those earlier passages, forbidding *any* employment practice that would "discriminate against any individual" because of that individual's race. To add that prohibition yet again, in 703(j), would have been entirely redundant — and more importantly, it might have diluted the intended force of that particular passage, aimed narrowly at the objection that racial preference would otherwise someday be imposed by government.

That it was so aimed is made exquisitely clear by the difference in the phrasing of 703(j) from that of the earlier, central sections of the title. The earlier sections, prohibiting racial discrimination in employment universally, are directed specifically at the employer and therefore begin: "It shall be an unlawful employment practice for an employer..." Section 703(j) is directed specifically *at possible federal enforcement agencies,* commissions, or courts, and therefore begins with language indicating that kind of target: "Nothing contained in this subchapter shall be interpreted..." Now to infer, from the fact that this section does not repeat the prohibition already several times explicit in earlier sections, that it was the intention of Congress *not* to prohibit racial preference, is transparently unsound.[61]

Lest there be any doubt about the intent of the Congress *after* the addition of 703(j), we can return to the debate itself. Senator Saltonstall, defending the Dirksen-Mansfield amendment including 703(j), says of it, very plainly; "The legislation before us today provides no preferential treatment for any group of citizens. In fact, it specifically prohibits such treatment."[62]

And yet again, in defending the amended bill against Senator Ervin's criticism that it "would make the members of a particular race special favorites of the laws," Senator Clark answers: "The bill does not make anyone higher than anyone else. It establishes no quotas." Employers, labor unions, employment agencies, remain free, Clark points out, to use normal judgment in their business activity — but:

> All this is subject to one qualification, and that qualification is to state: "In your activity as an employer, as a labor union, as an employment agency, you must not discriminate because of the color of a man's skin ..." That is all this provision does. ... It merely says, "When you deal in interstate commerce you must not discriminate on the basis of race."[63]

In the event this be somehow misunderstood, he repeats himself in that speech: "All it [Title VII] does is to say that no American, individual, labor union, or corporation, has the right to deny any other American the very basic civil right of equal job opportunity."[64]

Senator Cooper, anxious to make the force of what was soon to become law unmistakably clear, also responds to Senator Ervin's concerns, saying:

As I understand Title VII, an employer could employ the usual standards which any employer uses in employing — in dismissing, in promoting, or in assigning those who work for him. There would be only one limitation: he could not deny a person a job, or dismiss a person from a job, or promote on the sole ground of his color, or his religion, other factors being equal.[65]

X

But how, one asks, can the Court majority not have been fully aware of all this? They must have seen the draft of Justice Rehnquist's dissent, which makes the same points vividly. Did they, perhaps, find other evidence within the record of the debates in Congress, evidence that has here been left unmentioned, which might somehow permit a reading of congressional intent to permit racial preference? No, no evidence has been suppressed here. Like Francis Vaas[66] and Justice Rehnquist, upon whose guidance I have relied, I have scoured the pages of the *Congressional Record;* like them I have registered only a fraction of the evidence against the majority's interpretation. If, in all those pages, there were evidence that *any* Senator or Congressman had the intent that the majority ascribes to the whole Congress, we may be certain it would have been dug up and registered within the majority opinion. No such evidence appears there. Here is a negative pregnant upon which we may rely. In this majority opinion, any quotation from the congressional debates that might contribute, in any way, to its strained interpretation of congressional intent, would surely be presented. The total absence of any passages that express that intent is therefore very revealing.[67]

The plainest proof that the members of the majority in Weber cannot have been in ignorance of the actual intent of Congress is given by Justice Marshall himself. In a 1976 opinion, writing for the Court, he presented a careful analysis of the intent of Congress in Title VII. He quotes Representative Celler, saying Title VII was intended to "cover white men and white women and all Americans."[68] He cites Senator Humphrey, Senator Clark, Senator Case, and Senator Williams in passages like those quoted above. Justice Marshall concludes that "Its [Title VII's] terms are not limited to discrimination against members of any particular race."[69] He then substantiates this judgment by extended reference to the interpretation of Title VII given by the Equal Employment Opportunity Commission:

> The EEOC, whose interpretations are entitled to great deference, ...*has consistently interpreted Title VII to proscribe racial discrimination in private employment against whites on the same terms as racial discrimination against non-whites,* holding that to proceed otherwise would "constitute a derogation of the Commission's Congressional mandate to eliminate all practices which operate to disadvantage the employment opportunities of any group protected by Title VII, including Caucasians."[70]

Justice Marshall, there representing the Court, observes that the history of legislative intent in adopting Title VII is "uncontradicted."[71]

Members of the House and Senate are quoted by the majority, to be sure. But the quotations serve to establish matters only tenuously related to the central point at issue. Repeated citations from the debates are given to establish that it was the larger purpose of Congress, in tackling this legislation, to promote employment opportunities for blacks. That is true, and is not at issue, and does not speak to the question of what prohibitions were intended. Several citations are given to show, correctly, that one major concern in the Senate when introducing Section 703(j), which precludes the requirement of racial preference by the enforcers, was to reduce the likelihood of federal interference with private business. That was an aim of many Senators; but showing that does not prove, or even tend to confirm the thesis that Title VII as a whole was designed to permit nongovernmental racial preference.

One other citation by the majority deserves attention. To give credence to the claim that the distinction between private racial favoritism and federally required racial favoritism was before the congressional mind, the majority quotes from the House Committee report favoring the original bill. The passage says that "the enactment of Federal legislation dealing with the most troublesome problems [of social discrimination] will create an atmosphere conducive to voluntary or local resolution of other forms of discrimination." The majority fastens on this sentence, even adds emphasis to the final phrase, suggesting that it proves that a voluntary racial quota in employment is one of those "other forms" for which the Civil Rights Act had created the atmosphere.[72]

Fallacious would be the gentlest way to describe this argument — in view of the failure, not likely to be accidental, to quote the lines immediately following the cited passage. An explanation is given there of the distinction between "the most serious types of discrimination" and those other varieties for which voluntary attention might be encouraged. The serious types, types this House report there suggests *will* be dealt with by this bill, specifically include voting, public accommodation, *and employment*. The omitted passage reads:

> It is, however, possible and necessary for the Congress to enact legislation which prohibits and provides the means of terminating the most serious types of discrimination. This H.R. 7152, as amended, would achieve in a number of related areas.... It would prohibit discrimination in employment.[73]

The forms of discrimination it was hoped might yield to voluntary action were those other than discrimination in employment, voting, and the like. Indeed, employment discrimination is mentioned repeatedly in the report as being of the most serious kind, the kind for whose prevention this legislation was specifically designed.

There is not a shred of evidence in this passage that the report actually envisaged voluntary racial *preference* of any kind, or that would have suggested to the House that such preference — especially in employment — was permissible under this act.

XI

One hates to flog a dead horse. But this horse came to life in an extraordinary opinion of a Supreme Court majority — so I report, finally, the understanding of the Civil Rights Act of 1964 as that understanding was registered in the final hours of debate on the Senate floor — after which it was returned to the House and approved as amended. The legislative decision was at hand. The advocates of the bill, now under cloture, had to give their final defenses and interpretations. On the point at issue here their remarks were unmistakably clear.

Senator Muskie:

It has been said that the bill discriminates in favor of the Negro at the expense of the rest of us. It seeks to do nothing more than to lift the Negro from the status of inequality to one of equality of treatment.[74]

Senator Moss:

The bill does not accord to any citizen advantage or preference — it does not fix quotas of employment or school population — it does not force personal association. What it does is to prohibit public officials and those who invite the public generally to patronize their businesses or to apply for employment, to utilize the offensive, humiliating, and cruel practice of discrimination on the basis of race. In short, the bill does not accord special consideration; it establishes equality.[75]

Very self-consciously, aware that it was making history, the Senate passed the amended Civil Rights Act on June 19, 1964, by 73 to 27. Every senator voted. The struggle in that body, as Vaas describes it, had been "titanic and protracted." The meaning and force of every line, every phrase in the bill had been intensely scrutinized and explained with scrupulous care. The legislators knew precisely what they were prohibiting with this legislation, and we know exactly what they understood themselves to be doing because they took care, very deliberately, to put their explanatory accounts on record.

No impartial judge, attentive to the abundant evidence that establishes dispositively the intent of Congress, could honestly conclude that its "real" intent was to permit private racial preference in employment. Yet that is what the majority did conclude, in a decision that is, taken all in all, simply shocking.

XII

Are there no mitigating features of the majority's decision? Yes, there are some flowing from the explicit limitations imposed by the Court upon the impact of the decision. "We emphasize at the outset," writes the majority, "the narrowness of our inquiry."[76]

It is, indeed, narrow in a technical sense. The majority explicitly decided the case entirely as one of *statutory* interpretation; they determined no more than that Title VII of the Civil Rights Act does not forbid the Kaiser quota plan. They restricted themselves to an interpretation of the statute, the majority said, because "this case does not present an alleged violation of the Equal Protection Clause of the Constitution."[77] It does not, they explain, because the racially preferential quota in question was entirely within "the private sector," and did not involve any "state action."[78]

This view of the Kaiser plan is at once reasonable and ironic. It is ironic because although the racial quota surfaced only in a labor-management agreement, it had been put there partly as a result of threats of contract cancellation by a federal enforcement agency. Threats why? Because Kaiser's workforce was not racially balanced. In the language of the Office of Federal Contract Compliance, minorities were being "underutilized" by Kaiser. By devising job-training racial quotas in submission to that threat, Kaiser and the union showed how well-grounded were the fears of those who had wished to preclude not only the federal requirement of racial preference, but the federal coercion of it. The addition of Section 703(j) sought to guard against the first of these dangers, the requirement. Now its very language is used to realize the second, coercion, accomplishing indirectly what that language was designed to prevent directly.

In a historical aside that would be amusing if it did not reflect upon the highest court in the land, Justice Rehnquist cites a remark by Senator Sparkman in projecting the uses to which Title VII may one day be put: "Certainly the suggestion will be made to a small business that may have a small government contract ... that if it does not carry out the suggestion that has been made to the company by an inspector, its government contract will not be renewed."[79]

Yet the Court's distinction between state action and private action remains reasonable. However pernicious racial discrimination may be, it is right to distinguish between immoral acts done by private parties and the same acts done directly by a representative government. To accept that distinction is not to suggest that the majority is correct in holding this private racism lawful. Under any plausible reading of the Civil Rights Act, it is not. But not all private nastiness is public business, and we are wise to agree that, where state action *is* clearly involved in racial preference, the problem rises to a different and higher level of gravity.

Because the *Weber* majority puts substantial emphasis on the distinction between public and private employment, limiting its decision to the latter, it is reasonable to conclude that its opinion does not cover public employers at all. Government agencies, public universities, municipalities — public employers of every kind cannot rely in any way upon the permission to discriminate here being given to a private employer. And private employers may reasonably decide, as a matter of morality, to refrain from engaging in practices forbidden to public employers. There is an odious quality in conduct held narrowly lawful but which, if engaged in by government, would violate constitutional rights.

The majority opinion is narrow in the further sense that it gives almost no guidance to those private employers who do wish to give preference by race. No principles of acceptability for racial preference are advanced. The majority explicitly refrains from defining or describing the line of demarcation between permissible and impermissible affirmative action plans. It holds only that this plan, which gives preference to blacks over whites for job-training opportunities (but not for employment itself) in this particular setting falls on the permissible side of the line.[80] In *Weber* we learn that the Supreme Court in 1979 held this precise plan not forbidden by Title VII of the Civil Rights Act of 1964 — no more than that.

Weber was decided by a vote of five to two, two justices not participating. Justice Stevens, author of the opinion in support of Allan Bakke in that analogous case, recused himself because he had once served as an attorney for Kaiser. Justice Powell was kept from presence at the oral argument by illness and took no part in *Weber*. The author of the majority opinion, Justice Brennan, and all four justices who joined him (Marshall, Stewart, White, and Blackmun) are (in 1995) no longer members of the Court. Some of their replacements are plainly hostile to naked racial preference. The author of the most telling dissent in *Weber* has become chief justice. When the fundamental issues of this case arise again in a context obliging a full-blooded constitutional response by the full Court, we may hope for a wiser result.

XIII

The *Weber* decision may eventually provoke a response from Congress, since the majority opinion hangs entirely on its interpretation of congressional intent. Our legislature may one day register its true intent so clearly that no judge could fail to perceive it. Justice Blackmun, exhibiting troubled reluctance in his concurring opinion, and reiterating his hopes for an early end to affirmative action preference that he had himself (in his *Bakke* opinion) called "ugly," concludes his opinion with an explicit invitation to the Congress: "And if the Court has misperceived the political will, it has the assurance that because the question is statutory Congress may set a different course if it so chooses."[81]

The intent of Congress to forbid all racial preference in employment already appears in the unambiguous words of Title VII, Section 703(a), quoted above. That is indisputable. Yet it is possible that formal congressional reemphasis of its intent might prevent judges from rewriting to their own taste legislation that flatly forbids racial discrimination.

Another provocative aspect of the majority opinion in *Weber* is the callousness it displays toward the interests of ordinary working-class people. Allan Bakke was ordered admitted to the Medical School at Davis; blatant racial discrimination against him was not tolerated. Brian Weber, a working man without skills or influence, and without the organized support of the intellectuals, was left to bear his burden even though he was *admittedly* discriminated against. The majority is explicit on this point. To advance the racial balancing they think good it may be necessary, they say, to *"trammel the interests of the white employees."*[82]

Five members of the Supreme Court found this an acceptable position in which to rest; many elected legislators will not. By egregiously misreporting the intent of Congress, and then boldly expressing their own willingness to sacrifice the interests of one race to advance the interests of another, the majority in *Weber* may have taken provocative steps that will lead eventually to more emphatic legislative insistence upon the equal protection of the laws.

NOTES

1. *Steelworkers v. Weber*, 443 U.S. 193 (1979).

2. The *Weber* majority was constituted by Justices Brennan, Marshall, Blackmun, Stewart, and White. All five have left the Court.

3. The Civil Rights Act of 1964: Title VII, Section 703, Subsection (a).

4. Subsection (a) of Sec. 703 reads: "It shall be an unlawful employment practice for an employer —

(1) to fail or refuse to hire or discharge any individual, or otherwise to discriminate against any individual with respect to his compensation, terms, conditions, or privileges of employment, because of such individual's race, color, religion, sex, or national origin; or

(2) to limit, segregate, or classify his employees or applicants for employment in a way which would deprive any individual of employment opportunities or otherwise adversely affect his status as an employee, because of such individual's race, color, religion, sex, or national origin" [42 U.S. Codes 200e-2(a) (1970)].

5. 42 U.S. Codes 2000e-2(d) (1970)(emphasis added).

6. See *Franks v. Bowman Transportation Co.,* 424 U.S. 747 (1976).

7. 653 F. 2d 216, 225 (1977). The Supreme Court has agreed. In a case arising from a plan devised to give remedy to school employees within a previously discriminatory system, the Supreme Court declined

review of a decision that, in view of the source and nature of that earlier injury, a minority worker may there be entitled to preferential treatment "not because he is black, but because, and only to the extent that, he has been discriminated against"[*Chance v. Board of Examiners*, 534 F. 2d 993, 999 (1976) cert. denied 431 U.S. 965 (1977)].

8. 653 F2d 216, 225.

9. Ibid., p. 226.

10. *New York Times Magazine*, 25 February 1979.

11. *Shelly v. Kraemer*, 334 U.S. 1, 22 (1948).

12. In the original trial of the *Bakke* case, the University of California defended the racial quotas at the Davis Medical School as being for all "disadvantaged" students. When the court noted that not a single disadvantaged person who was not of an ethnic minority had been admitted in all the years of that program's operation, the university conceded the misdescription.

13. 30 *Fed. Reg.* 12319 (1965).

14. Sect. 703(d); cited above, p. 88.

15. 653 F. 2d 216, 227.

16. *Associated General Contractors of Massachusetts Inc. v. Altshuler* 490 F.2d 9, 17-18 (1973).

17. Associated unions, brief *amici*, p. 13.

18. Ibid.

19. 653 F. 2d p. 216, 230 (emphasis added).

20. *Alexander v. Gardner-Denver Co.*, 415 U.S. 36, 51-52 (1974) (emphasis added).

21. The Supreme Court has written: "[T]he statutory power to represent a craft and to make contracts as to wages, hours, and working conditions does not include the authority to make among members of the craft discriminations not based on such relevant differences. Here the discriminations based on race alone are obviously irrelevant and invidious. Congress plainly did not undertake to authorize the bargaining representative to make such discriminations" [*Steele v. Louisville & Nashville R.R. Co.*, 323 U.S. 192, 203 (1944)].

22. *University of California Regents v. Bakke,* 438 U.S. 265, 307-309 (1978).

23. Ibid. (emphasis added).

24. ACLU and Society of American Law Teachers, brief *amici,* p. 11.

25. The inappropriateness of such population percentages in estimating fairness with respect to employment in the skilled crafts is so obvious, and has been so often remarked, that one is embarrassed for the ACLU to find such an argument presented. See Thomas Sowell, "Are Quotas Good for Blacks?," *Commentary,* June 1978.

26. Might an appellate court not reverse an inferior court because of its mistaken interpretation of the facts as appearing in the record? Only in those rare circumstances in which the treatment of the facts by the inferior court was "clearly erroneous." That claim would be untenable in this case.

27. *Humphrey v. Moore,* 375 U.S. 335, 346-47 (1964).

28. 653 F. 2d 216, 235.

29. 443 U.S. 193 (1979). Three related cases were consolidated and decided together: *United Steelworkers of America, AFL-CIO-CLC v. Brian F. Weber et al.; Kaiser Aluminum & Chemical Corporation v. Brian F. Weber et al.;* and *United States et al. v. Brian F. Weber et al.* There are four opinions in all: that of the majority written by Justice Brennan; a concurring opinion of Justice Blackmun; a dissent by Justice Burger; and a second dissent by Justice Rehnquist which Justice Burger joined.

30. Civil Rights Act of 1964: Title VII, Section 703, Subsection (a).

31. 443 U.S. 193, 204.

32. Ibid.

33. Ibid., p. 208.

34. 443 U.S. 193, 217.

35. *McDonald v. Santa Fe Trail Transportation Co.,* 427 U.S. 280 (1976).

36. Ibid., p. 283.

37. *Griggs v. Duke Power Co.,* 402 U.S. 424, at p. 429 and p. 431 (1971).

38. *Furnco Construction Corp. v. Waters,* 438 U.S. 567 (1978).

39. 443 U.S. 193, 221. Rehnquist here cites *United States v. Rutherford,* 442 U.S. 544 (1979).

40. The congressional debates appear in volume 110 of the *Congressional Record* of 1964, extending intermittently over exactly thirteen thousand pages (from page 1,511 to page 14,511) of ten massive tomes. The committee reports appear in *House of Representatives Reports,* No. 914, 88th Congress, First Session, 1963. With the majority and minority reports are printed additional views of particular members of the Judiciary Committee, and views of groups of Representatives, on the bill being reported. The Senate having decided to take up the bill directly, it was not submitted to committee there, hence there are no Senate reports beyond the actual Senate debate, which was very long. The study referred to, used both by Justice Rehnquist and myself, is by Francis J. Vaas, "Title VII: Legislative History," in volume 7 of the *Boston College Industrial and Commercial Law Review,* pp. 431-58. Vaas records the tortuous path of the Civil Rights Act through Congress with meticulous attention to detail, and draws (on p. 444) this striking conclusion: "Seldom has similar legislation been debated with greater consciousness of the need for 'legislative history,' or with greater care in the making thereof, to guide the courts in interpreting and applying the law."

41. *H.R. Reports,* No. 914, p. 26.

42. 42 U.S. Codes 2000e-2(d) (emphasis added).

43. *H.R. Reports,* No. 914, pt. 2, p. 29; Francis J. Vaas, "Title VII: Legislative History," *Boston College Industrial and Commercial Law Review,* vol. 7, p. 437.

44. *H.R. Reports,* No. 914, p. 69.

45. 110 *Congressional Record,* p. 1518.

46. Ibid., p. 1540.

47. Ibid., p. 5423.

48. Ibid., p. 6549.

49. Ibid.

50. Ibid., p. 6564.

51. Ibid., p. 7213.

52. Ibid., p. 7207.

53. Ibid., p. 8921.

54. Ibid., p. 11848 (emphasis added).

55. 443 U.S. 193, 209.

56. 110 *Congressional Record,* p. 7213 (emphasis added).

57. Ibid., p. 7207.

58. See above, p. 127 (emphasis added).

59. 42 U.S.C. 2000e-2(j).

60. 443 U.S. 193, 206.

61. The argument called a "negative pregnant" is one having the form logicians call *modus tollens:* if p entails q, and q is false, then p must be false. This form is valid, of course. But the majority's use of this argument form (in either of two possible reconstructions of it) incorporates a false premise.

Version A: "If Congress had intended to forbid all racial preference they would have said that explicitly. They did not say that explicitly. Hence they did not intend that." In this version the second premise is plainly false; the congressional ban against racial preference in Section 703(a) is perfectly explicit.

Version B: "If Congress had intended to forbid all racial preference they would have expressed that intention explicitly in Section 703(j). They did not express that intention there. Hence they did not have that intention." In this version the second premise is true but the first is false. There was no need for Congress to repeat, in Section 703(j), the ban it had already made explicit earlier, and there was good reason not to do so.

Arguments relying upon false premises, even when valid in form, are not sound.

62. 110 *Congressional Record,* p. 12691.

63. Ibid., p. 13079.

64. Ibid., p. 13080.

65. Ibid., p. 13078.

66. "Title VII: Legislative History," pp. 431-58.

67. Again the valid argument is in the form of *modus tollens*, but here its premises are true: "If Congress had intended to permit private racial preference in employment there would have been clear expression of that intention by at least some defenders of the act in the course of lengthy debate. No such expressions appear. Hence Congress cannot be supposed to have had that intent."

There is nothing wrong with *modus tollens*; its effectiveness in argument, however, depends upon the truth of the premises relied upon.

68. 110 *Congressional Record,* p. 2578.

69. *McDonald v. Santa Fe Trail Transportation Co.*, 427 U.S. 273, 278.

70. Ibid., p. 280.

71. Ibid., p. 283.

72. 443 U.S. 193, 204.

73. *House of Representatives Reports*, No. 914, p. 18.

74. 110 *Congressional Record,* p. 14328.

75. Ibid., p. 14484.

76. 443 U.S. 193, 200.

77. Ibid.

78. Ibid.

79. 110 *Congressional Record*, p. 8618.

80. 443 U.S. 193, 208.

81. Ibid., p. 216.

82. Ibid., p. 208 (emphasis added).

D

Quotas, Goals, and Ethnic Proportionality
Wygant v. Jackson Board of Education

Preference by race, given apparent legitimacy by the *Weber* decision, became almost universal over the decade that followed. The mechanics by which preference is given are now generally hidden by schools or employers; details are difficult to uncover. Descriptions of affirmative action devices are presented to the public in language designed to obscure the racial favoritism they embody; what is really going on is put in writing only when circumstances require it. Institutions try to avoid allowing preferential practices of which they are not proud to become an addressable target.

With a self-righteousness that borders on duplicity, administrators will often announce that no consideration of race, sex, nationality, or the like is tolerated by them — *while* they are authorizing and executing schemes in which race, sex, and nationality are deliberately used as threshold considerations in admissions or employment. Vacancies are advertised in ways making it clear to persons who are not members of the preferred groups that it is virtually useless for them to apply. Affirmative action plans in colleges commonly channel minority applications to separate minority subcommittees. Where that device is abandoned as too blatant, too vulnerable to attack, other devices are introduced to insure that a lower standard is used for the evaluation of minority applicants. This cannot be admitted publicly so the meaning of "qualified" is commonly adjusted, permitting the proud announcement that all those admitted are fully "qualified." Admissions are determined in closed sessions, relying upon the discretionary decisions of committees that ostensibly weigh character and other traits, so that complainants find it almost impossible to document the racial preference given. Not a pretty business.

The defense of preference, when given at all, continues to be couched in terms of compensation, but it is evident that most of those now given preference have not themselves been discriminated against, and therefore cannot plausibly be said to deserve special treatment as compensation for the damage done to them by the white majority. And those among the majority who have been obliged to bear the burden of these "compensatory" plans, sometimes having to give up their jobs so that members of protected minorities do not lose theirs, are usually entirely innocent of any wrongdoing.

Compensation thus comes to be viewed as an entitlement of disadvantaged *groups*, not injured persons. Membership in certain groups becomes in itself sufficient grounds for preference, membership in other groups sufficient grounds for handicap. Whatever the language used to rationalize it, racial preference became, by the mid-1980s, a form of social engineering in which jobs, college admissions, and other social goods were to be redistributed in the light of some ideal ratio of ethnic groups. The chief architects of the redistribution were (and are) the affirmative action planners.

The social engineers agree with their lips that there must be no ethnic quotas. "Quota" early became a bad word, to be scrupulously avoided. To give ethnic preference and quantify its results, however, affirmative action could not possibly avoid using quotas in practice. It became a game of numbers, in which the ratios of black to white, the alleged underrepresentation of assorted ethnic groups, idealized racial proportionality, and so on, are central to employment and admission policies. Ethnic quotas became ubiquitous in the 1980s and remain so still, although they are so far as possible concealed. The actual word "quota," of course, is used only in mock horror.

Obfuscation is supported by an alleged contrast between "quotas" and "goals." Ethnic goals, we are told, do no more than "provide guidelines" for affirmative action, and help "to measure its effectiveness" — based upon the numerical proportions of racial groups in the population at large. It was only the unfortunate use of "rigid quotas" (the argument now goes) that led to the condemnation of the affirmative action program at issue in the *Bakke* case at the University of California. This claim is false, but it is repeated unendingly. If rigid quotas are avoided (the argument continues), we are authorized to go on giving preference. Numerical goals for ethnic groups cannot be wrongful, it is said, since a goal is not "rigid," and the failure to achieve it may be explained and excused. The key thing is that the instruments be "flexible."

Do those who argue in this way really believe what they are saying? When the job (or promotion) of a personnel officer, or an admissions officer, depends upon achieving some preestablished numerical outcome, that outcome or something close to it will of course be achieved. A failure by subordinates to reach the "goals" established by their superiors is not likely to be common. In real life, "goals" and "quotas" mean precisely the same thing for the persons displaced by them. And everyone knows that.

One premise, absolutely crucial, underlies goals and quotas equally: that the racial mix, in colleges or on the job, *ought* to manifest some antecedently determined proportionality. If admissions or hiring do not have that result, it is said, this is *prima facie* evidence of "institutional discrimination" in the system, requiring "affirmative action" to uproot.

Racial proportionality among the teachers in a public school system became the focus of a major Supreme Court case in 1986. In this case it was firing, not hiring, that brought Wendy Wygant and her colleagues to court. Ms. Wygant was one of a group of white teachers, perfectly innocent of any wrongdoing, who were laid off, losing employment benefits and seniority as well as income, as a direct result of the affirmative action plan agreed to by their school board and their union in Jackson, Michigan. The preferential plan they contested avoided all reference to "rigid quotas," of course. It simply established rules governing layoffs (unavoidable when a school board runs short of funds) based on a vision of ethnic proportionality. The result of those rules was — repeatedly — the removal of Ms. Wygant and her colleagues from the jobs they had held for years, in favor of minority teachers with much lower seniority. In the annals of affirmative action no case more fully deserves being described as "naked racial preference."

The chapter that follows, from which the title of this book is taken, first appeared in *Commentary* in March of 1986, while the case was under deliberation. Wendy Wygant was ultimately vindicated. The eventual Supreme Court decision[1] struck down the Jackson affirmative action plan because of its unlawful racial discrimination against her, and against others similarly situated.

The *Wygant* decision was a significant blow against racial discrimination in the workplace. But the discrimination forbidden by the *Wygant* decision remains widespread, because the designers of affirmative action plans have evaded the law. They have devised and applied other ways — other programs and numerical schemes discussed in part E below — to continue giving preference by race.

6

Naked Racial Preference*

The Board of Education in Jackson, Michigan, between 1972 and 1981, repeatedly laid off high-seniority white teachers to protect the jobs of others, with less seniority, who were "Black, American Indian, Oriental, or of Spanish descendancy." Those white teachers contend that they were discriminated against unjustly on the basis of their race, denied their constitutional right to the equal protection of the laws. Are they correct? This question — in the case of *Wendy Wygant, et al. v. Jackson Board of Education* — is now before the United States Supreme Court.[2]

All parties in this dispute agree that unjust discriminatory practices must be uprooted, and that affirmative steps to achieve that end remain in order. All parties agree that when persons have been directly injured by racial discrimination they are entitled to a remedy, and that to give such remedies the use of racial classifications may sometimes prove essential. Affirmative action in its wholesome forms is not at issue in this case. But the teachers whose jobs were protected in Jackson had not been discriminated against, and the teachers whose jobs were sac-

* This chapter was first published in *Commentary*, vol. 81, no. 3 (March, 1986). It is reprinted here with the kind permission of the editors.

rificed to protect them had not discriminated against anyone. What is here at issue is the species of affirmative action properly described as naked racial preference.

I

"Equal Justice Under Law" is the inscription carved into the frieze of the United States Supreme Court Building. The thrust of this principle is not merely that legal categories are to be applied fairly, but that some categories, intrinsically unfair, are not to be applied at all. Classifications by race (using "race" here as shorthand for the families of ethnic criteria — race, color, religion, national origin) are those chiefly to be guarded against. To be denied what one is otherwise entitled to on grounds of race violates the constitutional expression of that principle, appearing in the Fourteenth Amendment: "No state shall ... deny to any person under its jurisdiction the equal protection of the laws."

Because they are sometimes essential in giving appropriate remedy for racial discrimination racial classifications cannot now be precluded absolutely. So we ask: when does equal justice under law permit the uses of racial classification, and when does it forbid them?

The answers thus far given by the Supreme Court have been incomplete. Some principles are quite firmly established: racial classifications are invariably *suspect,* because their use tends to be, and traditionally has been, damaging and cruel. Jobs or other benefits in short supply given to some on the basis of their race must be taken from others on the basis of their race; hence no such racial distributions, whatever their alleged objective, can be "benign." Any use of racial classifications, therefore, must be subjected to what the courts have come to call "strict scrutiny." More lenient standards the Supreme Court has repeatedly rejected.

Thus it will not be sufficient justification for the use of racial categories that they are plausible devices to achieve worthwhile ends, or that they are used in programs agreed upon by a majority of those immediately concerned, or that the intention of their users is honorable, or that there is some rational basis for their use. No. For the defense of racial and other suspect classifications it must be shown that the governmental interest served in applying them is *compelling.* A satisfactory defense must also show that to serve that compelling state interest, the race-based instrument used is *necessary,* no alternative being available, and has been *narrowly tailored* to achieve the compelling objective in view.

Can a standard so high ever be met? Yes. If identifiable persons have been injured by racially discriminatory conduct, the need for a remedy that will make them whole is compelling. To determine the appropriate beneficiaries of the remedy devised — to right the wrongs done — the use of the racial categories that underlay the original injury may be necessary. And the racial instrument applied may be carefully designed to compensate all and only those injured in appropriate form and degree. The test of strict scrutiny is not insurmountable — but it was designed by the Supreme Court to ensure that racial classifications would be used only in very special circumstances. From the standard of strict scrutiny this much may be confidently deduced: the use of a racial classification that imposes a serious burden upon innocent persons cannot be justified if those who benefit from that use are not themselves the victims of identifiable racial discrimination.

II

How does the teacher layoff plan, adopted by the Jackson Board of Education and the Jackson teachers' union in 1972, fare when judged on these principles? To answer, the workings of that plan must be explained. It gave explicit preference by race, but in a way that partly obscured this fact. "Minority-group personnel" were defined as "employees who are Black, American Indian, Oriental, or of Spanish descendancy." A "goal" for "minority racial representation" was established: racial proportions among the faculty were to be the same as racial proportions among the students. Layoffs (when unavoidable) were determined by reverse seniority *"except that at no time will there be a greater percentage of minority personnel laid off than the current percentage of minority personnel employed at the time of the layoff."*[3]

The percentage of minority students in the Jackson schools was, and is, and for the foreseeable future will be, much higher than the percentage of minority teachers. The goal of equating them being unattainable, this plan operated inexorably as a contractual *ratchet* — the relative number of minority teachers is steadily raised, but it can never be lowered. Nonminority teachers, with seniority such that they would not otherwise have been laid off, have been laid off again and again. One of the eight white petitioners in this case was laid off eight separate times over nine years as a consequence of this device; another, Wendy Wygant, lost employment (and the seniority benefits that go with employment) for a total of more than three years. Under this contract in Jackson, keeping one's job as a teacher depends critically upon one's race.

No defense of this layoff plan is possible on the ground that it is a remedy called for by earlier discrimination against minority teachers in the Jackson schools. No one contends that any one of the minority teachers here given preference was ever discriminated against, or injured in any way, because of race. This is of central importance. The behavior of the Jackson School Board was scrutinized (in 1979) by a Jackson County court in the course of an entirely separate proceeding. Referring to the same contract in which the now-disputed layoff provision appears, that court concluded that "there is no history of overt past discrimination by the parties to this [labor] contract."

This finding has never been contravened. No court, no legislative body, no administrative agency — and no Jackson School Board — has ever found that the Jackson Board of Education engaged in unlawful racial discrimination. Justifying Jackson's racial preference now as redress for some earlier discriminatory injury is simply out of the question.

III

The ethnic numbers game is an ugly but pervasive element in this case. It is a game that ought not to be played at all — but if it is to be played the rules must be at least rational. When, in categories of employment traditionally segregated, the numerical "balance" of the races is at issue, the only rational standard for judging it is the existing racial proportions in the labor pool from which all employees in the disputed category must come. So said the Supreme Court explicitly in an earlier case.

The relevant labor pool for schoolteachers consists of all those receiving degrees in education, and who are certified teachers, in that state. In Michigan colleges and universities, blacks were awarded (in 1975-76) 10 percent of the degrees in education. In 1980-81, when blacks constituted 9.7 percent of the population of Michigan, and Wendy Wygant was laid off for the seventh time to protect minority teacher ratios, minorities constituted *13.5* percent of the teachers in the Jackson schools. In other words, the number of "minority-group personnel" *exceeded* their number in the relevant labor pool by at least 30 percent.

Nor do these figures tell the whole story. In the school year 1981-82, the percentage of minority administrators in the Jackson schools was 19.6; the percentage of minority coaches was 18.3; the percentage of minority teacher aides was 29.6. If preferential protection were justifiable in Jackson to compensate for numerical imbalance, that compensation would more justly have been given to whites. Wendy Wygant and her fellow nonminority teachers were the victims of racial favoritism so blatant that it is rightly called naked.

IV

If the Jackson layoff scheme cannot be justified as remedial, what might be offered in its defense? First proposed is a theory of contract. "This layoff provision is part of a collective-bargaining agreement" [argues the Board, in effect] "reached through a process in which the duly elected representatives of all the teachers participated. Eighty percent of the teachers in the negotiating union were white; they had the opportunity to reject that contract if they thought it unfair. From the results of the democratic process some gain and some lose. White teachers who wound up losers in this process cannot now claim to be exempt from the provision of a contract bargained for by their own union."

This argument fails utterly. Collective bargaining between employers and democratic trade unions is indeed a treasured process. But the constitutional guarantee of equal justice — the guarantee that certain highly suspect classifications will not be used with damaging result, save under the compelling need to give redress for injury — cannot be bargained away.

No organization has a more intense interest in preserving the authority of collective-bargaining agreements than the American Federation of Teachers (AFT), AFL-CIO. Although not a party directly involved in this case, the AFT submitted a brief *amicus* in support of Wendy Wygant and her fellow petitioners — and in it rejected categorically the claim that the constitutional injury done to them may be "insulated from judicial scrutiny" or "constitutionally justified because it is included in collective bargaining agreements." If all that were necessary to validate the use of racial classifications by a public employer were a vote of approval by employees, it is a virtual certainty that many American school districts now healthily integrated would be segregated still. "[A]n individual teacher's right to be free from employer decisions based on race," concludes the AFT, cannot "be waived by fellow employees."

The Jackson Board of Education is a public employer, from whom the highest standards of constitutional integrity may be demanded. Its conduct overriding the constitutional rights of employees cannot be defended on the ground of a bargain with a union. No defense of preferential instruments can be even minimally plausible unless it deals with the substance of those instruments, not merely the method of their adoption.

V

The substantive justification of racial preference proposed by the board (on its second theory) is the alleged need for *same-race role models*. Only the visible presence of minority-group members in positions of authority and esteem, it argues, can give minority school children the self-confidence they need to break out of the long continued cycle of socioeconomic depression.

This is an old argument, not entirely without merit; here it is invoked crudely. Social gain is likely when minority-group members are visible in the public schools. But the extent of that gain, even the reality of it, is quite uncertain; it has never been empirically established. There is no good evidence concerning the relationship between the success of students and the degree of race-match between them and their teachers. Even a systematic study of the effect of same-race role models on performance, contends one scholar, "does not appear to exist."[4]

In the context of this case, moreover, the role-model argument cuts two ways. Small psychological gains may be achieved by protecting the jobs of additional minority teachers; but such gains become losses when it is widely believed (and true) that those minority "role models" occupy their posts only as the result of special favor given to them because of their race. Even the stature of minority teachers who sought no racial favors and received none is eventually undermined by such devices. For role models that are truly positive and effective, naked racial preference is counterproductive.

Teachers *are* role models for their students. By example as well as instruction, they influence and motivate their students, imparting values as well as knowledge. A healthy public school system will employ teachers of differing races and cultural backgrounds. But what follows from all this? Of the many factors that contribute to the making of a role model, race is but one; in the making of a wholesome role model, the teacher's being of the same race as the student is of relatively little importance. More critical by far are those aspects of the teacher's character and conduct that bear directly upon school activity: intellect, effective speaking and writing, commitment to students, honesty and curiosity, fairness and absence of prejudice. Students are better served (as Justice Thurgood Marshall once suggested) by an excellent teacher role model of another culture than by a poor teacher role model of their own culture.

The same-race role-model theory — as federal courts have repeatedly pointed out — leads when extended (and traditionally did lead) to the general *segregation* of the races in public-school systems. Indeed, the heaviest reliance upon this argument in school-desegregation cases has been placed by those seeking to justify the segregation of minority faculty in primarily minority schools. The argument has been consistently, and rightly, rejected.

Finally, even if the benefits of same-race role models had been shown to be substantial in some school contexts (which is not the case), those could only be contexts in which previously there had been very little minority presence, or none at all. In settings like Jackson, where the percentage of minority teachers has for some time been greater than the minority percentage in the population at large, and markedly exceeds the minority percentage in the relevant labor pool, the preferential

protection of *additional* minority teachers against layoff on the ground
that they are essential as role models cannot be taken seriously.

In this case the persons advantaged by the preferential layoff plan
had never been racially hurt, and the persons hurt by the layoff plan had
never been racially advantaged. To justify the racially based constitutional injury done by such a plan, some utterly compelling governmental interest would have to be shown. An interest weighty enough to
serve that purpose is difficult even to imagine. The alleged need for
additional same-race role models cannot hope to serve as that compelling end.

In this case, both parties call upon the Supreme Court to pass judgment on the same-race role-model argument as a defense of racial preference in employment. The opinion handed down will greatly affect the
inclination of all employers, private as well as public, to rely upon that
argument in giving preference on the basis of race. The importance of
Wygant lies partly in this.[5]

VI

What plausible defense of the Jackson preferential layoff plan remains?
It is constitutionally justifiable, argued the federal district court, because
"minority teachers were 'substantially' and 'chronically' *underrepresented* on the Jackson School District faculty in the years preceding the
adoption of the affirmative-action plan."[6] The circuit court of appeals
agreed. We may call this third theory the argument from underrepresentation. It has only two failings: (1) its premise (that minority teachers
were underrepresented) is false; and (2) even if that premise were true,
it could not justify this racial preference.

How could the lower courts have reached the extraordinary conclusion that minority teachers were "underrepresented" in the Jackson
School District? In the ethnic numbers game the standard measuring
rod (as noted above) is the percentage of minority employees in the
relevant labor pool. On that standard, the figures given above plainly
show that the Jackson schools certainly were not discriminating against
blacks in 1980-81, although they may have been discriminating against
whites.

The lower courts noted this standard explicitly — but then refused to apply it. What numerical standard did they apply? The percentage of minority *students* in the school district! It did not matter how many black teachers were in fact available in Michigan, said the courts; minorities were "substantially and chronically underrepresented" because the ratio of black students to white students was greater than the ratio of black teachers to white teachers. And on what ground was this new standard defended? On the ground that teachers are role models for their students!

> [I]n the setting of this case, it is appropriate to compare the percentage of minority teachers to the percentage of minority students in the student body, rather than with the percentage of minorities in the relevant labor market. It is appropriate because teaching is more than just a job. Teachers are role models for their students. This is vitally important because societal discrimination has often deprived minority children of other role models.[7]

With superficially plausible passages like this one, well-meaning but confused, the seeds of racial bitterness are planted. The argument is a *non sequitur*. From the fact that minority children need positive role models it is inferred, uncritically, that only same-race role models will serve; but even if that oversimplification were true, it certainly would not follow that to provide such same-race role models the *proportion* of minority teachers must equal the proportion of minority students. Such a quota — and in use it was a quota in the strict sense, since persons in other racial categories lost their jobs as a consequence of its application — is nothing short of outrageous. The principle upon which it relies is that every ethnic subset, every national, religious, and racial minority in every school population, has a constitutional entitlement to a proportion among its public-school teachers equal to the proportion that subset constitutes among public school students.

This principle is not merely difficult to apply. It is also internally incoherent because of the mix and overlap of groups. The objective confusedly in mind is not merely distant, it is utterly unrealizable for reasons both logical and factual. Yet the conclusion that minorities were "underrepresented" among Jackson teachers could only have been reached with that principle and that objective assumed. Additional same-race role models had somehow to be shown to be a compelling need; their overpowering importance is therefore first asserted, and racial preference then defended on the ground that the critical function served by same-race role models can only be fulfilled when the number of minority teachers becomes proportional to the number of minority students. In Jackson, reasoning of this caliber cost teachers their jobs.

Proportionality by race among public-school faculties had previously been before the U.S. Supreme Court. In *Hazelwood School District v. United States,* in 1977, the claim that minority teachers were underrepresented was based on a comparison of the proportion of minorities among the teachers with the proportion of minorities among the general population.[8] That comparison was rightly rejected by the Court, and with its rejection went this warning: "When special qualifications are required to fill particular jobs, comparisons to the general population (rather than to the smaller group of individuals who possess the necessary qualifications) may have little probative value."[9] Gently put.

But if the probative value of racial proportions among the general population is low, how much lower is the probative value of racial proportions among student populations? Demographic factors bearing heavily upon the racial mix among students may have very little bearing upon teacher availability. The increasing departure of white families from the cities, and white students from the public schools, results in a steadily increasing proportion of minority students in urban public-school districts. In some cities, that proportion exceeds 70 and even 80 percent. But the flow of teachers, white and black, is largely determined by considerations of very different kinds.

So long as the percentage of minority students in the public schools exceeds that of minority teachers — an increasing, not decreasing inequality — those who would apply the numerical standard used by the lower courts in this case are like dogs chasing their tails. To match the ratio of black or Hispanic students in a given district, black or Hispanic teachers must be drawn away from other districts — either blocking the pursuit of the same objective in other well-integrated districts, or reducing the number of minority teachers in districts where the proportion of minority students is small. For universal application the standard is absurd; by means of naked racial preference it might be achieved in a few districts, but only at the cost of resegregating, or tending to resegregate, many others. Its general use would, in any event, undermine honest efforts to integrate all the public schools. Never was there a more painful case of zeal outrunning good sense.

Had the standard laid down in *Hazelwood* — that the appropriate comparison, if any, would be "between the racial composition of [the district's] teaching staff and the racial composition of the qualified public-school teacher population in the relevant labor market"[10] — been applied in the present case, the conclusion forced (as earlier noted) would be that, for mysterious reasons, minority teachers have been for some years overrepresented in the Jackson School District. But if the "relevant-labor-market" standard had been established by the Supreme Court, how could the lower courts have replaced it with a different standard of their own in this case?

The maneuver, technically tricky, went like this. Between the *Hazelwood* decision in 1977, and the District Court's decision in the present matter in 1982, yet another case of this kind — *Oliver v. Kalamazoo Board of Education* — had been tried, this one in the Western District of Michigan. There the trial court had accepted the percentage of black students in that district (Kalamazoo) as the basis for explicit hiring and layoff quotas. This decision was reversed upon appeal, its reliance upon percentages in the student population being manifestly in error.

But *Oliver* had not yet been reversed when *Wygant* was first decided, so the use of student percentages in *Oliver* was relied upon in this case by the Eastern District Court. By the time *Wygant* was argued on appeal, however, *Oliver* had been reversed — and yet the Sixth Circuit Court permitted, in Jackson, the use of student populations forbidden in Kalamazoo. How could it? It could, said the appellate panel, because in Kalamazoo the quota was imposed by a court, while in Jackson it was the product of a labor-management contract. Judicial remedies (said the court) are subject to stricter constitutional standards than are racially preferential programs devised by local governments.

The irony of this distinction is that a judicial remedy (even when mistakenly based on student populations, as in *Oliver*) is issued only where some formal finding of discriminatory wrongdoing has been made. In *Wygant*, where there was no such finding and could have been none, a racially preferential device was approved that, by the appellate court's own reasoning, would certainly have been struck down if any lower court had ordered it as compensatory relief! In this upside-down condition the case of Wendy Wygant moved to the Supreme Court of the United States.

VII

Might the case for minority underrepresentation in Jackson be made hypothetically by showing that if the layoff plan were not in effect, the decline in the number of minority teachers would result in their being inadequately represented? During oral argument before the Supreme Court the attorney for the board made that try. Justice Sandra Day O'Connor, after observing that the Court would normally "look to see whether the government can demonstrate a compelling state interest to justify such a [racial] classification" went on to ask: "Now what is the compelling interest that the School Board asserts here? Is it to maintain a faculty-student ratio or is it some other purpose? What do you rely on today?" The board's attorney first replied by saying that two factors, the need for integration and the need for a diversified faculty, were equally important. The exchange continued:[11]

> *Justice O'Connor:* So the Board does rely essentially on a faculty-student ratio and the role-model rationale.
>
> *Attorney for the Board:* Justice O'Connor, I didn't say that and I didn't mean that. I think what I was looking at specifically was, was it their duty to integrate, how to go about that integration, and certainly at the same time — and we make no apology for it — educationally —
>
> *Justice O'Connor:* Integrate in hiring. You are talking about hiring employees?

This question the board's attorney first evaded by remarking upon the racial complexion of the Jackson school during the 1950s and 1960s, which, according to him, led in 1972 to "the allocation of the faculty." He then continued:

Attorney for the Board: Now, the reason it [race-based layoff] is addressed in Article XII is if you are not going to do something about layoffs is it going to be considered by the public as a good-faith effort to integrate?

Justice O'Connor: Maybe I can't get an answer, but I really would like to know what the compelling state interest is that you are relying on for this particular layoff provision in a nut-shell.

Attorney for the Board: ... to protect the gains made that was going to allow us to do that as we looked at what we certainly thought were some of the factors we ought to be looking at like faculty and wanting a diverse ethnic faculty, to protect that we had to have Article XII. [*sic*]

Justice O'Connor: To preserve a faculty-student ratio that the Board thought was appropriate?

Attorney for the Board: If you are not going to protect them in a layoff, you are really going through an exercise in futility in hiring in the first place. We wanted them there. We had to have a method of protecting them. ... If you are going to apply straight "inverse order [of seniority] to minorities" those gains were going to be long gone pretty quickly.

This is false. Years of experience in Jackson prove the contrary to be the case. Layoffs on a straight inverse-seniority basis were made in the very early 1970s, when the seniority of minority teachers was relatively lower than it was ten years later — and the percentage of minority teachers at that time steadily increased. Again in 1974, when seventy-five layoffs were made, the board refused to comply with the preferential provision in Article XII, whereupon the percentage of minority employees nevertheless went *up,* from 11.1 in 1974 to 11.4 in 1975. In 1981, had layoffs *not* been preferential, the minority-faculty proportion resulting would have remained at nearly 12 percent — higher than the percentage of minority teachers in the relevant labor pool. Racial preference cannot be defended here as necessary to protect integration already achieved. In every version, the argument from underrepresentation is hopeless.

VIII

The argument from underrepresentation fails for a deeper reason: it relies upon the seriously mistaken assumption that, absent discrimination, all ethnic groups would be randomly distributed among all categories of employment. With this conviction tacitly in mind, every departure from random distribution is held explainable only by some form of ethnic oppression. A just society, on this view, will be a homogenized society. Reformers find, of course, that reality does not approximate their vision; having confounded equal treatment with numerical proportionality, they cannot rest content until the latter is achieved, since its absence is, for them, the sure mark of injustice. Statistical "underrepresentation" thus becomes the warrant for racially preferential instruments to set things right.

This vision underlying the argument from underrepresentation is not merely unrealistic, it is unwholesome. Even where discrimination is wholly absent, patterns of employment (or recreation, or education, etc.) are rarely random across ethnic groups, and for good reasons. Human beings commonly work and play, live and study, with fellow members of the groups — religious, racial, national — with which they most closely identify themselves. Ethnic clumps, the natural product of what we regard with pride as "cultural pluralism," may be broken up by force, but they will re-form as soon as the external pressure is removed. The evidence for this is overwhelming, both from the social sciences and from everyday experience. Decades of studies, sociological and historical, by scholars around the globe who have carefully noted and discounted discriminatory factors, leave the matter in no doubt. Cultural homogeneity — numerical proportionality in employment and other critical spheres — never can be real, never should be thought ideal.

The error is dangerous. If the numerical "representation" of Jews or blacks is taken to be no more than a factual report of the frequency with which the members of those groups are found, or not found, in certain employments (or other spheres) the numbers may be innocuous. When those reports are so framed as to imply that random distribution is a *moral* standard and that departures from it therefore indicate the presence of "societal discrimination," the use of numbers proves insidious. Even if (as was not the case in *Wygant*) comparisons are made with the "relevant labor pool," statistically even distributions are not to be expected. Living and working patterns among Mormons and Episcopalians are likely to prove very different; so also will be the workforce distributions of Italians and Swedes. Numerical proportionality in the outcome is not simply a crude standard, it is a wholly unsuitable standard by which to judge the fairness of a social process.

Of course some ethnic patterns *are* the result of discrimination, overt and covert; the deliberate exclusion of blacks, Jews, and others has been commonplace. To suppose that invidious maltreatment never had a role in creating ethnic clusters would be as wrongheaded as to suppose that all clustering entails such maltreatment. Causal factors in this sphere are exceedingly tangled. Nothing could be clumsier, or more obtuse, than social instruments designed on the assumption that one factor, invidious racial discrimination, is the paramount cause of every nonrandom ethnic distribution. Yet it is precisely upon such an assumption that racially preferential programs — in *Wygant* and in uncountable other contexts — are founded.

Ironically, the drive to achieve racial "balance" has consequences the very reverse of those hoped for. Wanting racial justice, the advocates of group proportionality do racial injustice; seeking to eliminate discrimination by race, they encourage and even employ it. The racial bitterness it has taken our country decades to reduce is now recreated and exacerbated by deliberate racial favoritism.

IX

The premise of the argument from underrepresentation is plainly false. In Jackson the numbers show it false on its face. And even if that were not so, the argument wrongly supposes that nonrandom ethnic distributions entail "societal discrimination" as their cause. But the lower courts in *Wygant* erred more profoundly still. Not only did they use the wrong numbers, and then go on to draw unwarranted conclusions from the numbers they did use — they did all this relying upon a distorted conception of constitutional and moral rights.

The lower courts argued in effect: "The failure to achieve the correct ratios in the Jackson schools proves societal discrimination. Those hurt by this discrimination are off the stage and cannot be compensated; those who did the hurting are also long gone and cannot make restitution. But because minority groups have been unfairly treated over generations, those groups are entitled to favored treatment now. Race-based layoffs, protecting low-seniority members of such groups who have not themselves been discriminated against, are but one device to accomplish this."

The burden imposed by racially preferential devices, however, is not carried by a group; the majority feels nothing. It is individuals from whom the price is exacted — Wendy Wygant and unnamed others who are made to pay for wrongs they did not do, to persons who were not wronged.

Naked racial preference is ultimately grounded upon *groupthink*. But rights do not inhere in groups; they are possessed by persons, human beings, and it is deeply wrong to injure individual persons in pursuing the alleged interest of some racial class by advantaging its uninjured members. The equal protection of the laws is a guarantee upon which no qualification by race, or religion, or nationality can have any bearing whatever. In our Constitution, that protection is explicitly afforded in the *singular,* to "any person." As the Supreme Court has repeatedly affirmed, "The rights created by the Fourteenth Amendment are, by its terms, guaranteed to the individual."[12]

Blacks, Asians, Jews, and many other groups have been historically discriminated against, often brutally. It simply does not follow, in morals or in law, that individual blacks, or Asians, or Jews, who were not damaged are entitled now to special favor in the name of group redress. In this Republic, happily, that theory of collective rights has been rejected. The *Wygant* case gave to the Supreme Court the opportunity to reaffirm this rejection in terms so clear and so forceful as to put an end, unambiguously, to groupthink in American law.

X

Finally, who is a member of what race? Homer A. Plessy was the central figure in the infamous case of *Plessy v. Ferguson* in which the "separate but equal" doctrine was approved by the Supreme Court in 1896.[13] Plessy was seven-eighths white and one- eighth black, and "the mixture of colored blood was not discernible in him." He was a black man under Louisiana law; in other states he would then have been classified as white. How would the Jackson Board of Education classify him today? If black, such a person stands to enjoy a valuable employment benefit. If he claims it, who shall determine whether he is entitled to it? And by what criteria shall they decide?

Embarrassing these questions may be, but rhetorical they are not. In New York City in the autumn of 1985, when racial quotas were used in making police-department promotions, a rash of petitions was received from individual officers seeking to change the racial designation in their employment records to that of some minority. By such matters are we confronted unavoidably when once we begin, as a society, to "think with our blood."

"Orientals" are given preference in the Jackson schools, presumably because they were once discriminated against. The substantial Finnish community in Michigan is still discriminated against in some quarters — but Finns do not qualify for special treatment in Jackson, probably because not many of them remain there. There are not very many Orientals in Jackson either, but a third-generation Chinese-American, whose mother and father may be university professors, will have his or her job specially protected in the Jackson schools because he or she is, in the parlance of affirmative action officers, "a minority."

As for "Spanish descendancy" — who can say? If one's grandfather's name were Gonzales one is likely to be entitled to special protection in Jackson — unless that happened to be one's maternal grandfather, in which case the rules are not clear. Between Supreme Court Justice Powell and the attorney for the Jackson Board of Education there took place, during oral argument, the following colloquy:

> *Justice Powell:* I was interested in the fact that minorities described in the collective bargaining agreement include blacks, American Indians, Orientals, or persons of Spanish descendancy. How in the world would you determine who is a person of Spanish descendancy?

> *Attorney for the Board:* Well, I didn't write that.

> *Justice Powell:* Pardon me?

> *Attorney for the Board:* I didn't write that. Hispanics may have been a better term. I guess we just didn't think about it, Justice Powell, at that point. I think we were looking at Hispanic people.[14]

Wherever racial preference is given there must be rules — required mixtures of blood, and required epidermal hues, black or brown or whatever — to determine racial membership. There must also be public officials with the authority to apply those rules. In the Jackson, Michigan schools today, as in the Jackson, Mississippi schools of an earlier day, such rules are no doubt applied with scrupulosity. Now, as then, it is a nasty business.

Here is the lesson of *Wygant:* the equal protection of the laws requires not merely the evenhanded application of legal categories; it requires that every single person be protected against the invidious use of some categories. Above all, the categories to be abjured are those of race. If that is done, *Wygant v. Jackson Board of Education* may become a true landmark in American constitutional history.[15]

NOTES

1. *Wygant v. Jackson Board of Education*, 476 U.S. 267 (1986) is discussed on pp. 177-80.

2. Wygant and seven other tenured teachers lost in the Eastern District Court of Michigan in 1982 (546 F. Supp 1195), and lost again in the Sixth Circuit of Appeals in 1984 (746 F. 2d 1152). The case was argued orally before the Supreme Court (#84-140) on 6 November 1985. The Supreme Court decision in this case was issued finally on 19 May 1986, three months after this essay was written: *Wygant, et al. v. Jackson Board of Education,* 476 U.S. 267.

3. Article XII, Section B.1, of the Jackson Schools teacher contract (emphasis added).

4. M. W. Clague, "Voluntary Affirmative Action Plans in Public Education: Matching Faculty Race to Student Race," 14 *Journal of Law and Education* No. 3, July 1985.

5. The same-race role-model justification of preference was, indeed, rejected flatly: 476 U.S. 267, pp. 274-76.

6. 746 F. 2d 1156 (emphasis added).

7. Ibid.

8. 433 U.S. 299.

9. Ibid., p. 308.

10. Ibid., p. 307.

11. These passages are quoted from the *Official Transcript of Proceedings Before the Supreme Court of the United States*, 6 November 1985, Case #84-1340, pp. 30-33.

12. *Shelley v. Kraemer,* 334 U.S. 1, 22 (1948).

13. 163 U.S. 537.

14. *Official Transcript,* pp. 42-43.

15. Wendy Wygant and her colleagues did prevail (476 U.S. 267). The decision in that case is examined in part E.

E

Heads of the Hydra

From *Firefighters* to *Adarand* (1984 - 1995)

Hercules was assigned twelve labors as penance for his misdeeds; as the second of these he was obliged to kill the Hydra, a beast with nine heads. The task appeared impossible; one of the nine heads was immortal, and of all the other heads, when Hercules cut off one, two grew up in its place. Finally he did succeed, using a burning brand with which he seared the neck of each head as he cut it off anew. The last head could not be killed, of course, but was permanently disposed of by being buried securely under a great rock.

Eliminating racial preference will require Herculean tenacity. When racial preference in hiring was cut off by the Civil Rights Act of 1964, it emerged in other forms as preference in layoffs and promotions. When racial preference for minority businesses in the form of "set-asides" was cut off (in *City of Richmond v. Croson*, 1988[1]) it reappeared in the preferential policies of federal agencies. And when racial preference in university admissions was cut off (in *Regents v. Bakke*, 1978[2]) it reemerged in a variety of preferential affirmative action programs at colleges and universities across the country. Racial preference has many heads.

In *Bakke* the Supreme Court had held that colleges may not give preference simply to insure that their student bodies manifest some specified percentage of some ethnic group(s). Racial preference for that

purpose the Court called "discrimination for its own sake" and held to
be "facially invalid."[3] Nor may preference be given to counteract the
effects of "societal discrimination" because (said the Court) to prefer
persons of one race at the expense of persons of another race requires
the authoritative finding that some law had earlier been violated — a
finding that neither universities nor employers are authorized to make.
Admissions committees and personnel departments may not, therefore,
set themselves up as courts in equity.

New forms of racial preference were devised to evade this restriction. One such device in the sphere of employment was the firing of
more-senior white employees on the basis of race to protect the jobs of
less-senior employees who were black. This head of racial preference
was first cut off by the Supreme Court in 1984 in *Firefighters v. Stotts*.[4]
The beast remained very much alive. In Jackson, Michigan, white public school teachers continued to be laid off to protect the jobs of less
senior black teachers. Racially preferential firing was once again cut off
in 1986, in *Wygant v. Jackson Board of Education*,[5] and that case became
a landmark, not only because a brand was used to sear the neck of this
device, but because in *Wygant* the Supreme Court formulated unambiguously the standard against which, thenceforth, every race-based preference would have to be judged: Was the preference justified by some
compelling governmental interest? And, if so, was the preference *narrowly tailored* to achieve its *remedial* purpose?

After *Wygant*, advocates of racial preference had to prove that their
goals were in fact compelling. They are compelling, said some, because
racial injuries had earlier been inflicted by governments themselves,
and this is proved (they alleged) by the statistical disparities between the
ratio of whites to minorities in the general population, and that same
ratio in many specific employment contexts. This defense of preference
was emphatically cut off in 1993, in *Maryland Troopers Association v.
Evans:* no racial wrong (said the court) may be inferred from the bare
fact that persons in various ethnic groups manifest their work preferences in ways that are statistically lumpy and clustered, rather than racially "balanced."[6]

While preference in *employment* was at issue in the preceding set of cases, preference in the form of racial *set-asides* had become the focus in another set of cases. A set-aside incorporated in a federal statute had been approved in 1980 in *Fullilove v. Klutznick*, the Supreme Court there deferring to the special authority of Congress.[7] Local governments around the country thereupon sought to do what Congress had done, giving racial preferences by setting aside percentages of their contracts for minority-owned business enterprises. In *City of Richmond v. Croson,* the most important case in this arena since *Wygant*, this head of racial preference was cut off and with very strong language its neck too was seared.[8] The Court explicitly reaffirmed the standard established in *Wygant*: Is the interest pursued compelling? Not unless it can be shown that an identifiable racial injury had been done by the government now seeking to give remedial preference by race. And (assuming such a compelling interest could be specified) are numerical set-asides based upon race narrowly tailored remedies for those earlier injuries? On the *Wygant* standard, the Richmond preferences were struck down; set-asides are not likely to meet the constitutional standard for equal protection of the laws.

The fact that the Supreme Court had earlier deferred to the authority of Congress in one case led to the adoption of racially preferential policies by some federal agencies, defended as preferences indirectly authorized by Congress. The Federal Communications Commission, in its award of broadcast licenses, gave preference to "Minority Business Enterprises" for the sake of programming diversity. When this policy confronted the Supreme Court in *Metro Broadcasting v. FCC* in 1990,[9] no majority of the Court could be gathered; the preferential policies of the FCC, viewed by a plurality as having the imprimatur of Congress, were approved.

Since 1990 the membership of the Supreme Court has changed significantly. Justices Brennan, Marshall, and White, all of whom had supported racial preferences of the FCC in *Metro Broadcasting*, are no longer on the Court. But the dissenters in that case (Justices O'Connor, Scalia, Kennedy, and Chief Justice Rehnquist) remained as members of the Court in the autumn of 1994 when racial preference by a federal agency was once again accepted for adjudication in the case of *Adarand Constructors v. Pena.*[10] Between the earlier decisions in *Weber* and *Metro Broadcasting* on one side, and the decisions in *Wygant* and *City of Richmond* on the other side, there is a tension that demands resolution. Even the power of Congress to give naked preference by race may soon be buried, by the Supreme Court, beneath a great rock.

7

Preference as a Remedy for Racial Injury

Firefighters v. Stotts (1984)

The race-based practices of the Fire Department in the City of Memphis had created an ugly and tangled situation. To settle earlier complaints of discrimination against blacks, the city had agreed in 1980 to a consent decree, issued by a federal district court, governing Fire Department promotion practices with respect to race. When financial constraints later forced layoffs in the department, that court issued an injunction in 1981 requiring white employees with greater seniority to be laid off when the otherwise applicable seniority system would have called for the layoff of black employees with less seniority. This explicit preference, protecting the jobs of some employees simply because of their race, was rejected by the Supreme Court in 1984.[11]

Employees must often vie with one another for more desirable assignments or to avoid layoff; the established "competitive seniority" list normally resolves such rivalries. Courts will not upset established seniority systems of this kind by awarding additional seniority to some plaintiff unless (as the Supreme Court has directed) the beneficiary of such intervention has been proved to be a victim of earlier illegal discrimination by that employer. Race-based seniority assignments may be defended only by a narrowly specified remedial purpose.

Naked preference was thus to be precluded. Where preference is genuinely remedial "make-whole relief" may be awarded, but it may be awarded only to those who deserve to be made whole, who have themselves been injured by unlawful discrimination. The consent decree in Memphis was not like that; it protected black employees who had not been injured, and did so at the expense of white employees who had done no injury; it transformed an earlier remedy into an outright preference for all persons of a given race. That consent decree was cut off.

Reviewing the congressional debates at the time the Civil Rights Act was enacted in 1964, the Court noted that the remedies possible under the act were sharply limited, and those limitations were repeatedly emphasized by the *proponents* of the law. Opponents had contended that under the Civil Rights Act employers might be ordered to hire and to promote persons in order to achieve a racially balanced workforce, even though the beneficiaries of such orders had not been the victims of illegal discrimination. Replied the bill's sponsors: Never; *that could not happen*; no such racial balancing could be ordered by any court, and there would be no authority for any race-based remedy without proof of earlier injury suffered by those preferred.

Twenty years later the district court in Memphis did precisely what the authors of the Civil Rights Act said could never be done. The Supreme Court decision in *Firefighters* quotes the floor manager of the Civil Rights Act, Senator Hubert Humphrey:

> No court can require hiring, reinstatement, admission to membership, or payment of back pay for anyone who was not fired, refused employment or advancement or admission to a union by an act of discrimination forbidden by this title. This is stated expressly in the last sentence of Section 707(e).... Contrary to the allegations of some opponents of this title there is nothing in it that will give any power to the [Equal Employment Opportunity] Commission or to any court to require

... firing ... of employees in order to meet a racial "quota" or to achieve a certain racial balance. That bugaboo has been brought up a dozen times but is nonexistent.[12]

Assurances to exactly the same effect came repeatedly from all sides: racial balancing (ordered by the lower court in Memphis in 1981) was precisely what the Civil Rights Act would *forbid*. The Republican sponsors of the Civil Rights Act in the House of Representatives published a memorandum explaining the remedial powers given by the bill to the courts. They wrote:

Upon conclusion of the trial, the federal court may enjoin an employer or labor organization from practicing further discrimination, and may order the hiring and reinstatement of an employee, or the acceptance and reinstatement of a union member. But Title VII does not permit the ordering of racial quotas in business or unions.[13]

Making the same point, the Senate sponsors of the Civil Rights Act distributed a bipartisan newsletter during the debate in the Senate, explaining that:

Under Title VII, not even a Court, much less the [Equal Employment Opportunity] Commission, could order racial quotas or the hiring, reinstatement, admission to membership or payment of back pay for anyone who is not discriminated against in violation of this title.[14]

Senators Case and Clark, the bipartisan floor captains of Title VII, issued yet another memorandum, reemphasizing the restriction on remedies:

No court order can require hiring, reinstatement, admission to membership, or payment of back pay for anyone who was not discriminated against in violation of [Title VII]. This is stated expressly in the last sentence of section 706(g).[15]

A careful examination of the language of Title VII of the Civil Rights Act of 1964, and of the spirit with which it was enacted by the Congress, makes it very clear that the 1981 order of the district court in

Memphis did precisely what federal law forbids. A normal seniority system in the Memphis Fire Department was wrongly replaced by a system specifically designed to give preference by race to persons who had not themselves been discriminated against. Of course that order could not stand. Justice White, delivering the opinion of the Supreme Court, made it unmistakably clear that "mere membership in the disadvantaged class is insufficient to warrant a [preferential] seniority award; each individual must prove that the discriminatory practice had an impact on him."[16] *Firefighters* makes it clear that a genuine remedy cannot possibly entail giving preference to the whole of a racial class. And therefore a court may use its remedial powers, as Justice O'Connor wrote there, "*only to prevent future violations and to compensate identified victims of unlawful discrimination.*"[17]

8

When Is a Racial Remedy Justifiable?

Wygant v. Jackson Board of Education (1986)

Wholesale racial preference was not to be permitted; the decision in *Firefighters* made that clear. But a response had not yet been given to a more general question: By what *standard* can we determine when, if ever, a race-conscious preference would be permissible?

In the context of college admissions the question had been addressed eight years before in *Bakke*. But a standard derived from the Constitution and applicable to all settings in employment as well as in education, was wanting. Two years later in the case of *Wygant v. Jackson Board of Education*[18] that standard was formulated. Once again Justice Powell wrote for the Court.

The standard by which the equal protection clause is to be applied, said the Court, has two prongs: First, any proposed racial classification must be justified by "a compelling governmental interest"; *and* second, the preferential means chosen by the state to effectuate its purpose must be "narrowly tailored to the achievement of that goal."[19]

This was meant to be a standard difficult to meet. Race (like national origin and religion) is always a *suspect* category. The only interest compelling enough to justify its use by government is that of doing justice, giving redress for an identified racial injury. For racial preference to be constitutionally permissible, therefore, the governmental unit giving preference must itself have been guilty of earlier racial discrimination, discrimination for which the proposed race-based measures might provide appropriate remedy.

In the Jackson schools (as in most settings where preferential affirmative action has been introduced) nothing of that kind could be shown; the school board's preferential system was thrown out. A school board, aiming at racial proportionality by forcing the layoff of white teachers with greater seniority in order to retain minority teachers with less seniority, violates the equal protection clause of the Fourteenth Amendment of the U.S. Constitution.[20]

The several kinds of justification that had been proffered by the school board were examined and rejected in turn:

1. The "role model theory." Although used by some to defend racial preference, such a theory (said the Court) bears no relationship to any alleged harm caused by prior discriminatory practices.[21] Were we to accept the claim that black students are better off with black teachers, it could be similarly argued that white students are better off with white teachers; a very small number of black teachers might then be justified by the small number of black students. A role model theory could thus be used as a device to *evade* an obligation to give remedy where remedy is due. The premise that students need as "role models" teachers of a certain race, said Justice Powell, "could lead to the very system the Court rejected in *Brown v. Board of Education*.[22] Role model theories for the justification of racial preferences were rejected without qualification.

2. "Societal discrimination." This is an amorphous and totally unsatisfactory ground for racial preference. "No one doubts that there has been serious racial discrimination in this country," Justice Powell wrote. "But as the basis for imposing discriminatory *legal* remedies that work against innocent people, societal discrimination is insufficient and

overexpansive."[23] Particularized findings of discrimination by the agency in question are what must be shown; without such findings racially preferential remedies based on "societal discrimination" could be "ageless in their reach into the past, and timeless in their ability to affect the future."[24]

3. Discrimination by the school board itself. Anticipating that the defense of their racially preferential program would be sustained by the Supreme Court only if it could be considered a remedy for proved discriminatory practice, the Jackson School Board belatedly sought to persuade the Court that, if given an opportunity, it could establish the existence of prior discrimination on its own part. No such proof was in fact offered. Indeed, that very issue had been years in litigation, and in three separate lawsuits the Jackson School Board had repeatedly *denied* the existence of prior discriminatory hiring practices on its own part. This hypothetical justification was discarded with the others.

In sum: no compelling governmental interest to justify racial preference was shown or could be shown in this Michigan case. The school board's discriminatory plan fails on the first prong of the *Wygant* standard.

It fails also on the second prong, since it certainly could not be shown, even had its ends been considered compelling, that the means chosen by the board to achieve them were "narrowly tailored." On this aspect of the standard the case against the board was overwhelming. The record of the case established conclusively that the board's preferential layoff provision was directly tied to a goal of racial *proportionality*, not remedy. Moreover the racial proportions aimed at could have nothing whatever to do with earlier discrimination by the board, if there had been any, because the plan's numerical targets were determined not by the percentage of qualified minority teachers within the relevant labor pool, but by the percentage of minority students in the Jackson school district! This is a proportionality that bears (as Justice O'Connor wrote in a concurring opinion) "no relation to the remedying of employment discrimination."[25]

Layoffs determined by race are a particularly ill-suited means to any governmental end, Justice Powell observed, because they "impose the entire burden of achieving racial equality on particular individuals, often resulting in serious disruption of their lives. That burden is too intrusive."[26] Therefore, even if the purposes of the plan had been truly compelling (which they were not) the preferential layoffs introduced could not be adjudged "narrowly tailored" to their achievement. Racial preference as manifested in the employment practices of the Jackson School Board — practices mirrored in school boards and other governmental agencies across the country — could not possibly satisfy the constitutional demands of the equal protection clause.

9

When Is a Governmental Interest Compelling?

Maryland Troopers Association v. Evans (1993)

Any justification of preference by race must begin with the showing that the government interest served by it is compelling. That principle, laid down clearly in *Wygant* and in *Firefighters*, was inescapable. And the only interest that will serve, that is sufficiently compelling, is that of giving remedy to persons earlier injured by race. Therefore, those determined to save racial preferences were forced to prove some earlier discriminatory injury to the racial class now to be preferred. But how do that? What evidence can establish such wide-scale victimization?

"Numerical disparities" was the device relied upon. In the employment patterns of blacks and whites (and other ethnic groups) there are, of course, many disparities. The ratio of blacks to whites in some profession or trade, or employed by some unit of government, may differ greatly from the ratio of blacks to whites in the population at large. The causes of these disparities are many and complex.[27] Advocates of preference contended that these numerical disparities constitute *prima facie* proof of racial discrimination. Since (they argued) these disparities show that an entire racial class has been victimized, every member of that class minimally qualified for some specific employment or promotion must now be entitled to the preferential remedy.

Numerical disparities sometimes are the product of racial discrimination, but in many contexts such disparities have nothing to do with discrimination. In these times, one who suggests that the cause of those disparities may be something other than discrimination is likely to be charged with racism because, if that were so, the needed victimhood is rendered doubtful and the case for preference undermined. However unfair it may be, the charge of racism is seriously damaging; the safest course for threatened bureaucrats is to accept the claims of victimhood and give the preferences demanded.

In 1990 the Maryland State Police had adopted a plan under which they agreed to hire and promote certain percentages of black troopers at each rank. The Troopers Association called foul, arguing that these racial preferences violated the equal protection clause of the Constitution. The State of Maryland rejoined that the hiring and promotion preferences adopted were justified by statistical disparities between the numbers of minorities in the state police and the numbers of minorities minimally qualified to be state troopers — disparities that allegedly proved that the state police had long discriminated against blacks.

This evidentiary claim was at first accepted by a district court, which agreed that the gap between the percentage of black troopers at various ranks and the percentage of Maryland residents between twenty and fifty-eight years old with a high school diploma, proved that black officers had been "the victims of past discrimination in promotions." But when the Federal Court of Appeals, in *Maryland Troopers v. Evans*,[28] subjected the numbers underlying this argument to careful scrutiny, that decision was reversed and the preferential scheme for promotion and hiring was jettisoned.

Past discrimination against blacks in Maryland was not at issue; a history of general societal discrimination, said the Court, cannot justify race-conscious relief. To defend race-based programs, the state must identify the specific racial discrimination it purports to remedy. If a preferential plan is then adopted it must be shown "narrowly tailored" to redress those injuries earlier identified. And such preferences, if justified, "may remain in effect only so long as necessary to remedy the discrimination at which they are aimed; they may not take on a life of their own."[29]

The argument of the State of Maryland, crudely statistical, could not possibly satisfy this *Wygant* standard. The Court wrote:

> Inferring past discrimination alone [as the cause of disparities] assumes the most dubious of conclusions: that the true measure is always to be found in numeric proportionality. The Fourteenth Amendment does not embody that view....There is no reason here, for example, to assume that well-qualified minority applicants prefer police work to the spectrum of other public and private employment opportunities available to them. Thus, only when there are "gross statistical disparities" between the racial composition of the employer's workforce and the racial composition of the relevant qualified labor pool may a court infer that the employer has racially discriminated.
>
> The record in this case is devoid of anything approaching the "gross disparity" that must be present when statistics are offered as a predicate for race-conscious relief. A race-conscious remedy is simply too drastic a measure to rest upon the slender reed of appellee's [the state's] statistical comparisons.
>
> Appellees cannot escape the reality that these preferences will deny some persons the opportunity to be a state trooper or to advance as a state trooper solely because they belong to a certain race. The Constitution simply will not allow opportunity in employment to be compromised on so invidious a ground.[30]

The State of Maryland had also argued that race-based preferences must be retained indefinitely, in spite of the fact that a substantial number of blacks had become state troopers in recent years. Why? To prevent backsliding. The Court of Appeals dismissed this argument with a warning too seldom respected:

> Finally, we reject appellees' argument because it presumes that race-conscious relief must end later rather than sooner, and be-

cause it postpones the day when the constitutional promise of equality before the law can be achieved. The case against race-based preferences does not rest upon the sterile assumption that American society is untouched or unaffected by the tragic oppression of its past. Rather, it is the very enormity of that tragedy that lends resolve to the desire never to repeat it, and to find a legal order in which distinctions based on race shall have no place.[31]

10

Racial Preference through Set-Asides

Fullilove v. Klutznick (1980)
City of Richmond v. Croson (1988)

I. How Set-Asides Work

In 1983 the City of Richmond, Virginia, adopted a "minority business utilization plan" which required prime contractors to whom the City awarded construction contracts to subcontract at least 30 percent of the dollar amount of the contract to one or more "minority business enterprises" (MBEs). An MBE was defined as "a business at least fifty-one percent of which is owned and controlled ... by minority group members." And "minority group members" were defined as "citizens of the United States who are Blacks, Spanish- speaking, Orientals, Indians, Eskimos, or Aleuts." On one contract the J. A. Croson Company was the only bidder, yet it was denied the contract (the project was subsequently rebid) pursuant to the minority set-aside ordinance. Croson sued for damages. This notable case, *City of Richmond v. Croson*,[32] reached the U.S. Supreme Court in 1988.

The Richmond City Council, a majority of which was black, had defended the set-aside as a remedy for past discrimination in the construction industry, in Richmond and countrywide. But the evidence supporting the claim that there had been discrimination against minority contractors in Richmond was scant, and convincing proof was given by local contractors that they had never discriminated against minority firms. Moreover, the number of MBEs in the City of Richmond could not possibly satisfy the 30 percent set-aside requirement, since at that time only 4.7 percent of all construction firms in the United States were minority owned, and of these nearly half were in four large states and Hawaii.

Croson's complaint was at first (in 1985) rejected. But when the preferential ordinance was again reviewed by the Fourth Circuit Court of Appeals in 1987, the governing standard was that established by the Supreme Court in *Wygant* a year earlier. The Richmond set-aside plan was thrown out completely. "A municipality that wishes to employ a racial preference," said that Court, "cannot rest on broad-brush assumptions of historical discrimination" to establish the compelling need for remedy.[33] "Findings of *societal* discrimination will not suffice; the findings must concern 'prior discrimination *by the government unit involved*.'"[34]

Statistics comparing the percentage of blacks in the Richmond population and the percentage of contracts awarded to blacks in Richmond had no argumentative merit, said the court of appeals; even proposing those numbers as proof suggested "more of a political than a remedial basis for the racial preference."[35] The claim that there was a compelling governmental interest justifying the Richmond set-aside was far-fetched. "If this plan is supported by a compelling governmental interest [wrote the appellate court], so is every other plan that has been enacted in the past or that will be enacted in the future."[36] And even if one assumed some compelling governmental interest in the case, the race-based quota in the form of a 30 percent set-aside makes it evident that the Richmond plan could not have been "narrowly tailored" to accomplish any remedial purpose.

The United States Supreme Court affirmed this rejection of the Richmond set-aside. Six members of the Court, in four separate and largely concurring opinions, condemned the plan in language strong enough to be called a burning brand; of the three dissenting justices, none remain on the Court. The principles in *Wygant* were once again applied; the law of the land with respect to racial preference through municipal set-asides was made crystal clear.

II. The Federal Precedent

A racial preference as blatant as that in Richmond could be defensible only if the city were believed to have extraordinary authority to determine when earlier discrimination had taken place, and had the authority to determine what may serve as appropriate remedy for it if it had. Such authority is given to the Congress of the United States by the Constitution; and in 1977, Congress, as part of its Public Works Employment legislation that year, had set aside 10 percent of each grant under the act for minority business enterprises.

When that set-aside had come before it in 1979 (in *Fullilove v. Klutznick*[37]), the Supreme Court had felt bound to defer to Congress, a coequal branch charged by the Constitution with the power to "provide for the general Welfare" and authorized specifically by the Constitution to "enforce by appropriate legislation" the equal protection guarantees of the Fourteenth Amendment. The federal set-aside was not struck down, and because it was not, Richmond and many other municipalities came to believe that they might do as Congress had done. But the authority of cities and states differs vastly from that of the Congress.

The majority opinion in *Fullilove* was written by Chief Justice Burger, asking and answering two key questions:

1. Were the objectives of the legislation in that case within the power of Congress? Answer: Yes. Under its specific power to enforce the Fourteenth Amendment, and under its constitutional powers to regulate commerce, Congress — but not any lesser governmental unit, of course — had the power to enact that 1977 set-aside. In the Congress at that time the set-aside provision had been described as "designed to begin to redress

this grievance that has been extant for so long."[38] Chief Justice Burger concluded that the bill was enacted by Congress "as a strictly remedial measure."[39]

2. Was the use of racial and ethnic criteria a permissible means for Congress to carry out its objectives within the constraints of the Constitution? Answer: Yes. "[I]n no organ of government, state or federal, does there repose a more comprehensive remedial power than in the Congress, expressly charged by the Constitution with competence and authority to enforce equal protection guarantees."[40]

Concurring, Justice Powell observed that any interest in creating a race-conscious remedy is not compelling, and any purported race-conscious remedy therefore not permissible, *unless* an appropriate governmental authority had made specific findings of constitutional or statutory violations. Our national legislature is authorized to do this, he argued, and did so in this case. Powell contrasts this congressional device with the race-conscious admissions system struck down in *Bakke*, where the University of California did not make specific findings of constitutional or statutory violations, did not have the authority to make such findings, and in any case did not have the authority to give remedy if they had made them.[41]

The approval of the set-aside in *Fullilove* met with substantial constitutional objections. Congress has broad powers under the Constitution, to be sure — but even Congress, in the exercise of its powers, must obey the Constitution. Justice Stewart wrote in biting dissent: "If a law is unconstitutional, it is no less unconstitutional just because it is a product of the Congress of the United States."[42]

Although the *Fullilove* majority sought to characterize it as remedial, the set-aside cannot be honestly described as redress for injury. To be that, the legislature enacting it must have functioned as a court in equity, which it never did or can. There is no serious possibility that race-conscious remedies can be devised, by statute, for some generalized discrimination in an industry. And even if Congress were to act as though it could serve as such a court, it would need (to justify its set-aside as remedy) some evidence that Congress *itself* had engaged in racial discrimination in the disbursement of federal contracting funds. That is the evidence that a judicial decree would have required, but there was no such evidence in this case. And Congress has no greater authority than the judiciary when it imposes burdens based upon race.

III. Municipal Set-Asides Condemned

Cities and states around the country, learning a very bad lesson from Congress, undertook ethnic engineering by set-aside. But when such state-authorized set-asides finally reached the Supreme Court in *City of Richmond* in 1988 that lesson had to be unlearned; the states certainly do not have the authority to use such preferential devices. Said the Court:

> That Congress may identify and redress the effects of society-wide discrimination does not mean that, *a fortiori*, the states and their political subdivisions are free to decide that such remedies are appropriate. Section I of the Fourteenth Amendment [guaranteeing the equal protection of the laws] is an explicit constraint on state power, and the States must undertake any remedial efforts in accordance with that provision. To hold otherwise would be to cede control of the content of the Equal Protection Clause to the 50 state legislatures and their myriad political subdivisions. The mere recitation of a benign or compensatory purpose for the use of a racial classification would [in that case] essentially entitle the States to exercise the full powers of Congress ... and insulate any racial classification from judicial scrutiny. ...[S]uch a result would be contrary to the intentions of the Framers of the Fourteenth Amendment, who desired to place clear limits on the States' use of race as a criterion for legislative action, and to have the federal courts enforce those limitations.[43]

Justice Stevens, joined by Justices Stewart and Rehnquist, found the description of the Richmond set-aside as a "remedy" to be plainly incorrect;[44] and even if it were a remedy, they pointed out, a set-aside that benefits a narrow subclass of minority entrepreneurs most of whom had not themselves been injured cannot possibly be viewed as an appropriately tailored remedy. The racial set-aside, said they, is a clear instance of invidious discrimination by race alone, without genuine remedial functions, and therefore a clear violation of the Constitution.

In fact that set-aside was patently not remedial, even though it declared itself to be so. A disparity between the percentage of prime contracts awarded to minority firms and the minority percentage in the population of Richmond proves nothing, as the court of appeals had said. Construction contractors are highly specialized, and it must not be assumed that "all citizens are fungible for purposes of determining whether members of a particular class have been excluded."[45] The city council did not even know how many qualified minority business enterprises there were in Richmond at the time; nor did they know what percentage of city construction dollars went to minority firms as prime or subcontractors. The Supreme Court opinion puts the matter bluntly: "The 30% quota cannot in any realistic sense be tied to any injury suffered by anyone."[46]

If the set-aside had been genuinely remedial, there would have to have been proof of some "identified discrimination" by the City of Richmond whose redress might constitute the compelling government interest required. There was no such proof, because there was no such discrimination. "Societal discrimination" against blacks there surely has been — but that generalization cannot serve as the needed "compelling interest" because if it did (the Court notes) that "would give local governments license to create a patchwork of racial preferences based on statistical generalizations about any particular field of endeavor."[47]

By the first prong of the *Wygant* standard, therefore, the Richmond set-aside plan is devastated. By the second prong of that standard — that the race-based measure be narrowly tailored to achieve its end — that devastation is made complete. The contract quotas in Richmond could not be "narrowly tailored" because those quotas bore no relation to the injuries they were alleged to address. Consider:

1. A set-aside requires the employment of minority firms without regard to the actual history of those firms' past treatment. No

inquiry regarding any injury a minority business enterprise may or may not have suffered from previous discrimination by the City of Richmond or by prime contractors was ever undertaken. Whether the "remedy" went to those deserving remedy (if any) was a question never even asked.

2. A racial set-aside based on percentages cannot be "narrowly tailored" since it rests upon the false assumption that minorities will choose a particular trade in lockstep proportion to their representation in the local population — an assumption the Supreme Court called "completely unrealistic." The only goal to which the 30 percent set-aside in Richmond could have been tailored was, Justice O'Connor observes, "outright racial balancing."[48]

3. The class of persons benefited by a racial set-aside is not limited to the victims of alleged past discrimination, but is bound to include persons who were never so injured. Persons who had never been in business in Richmond, persons who themselves may have discriminated against other minority groups or may have prospered because of that discrimination, persons who had never even been in Richmond — all stood to benefit from the Richmond set-aside.

4. Set-asides are commonly made ridiculous by the inclusion of categories of beneficiaries whose suffering from past discrimination by that government unit is highly improbable. In Richmond the preference was given to "Spanish-speaking, Oriental, Indian, Eskimo, and Aleut" persons. The Eskimo population in Virginia is likely to have been small; whether any single Aleut ever lived in Richmond is very doubtful. The city council had simply copied the words of the federal statute that had passed muster in *Fullilove* years before. But if this set-aside were an honest remedy for past discrimination in Richmond, why must those deserving the remedial relief share it with an Aleut citizen who moves to Richmond tomorrow? The unthinking inclusion of Aleuts, Eskimos, and so on, is good evidence that the set-aside was adopted without any

serious attention to specifiable injury for which redress was to be designed. Said Justice O'Connor: "Under Richmond's scheme a successful black, Hispanic, or Oriental entrepreneur from anywhere in the country enjoys an absolute preference over other citizens based solely on their race. We think it obvious that such a program is not narrowly tailored to remedy the effects of prior discrimination."[49]

5. Set-asides give no consideration whatever to the persons obliged to bear their burden. In Richmond the white contractors who bore the burden may well have included some who were in fact guilty of past discrimination against blacks, but, as Justice Stevens writes, "it is only habit, rather than evidence or analysis, that makes it seem acceptable to assume that every white contractor covered by the ordinance shares in that guilt."[50]

Even worse than the burden upon the disadvantaged class is the burden the preference imposes upon those who were to be given special advantage. Justice Stevens continued:

Although [legislation of this kind] stigmatizes the disadvantaged class with the unproved charge of past racial discrimination, it actually imposes a greater stigma on the supposed beneficiaries [because] a statute of this kind inevitably is perceived by many as resting on an assumption that those who are granted this special preference are less qualified in some respect that is identified purely by their race.

When [government] creates a special preference, or a special disability, for a class of persons ... defined in racial terms [there are] only two conceivable bases for differentiating the preferred classes from society as a whole: (1) that they were the victims of unfair treatment in the past and (2) that they are less able to compete in the future. Although the first of these factors would justify an appropriate remedy for past wrongs, for reasons I have already stated, this statute is not such a remedial measure. The second factor is simply not true.[51]

The Richmond racial set-aside was held a clear violation of the Fourteenth Amendment of the U.S. Constitution. When Justice O'Connor, writing for the Court, cites that famous passage guaranteeing equal protection, she adds emphasis to two of its words: "No state shall ... deny to *any person* within its jurisdiction the equal protection of the laws." Another famous passage interpreting that clause, many times repeated in rejecting race-based remedies, she emphasizes as well: the rights created by that clause of the Constitution are expressly guaranteed to *individual* persons; they are *personal* rights.[52]

By denying some the opportunity to compete for a fixed percentage of public contracts simply because of their race, the Richmond plan violated their personal rights. There is indeed a moral difference between racial preference motivated by selfish convictions of racial superiority, and racial preference motivated by the desire to achieve greater equity. But race preferences of every kind are ugly; they always do stigmatize; they always do promote notions of racial inferiority; and they often are the product of what Justice O'Connor called "racial politics."[53] However benign the motives of the City of Richmond, its preferential set-aside plan was racism, plain and undisguised.

On every aspect of every reasonable standard for the use of racial classifications by government, the Richmond set-aside fails, as every racial set-aside with the same essential features must fail, to satisfy the constitutional demand that every person be guaranteed the equal protection of the laws.

11

Racial Preference by Federal Policy

Metro Broadcasting v.
Federal Communications Commission (1990)

I. Racial Preference in Another Shape

The real objective of most current affirmative action programs is ethnic proportionality, racial balance. The use of numerical targets (or goals, or quotas) to achieve that objective generally fails to meet constitutional standards because the "targets" are not designed to remedy a discriminatory wrong. It is *claimed* that they are instruments of redress — because only if that were true might they be permissible under the Constitution. University admissions based on race are certainly not giving redress to injured applicants, any more than contractors benefiting from racial set-asides are being compensated for damage done to them. Calling these devices remedies is an error or a lie. Race-based employment preferences can be honestly defended as remedies only in rare circumstances. So other devices to advance ethnic proportionality came to be tried.

Preferential policies by federal agencies is one of these. This form of preference is difficult to cut off because, since the rule-making agency was established by Congress, its policies are claimed to have congressional authorization. The standard formulated by the Supreme Court in *Wygant*, and since reaffirmed repeatedly, bars racial preference in most spheres, but the application of that standard has been vacillating where *federal* policies are involved.

There are very many such federal policies, taking a great variety of forms. They are to be found in the official regulations of the federal Departments of Agriculture, Commerce, Defense, Education, Energy, Health and Human Services, Housing and Urban Development, Interior, Justice, Labor, State, and Transportation. Federal policies giving preference by race appear also in laws pertaining to banking, communications, the environment, small businesses, veterans affairs, and especially federal grants and procurement. The Congressional Research Service of the Library of Congress identified, in 1995, *one hundred sixty-nine* specific instances in federal statutes, regulations, programs, and executive orders in which explicit provision is made for preferences to be granted to individuals on the basis of race, sex, national origin, or ethnic background.[54] Such preferences include, but are not limited to, affirmative action goals, timetables, set-asides, and quotas.

Among the most egregious of these many preferences are policies of the Federal Communications Commission having a direct and plainly injurious impact upon nonminority broadcasters who are not preferred; these have become the focus of far-reaching litigation. The FCC gives preference by race in the following ways: (1) In the competition for new broadcast licenses substantial minority preference is given; a "quality enhancement credit" for minority ownership is awarded by the FCC when faced with mutually exclusive applications for the same broadcast channel.[55] (2) Under the "distress sale policy" of the FCC, existing licensees in jeopardy of having their licenses revoked are given the option of selling their license — but only to a minority owned or minority controlled firm — for up to seventy-five percent of their fair market value.[56] These policies came before the Supreme Court in 1990, in *Metro Broadcasting v. FCC*[57]; the preferences were sustained by a plurality of the Court, but no majority rationale for them could then be agreed upon.

The preferential policies of the FCC are certainly not remedial. No earlier race-based injury by that agency can be identified, and even if it could, those benefiting from the current preferences are very certainly not those who may earlier have suffered. How then might the FCC policies be justified? Everything depends upon the standard under which they are reviewed. The defenders argued that the standard of review ought to be lower than elsewhere, because Congress had a role in the adoption of those policies. In this sphere, even the Supreme Court found it difficult to agree upon the appropriate criteria for judgment.

The preferences work like this: Metro Broadcasting, Inc., would certainly have been awarded the new television license for which it competed in the 1980s, but for the fact that its competitor was minority-owned. Metro was actually awarded the license in the first competition held by the FCC, but that result was overturned by the commission's Review Board, which gave to the competitor's application a *"substantial* enhancement" on the ground that it was 90 percent Hispanic-owned, while Metro had only one minority partner who owned 19.8 percent of the enterprise. Metro was locally owned (in Orlando, Florida) and the competitor was not; Metro was admittedly superior in "civic participation." All Metro's merits were outweighed, however, by the competitor's "minority credit."[58] Metro lost out.

Shurberg Broadcasting, Inc., was denied consideration for the acquisition of a broadcast license under the FCC distress-sale policy that requires licenses so disposed of to go to minority applicants only. The D.C. Court of Appeals invalidated the preferential distress-sale policy in the Shurberg case, holding that it unconstitutionally deprived Shurberg of equal protection rights. Because the policy gives absolute preference to minorities, said the appeals court, it "unduly burdens Shurberg, an innocent nonminority, and is not reasonably related to the interests it seeks to vindicate."[59] Both Metro and Shurberg contended that they were denied the equal protection of the laws; on appeal to the U.S. Supreme Court the two cases were consolidated in *Metro Broadcasting v. The FCC.*

II. The New Defense of Racial Preference

A plurality opinion of the Court authored by Justice Brennan decided this case. The decision was grounded chiefly on the claim that the FCC is empowered by Congress, which is authorized to adopt such policies. The justifiability of the preferences on their merits remained in controversy.

Brennan's argument was in essence this: The policies in question do not violate equal protection because (1) although not themselves adopted by Congress, they "bear the imprimatur of long-standing Congressional support," and because (2) they are "substantially related to the achievement of the important governmental objective of broadcast diversity."[60]

It was the "lesson of *Fullilove*" on which the plurality opinion was grounded: "race-conscious classifications adopted by Congress to address racial and ethnic discrimination are subject to a different standard than such classifications prescribed by state and local governments."[61] Racial classifications are suspect; the standard for the judgment of suspect classifications is normally that of *strict scrutiny*, the highest standard by design. But where, as in this case, congressional authority is involved (on this view) that standard need not be applied.

What standard should replace strict scrutiny here? The test, Brennan answers, should have two parts: First, do the minority ownership policies in question serve some "important governmental objective"? He finds that they do. Second, are the preferential policies "substantially related to the achievement of that objective"? He finds that they are.

The important government objective that racial preference is here claimed to serve is *broadcast diversity*. The plurality disclaims the remedial justification:

Congress and the [Federal Communications] Commission do not justify the minority ownership policies strictly as remedies for victims. ... Rather, Congress and the FCC have selected the minority ownership policies primarily to promote programming diversity. And they urge that such diversity ... can serve as a constitutional basis for the preference policies. We agree."[62]

"Diversity" is the key. In *Bakke* it had been held that a "diverse student body" contributed to a "robust exchange of ideas" and that some race-conscious programs may be justified, in universities, to advance that First Amendment value.[63] The diversity of views and information on the airwaves, Brennan argues, serves the same important value. All members of the community, not the favored minority only, benefit from a wider range of information sources. This objective is surely one of great importance.

Preferring minorities for the ownership of broadcast stations, Brennan holds, is "substantially related" to the achievement of that government objective. Whether this is really true is a question of fact, and not of law, as Brennan himself points out. But when analyzing "the nexus between minority ownership and program diversity," great weight must be given to the judgments of Congress and the experience of the commission. The FCC adopted these policies after having sought broadcast diversity for a long time; Congress made clear its view that the minority ownership policies of the FCC do advance the goal of diverse programming. These determinations may be accepted as the answer to the factual question regarding the connection between minority ownership and program diversity.

The policies also have a remedial aspect, he holds. The barriers minorities face in entering the broadcasting industry are just what these preferential policies aim to overcome: a lack of adequate financing, paucity of information regarding license availability, and broadcast inexperience. It is true that the policies impose a burden on nonminority applicants, but such burdens are slight, Brennan concludes, because the number of licenses distributed under these policies is quite small.

In sum: the aims of the preferences are important, the FCC policies are suited to those aims, and the authority to adopt such policies is legitimate. Here racial preference may stand.

III. Racial Preference Condemned Once More

It may. But at the opening of the autumn term of the Supreme Court in 1994, four of those supporting the FCC in *Metro Broadcasting* (Justices Marshall, Blackmun, White, and Brennan himself) had left the Court. And the four whose dissent was sharply critical of that outcome (Justices O'Connor, Scalia, Kennedy, and Chief Justice Rehnquist) remained on the Court, joined by others who have made their opposition to racial preference quite clear. If the position of the dissenters in this case one day becomes the law of the land, naked racial preference, regardless of its authorizing body, may be strictly forbidden.[64]

Justice O'Connor begins the dissent by highlighting the fundamental premise of the Constitution upon which the guarantee of equal protection rests: that our government must treat citizens "as *individuals*, not as simply components of a racial, religious, sexual or national class."[65] It was upon this same premise that preferential set-asides had been cut off in *City of Richmond*. The constitutional standard formulated in *Wygant* is its corollary: racial measures are permissible only if grounded upon a compelling government interest, and then only if they are narrowly tailored to achieve that compelling end. On this standard, she concludes, the preferences of the FCC ought also to be cut off.

A. Racial Preference on Whose Authority?

Is the standard of judgment rightly lowered because the FCC acts as an agent of the Congress? Certainly not. The principles of justice that apply to the states and to all lesser governmental units in judging racial classifications must apply to Congress as well. The FCC gives benefits to some members of society, and denies benefits to others, based on their race or ethnicity. This is precisely what the equal protection of the laws forbids. Long experience has exhibited the dangers of such race-based thinking: it erodes individual dignity; it opens the door to discriminatory actions against other minorities in the interest of allegedly worthwhile goals; it embodies stereotypes that treat persons not as individuals but as tokens of their race. Racial classifications, whether intended to benefit some or to burden others, "stigmatize those groups singled out for differential treatment." They undermine our national commitment to evaluate individuals on their individual merit.

So harmful are classifications based on race, and so seldom appropriate as instruments of justice, that any defense of them must be unquestionably compelling. That is what the constitutional guarantee of equal protection demands. Neither the states, nor the Congress, may distribute benefits or burdens among individuals based on stereotypical assumptions about how members of a given race or ethnic group will think or act. The fact that there may have been some congressional involvement in the adoption of the FCC policies therefore cannot justify the application of a lower standard of review.[66]

Brennan's lower standard (Is the preference "substantially related" to an "important government interest"?) rested essentially upon the precedent in *Fullilove*,[67] where the lower standard was justified by the special authority of the U.S. Congress. But *Fullilove* cannot justify these FCC preferences, for two compelling reasons:

First, the authority of Congress was upheld (in *Fullilove*) only because the set-asides there were (allegedly) enacted specifically as *remedial* measures to compensate for past identified discrimination. But the preferential policies of the FCC were plainly not adopted for remedial purposes, and are not remedial in any sense. In oral argument before the Court the FCC admitted that its policies embodied no remedial purpose, and insisted that there had been no past discrimination by the FCC in the allocation of licenses. The language of those policies appeals to no remedial purpose whatever; the rationale given (by the FCC and by congressional reports) is clearly the promotion of "diversity." Even the Court plurality approving the FCC preferences makes no claim for their remedial purpose. It is therefore certainly the case that these policies cannot be upheld as remedial measures, and that therefore *Fullilove* cannot apply.

Second, in *Fullilove* the racial preferences given were held justifiable only as an exercise of powers specifically granted to Congress under Section 5 of the Fourteenth Amendment, which reads: "The Congress shall have the power to enforce by appropiate legislation, the provisions of this article." This one sentence in the Constitution, a grant of special remedial authority to the Congress specifically, is an authorization that certainly does not empower the Federal Communications Commission.[68]

The dispute between the Brennan group and the O'Connor group over the appropriate standard for judgment is of the highest importance. The standard of review, as Justice O'Connor writes, "establishes whether and when the Court and the Constitution allow the Government to employ racial classifications. A lower standard signals that the Government may resort to racial distinctions more readily."[69] The standard must not fluctuate with context; it is not dependent upon the race of those benefited or burdened (as noted in *City of Richmond*[70]); nor ought it shift with the unit of government whose preferences are in question. Said Justice Stevens in *Fullilove*: "Racial classifications are simply too pernicious to permit any but the most exact connection between justification and classification."[71] *Strictest scrutiny* is in every case the standard to be applied.

B. Racial Preference to Advance What Compelling Interest?

Under strict scrutiny, the government's use of racial classification may be supported only by a compelling interest. But the established law of equal protection, Justice O'Connor observes, recognizes only one such interest: remedying the effects of past racial discrimination.[72]

However "important" other interests may be thought, they cannot serve to justify imposing burdens by race. Even the interest in remedying general societal discrimination cannot be considered compelling because (again as noted in *City of Richmond*) it has "no logical stopping point" and would support unconstrained uses of racial classification.

Providing minority role models in a public school system to alleviate societal discrimination (as noted in *Wygant*) certainly cannot be considered compelling; it is an aim far too amorphous, and would allow "remedies that are ageless in their reach into the past, and timeless in their ability to affect the future."[73] And if the claimed objective is "representativeness" or ethnic proportionality, the distribution of goods "according to the demographic representation of particular racial and ethnic groups," that objective is to be condemned.

The purpose of the FCC — to increase the diversity of broadcast viewpoints — is certainly not compelling in the critical sense. Like the "role model" objective, it is, as Justice O'Connor writes, "simply too amorphous, too insubstantial, and too unrelated to any legitimate basis for employing racial classifications."[74] Even Justice Brennan, defending the preferences in *Metro Broadcasting,* never claimed the FCC's objective was compelling. He sought to bypass the need to make that claim by devising a new standard under which the term "compelling" drops out, and only "important" government interests are required. This is dangerous. Racial classifications are "so harmful that unless they are strictly reserved for remedial settings, they may in fact promote notions of racial inferiority and lead to a politics of racial hostility."[75]

The politics of racial hostility has at times been the ground of the government's use of racial classifications, to our national shame. When the Brennan plurality approved of race-conscious measures that are "not designed to compensate victims of past governmental or societal discrimination" but that "serve important governmental objectives ... and are substantially related to achievement of those objectives,"[76] the policy they proposed was not new to our country. That justification precisely had defended the old Louisiana law that required "equal but separate accommodations" for "white" and "colored" railroad passengers in 1896. The Supreme Court asked then — in *Plessy v. Ferguson*[77] — just as the Brennan plurality asked in *Metro Broadcasting* in 1990, whether the measures used were "reasonable." In that infamous old decision the Court went on to say: "In determining the question of reasonableness, [the legislature] is at liberty to act with reference to the established usages, customs, and traditions of the people, and with a view to the promotion of their comfort."[78] "Separate but equal" was the doctrine that argument yielded; it burdened American society for half a century because an invidious racial classification served the governmental interest of increasing the riding pleasure of railroad passengers.

In 1990 the interest to be advanced was not riding pleasure but listening pleasure; to promote broadcast diversity, we are told, the government may go so far as to discriminate among persons on the basis of their race. Justice Kennedy's dissent in *Metro Broadcasting* is disdainful, in places angry. The approval of the FCC preferences, he writes, exhumes *Plessy*'s deferential approach to racial classifications."[79] Once untie racial classifications from any goal of addressing past racial discrimination and there is no stopping any future legislature. "All that need be shown under the new approach … is that the future effect of discriminating among citizens on the basis of race will advance some 'important' governmental interest."[80]

Having linked the race of station owners to their stations' content, the government will be obliged to continue to determine which races to favor and which to disfavor. Many ethnic minorities have not been so fortunate as to make the FCC list of favorites — and there is no telling to whom the favor will or will not be given next. Even the *strictest* scrutiny did not block some convenient racial discriminations when the government held compelling the alleged need to put American citizens of Japanese descent into concentration camps during the Second World War. Now it is argued that we ought to reduce the level of scrutiny and seek only some "important" governmental interest. Racial preferences employed by the FCC might well be defended with a formal statement of interest like the following, appearing in an official publication of government: "The policy is not based on the concept of superiority or inferiority [of any race] but merely on the fact that people differ, particularly in their group associations, loyalties, cultures, outlook, modes of life." The government issuing this defense of preference was that of South Africa defending apartheid in 1960.[81] We are warned by the history of invidious governmental uses of race. Racial classifications have dreadful consequences "*when they stray from narrow remedial justifications.*"[82] A government interest that may truly justify a race-conscious measure must be so clearly tied to earlier racial injury and so verifiable that it supports racial classification in a sharply limited and carefully defined way.

The measures adopted by the FCC certainly fail on this standard. No one can be confident that a particular viewpoint would be associated with a particular race, or even how one might assess the diversity of broadcast viewpoints. There is no constraint on the preferences that might be justified in pursuit of "broadcast diversity." Nor would there be any limit to their duration; the preference could be defended indefinitely "first to obtain the appropriate mixture of racial views and then to ensure that the broadcasting spectrum continues to reflect that mixture."[83] We are likely to hear the argument, later actually presented by the State of Maryland,[84] that preferences must be retained indefinitely to prevent backsliding! Outright racial balancing, Justice O'Connor observes, is a "core constitutional violation."[85]

"But racial diversity is an honorable ideal," the defenders of affirmative action reply, "and our pursuit of it, although using racial classifications, is not invidious but benign." The intent may be benign, Justice O'Connor answers, but the reality never is. "'Benign racial classification' is a contradiction in terms," she writes, echoing Justice Douglas and the Supreme Court of Washington in *DeFunis* twenty years before. "To the person denied an opportunity or right based on race, the classification is hardly benign."[86] And to those who believe that they can readily distinguish the good from the hurtful uses of racial criteria

> history should teach greater humility.... "[B]enign" carries with it no independent meaning, but reflects only acceptance of the current generation's conclusion that a politically acceptable burden, imposed on particular citizens on the basis of race, is reasonable. ... Divorced from any remedial purpose and otherwise undefined, "benign" means only what shifting fashions

and changing politics deem acceptable. Members of any racial or ethnic group, whether now preferred under the FCC's policies or not, may find themselves politically out of fashion and subject to disadvantageous but "benign" discrimination.[87]

On its theory the FCC may one day seek to advance "viewpoint diversity" by identifying what it conceives to be a "Black viewpoint," or an "Arab viewpoint," and so on; and it may then, using its determination of which viewpoints are underrepresented, mandate programming, or deny licenses to those deemed less likely to present the favored views. And it will prove impossible, Justice O'Connor writes, "to distinguish naked preferences for members of particular races from preferences for members of particular races because they possess certain valued views; no matter what its purpose, the Government will be able to claim that it has favored certain persons for their ability, stemming from race, to contribute distinctive views or perspectives."[88]

That is an ugly prospect because we accept the premise that American citizens think and act and live not as representatives of racial or ethnic groups, as blacks or whites or Hispanics, but as individuals above all. And "we are governed by one Constitution, providing a single guarantee of equal protection, one that extends equally to all citizens."[89] Broadcast diversity, held by the FCC to justify race-based preference, is certainly not a compelling government interest.

C. Racial Preference as Crude Instrument

And even if diversity were compelling, the preferential policies in question are wholly unsuited to its achievement. Recall that the test of a proposed justification of preference has two prongs, of which the second is the *suitability* of the remedy to the wrong. Suppose (what has certainly not been shown) that there had been a discriminatory injustice in the historical failure to have minority viewpoints represented on the airwaves. There is no likelihood, almost no possibility, that giving current preference to license applications by minority owners could address that alleged wrong. Far from being "narrowly tailored" to fit the purported end, the preferences are not even substantially related to the end in question.

The FCC license preferences rely upon the crudest sort of racial stereotyping — the assumption that there are distinct viewpoints inhering in persons of a given skin color, and that therefore applicants of a given race are more "likely to provide [that] distinct perspective"[90] in their managerial policy than other applicants. To represent "minority tastes" the FCC would change the structure of station ownership. Race alone is made the necessary and sufficient condition of the preference, because race is presumed to entail certain beliefs and behaviors associated with the minority in question. Racial thinking of this kind, said another federal court, is contrary to "one of our most cherished constitutional and societal principles ... that an individual's tastes, beliefs, and abilities should be assessed on their own merits rather than by categorizing that individual as a member of a racial group presumed to think and behave in a particular way."[91] *Groupthink* is again the foundation of the preferences here: the presumption that persons regularly act and judge in a manner characteristic of their race.

Groupthink had been rejected a dozen years before, in *Bakke*, when the University of California had argued that members of minority groups ought to be preferred in admission to medical school because they were more likely to serve minority communities specially needing medical care. That presumption was rejected flatly; we may not assume that the choices people make, in work or in recreation, are determined by their race.

The presumption that viewpoint is a function of race was softened by the plurality in *Metro Broadcasting* with the contention that the tie between race and viewpoint (upon which their argument depends) is to be found only "in the aggregate."[92] But that qualification serves only to obscure the stereotype. Similar reasoning has been used to defend the presumption that men are the primary supporters of their spouses and children — but that generalization about the sexes serves to "justify the denigration of the efforts of women who do work and whose earnings contribute significantly to their families' support."[93] We must not rely upon generalizations about behaviors in the aggregate when making decisions seriously affecting individuals. Inferences drawn about blacks "in the aggregate" are as bad or worse than analogous inferences drawn about women.

Stereotypes about the tastes and opinions of minorities have, as corollaries, stereotypes about majority whites, disfavoring them because of the assumptions made about their tastes and opinions. But (just as in deciding which medical school applicants are more likely to give medical service where it is needed) we are obliged to consider applicants as individuals, and to respect them as persons, not merely as representatives of their race or sex. Generalizations about races or religions or sexes sometimes do have statistical merit, but even where that is so, the Supreme Court wrote in 1978, it is "an insufficient reason for disqualifying an individual to whom the generalization does not apply."[94]

"We would not tolerate the Government's claim that hiring persons of a particular race leads to better service 'in the aggregate,'" the dissent in *Metro Broadcasting* remarks, "and we should not accept as legitimate the FCC's claim in this case that members of certain races will provide superior programming, even if 'in the aggregate.' The Constitution's text, our cases, and our Nation's history foreclose such premises."[95]

Even if favoring license applicants by race did have the result of enhancing the viewpoints that the FCC finds underrepresented, such preference would be unacceptable so long as there remain other *race-neutral* means to achieve the same result. The FCC never determined that there is a need to resort to racial classification to achieve its asserted interests; it leaped to the use of race before race-neutral devices had been fully and vigorously tried.

What race-neutral methods might have been explored? Licensees could be required to offer programming of the kind that the FCC believes would add to viewpoint diversity. The commission claims that to have done that would have interfered improperly with First Amendment freedoms. But the FCC, as Justice O'Connor points out, cannot have it both ways. If the manipulation of programming is an objective that the First Amendment forbids the FCC to pursue directly, then the FCC may not seek to accomplish the same objective indirectly through racial preference; and if program diversity is an objective that is permissible in spite of First Amendment concerns, it must be pursued using race-neutral means, means that do not violate equal protection rights by giving crude ethnic favors.

To overcome the barriers of inexperience and underfinancing which have often inhibited broadcast station ownership there are many race-neutral means that might give greater access to persons, of whatever race or ethnicity, who have heretofore been excluded for financial or related reasons. But we ought not assume that station owners of one race can succeed in doing what owners of another race cannot succeed in doing. Station programming must compete in the broadcast market; black owners like white owners face the realities of that competition; black owners like white owners have only limited control over the content of the programming on their own stations.

If diversity of viewpoints is the end sought, and if it may properly be sought, then it should be sought directly rather than relying upon an impermissible categorization of applicants by race to achieve that end indirectly. If persons who have knowledge or experience of certain kinds are believed more likely to contribute to broadcast diversity, the FCC might directly inquire into the backgrounds of applicants, favoring those whose knowledge and experience are of the requisite sort — but giving that favor whatever their race, and not supposing, as present policies do, that the attitudes to be favored regularly accompany (or do not accompany) certain colors of skin.

In sum: There is no good excuse for the outright racism of the FCC policies here in question.

12

The Road to Hell Is Paved with Good Intentions

Racial preferences are commonly defended by decent people who mean to be just and to do good. But the use of racial classifications undermines the quest for social justice. Racial instruments are deeply flawed, and the results they produce are almost inevitably unjust, whatever the motives for their use. Deteriorating race relations across the country now drive this point home: racial preferences "foster intolerance and antagonism against the entire membership of the favored classes."[96]

Good intentions are not good enough. Of course those who defend racial favoritism do not mean to patronize minorities. But they do. Underlying all racial preference is the notion that members of certain minorities, needing favor, are inherently less able to compete on their own — whether in education, or in employment, or in construction, or in broadcasting, or elsewhere.

And the disfavored group, the white majority, is stigmatized as well because the charge of past racial discrimination is laid upon them all. The cardinal rule of the Constitution, that each citizen is protected as an individual and not merely as a member of a group, bars this presumption of racial guilt, but official preference nevertheless implies it, and the burden of guilt is borne by all members of the majority regardless of their actual past conduct. Some who acknowledge that racial preferences "trammel" the interests of majority citizens are willing to impose that penalty upon them (as Justice Brennan did explicitly) so long as rights are not trammeled "unnecessarily."[97] Very few today will think such trammeling by race is either fair or constitutionally permissible.

The first Justice Harlan, in his memorable dissent in *Plessy*, warned of the consequences of any formal rule dividing the races. Lamenting the approval of the "separate but equal" doctrine, he wrote in 1896: "The destinies of the two races, in this country, are indissolubly linked together, and the interests of both require that the common government of all shall not permit the seeds of race hate to be planted under sanction of law."[98] Now, one hundred years later, the seeds of race hatred have been replanted by institutionalized racial favoritism. Those seeds grow and fruit where wounds had begun to heal, as in our schools and universities where resentment, distrust, and hostility now thrive once more.

The American jurisprudent, Alexander Bickel, explained why racial preference invariably has this corrupting consequence. A system that favors or disfavors by race, he wrote

> derogates the human dignity and individuality of all to whom it is applied; it is invidious in principle as well as in practice. Moreover, it can easily be turned against those it purports to help. The history of the racial quota is a history of subjugation, not beneficence. Its evil lies not in its name, but in its effects: a quota is a divider of society, a creator of castes, and it is all the worse for its racial base, especially in a society desperately striving for an equality that will make race irrelevant.[99]

Concluding his biting dissent in *Metro Broadcasting*, Justice Kennedy notes with regret that "after a century of judicial opinions we interpret the Constitution to do no more than move us from "separate but equal" to "unequal but benign."[100] Some may rely upon a benevolent government to decide, on a case-to-case basis, which citizens shall be favored and which disfavored based on color of skin. But this enterprise, as Kennedy observes, is so very perilous that "the Constitution forbids us to undertake it."[101]

Racial hostilities are *engendered* by racial unfairness. The reason is this: race is a category having absolutely nothing to do with merit, or with genuine entitlement; its use in the distribution of goods — employment, promotion, licenses or contracts, admissions, or whatever — is therefore odious and by a good society repudiated. Racial favoritism first breeds resentment; resentment breeds distrust. Treatment perceived as unfair leads inevitably to anger, and the anger erupts in racial "incidents" — especially in schools and universities — which heighten tension and intensify racial hostility. Even when well meant, racism is nasty. Justice Stewart, dissenting in *Fullilove*, wrote: "There are those who think we need a new Constitution, and their views may someday prevail. But under the Constitution we have, one practice in which government may never engage is the practice of racism — not even 'temporarily,' and not even as an 'experiment.'"[102]

In those special circumstances in which we can ascertain that race was the ground of an earlier injury, and it is known by whom and to whom that racial injury was done, racial classifications can serve in the design of a fitting remedy. Such cases are very few. That is why our courts emphatically insist upon the standard of strict scrutiny in appraising any uses of race by the government — a standard made deliberately difficult to meet. No lesser standard ought be accepted; it should be difficult, very difficult, to justify any allocation on racial grounds. In a nation of equals race is a category whose use (however honorable the motive) is a signal of great danger.

With rare exceptions, therefore, race-based measures *cannot* do justice. To hire — or to admit, or to award, or to promote — in order to reach some numerical racial targets is almost certain to take from some what they deserve, and to give to others what is not deserved. At their best, racial preferences are crude; at their worst, they are cruel; in almost every case, they are unfair and counterproductive.

Our government is therefore forbidden to use race as a "proxy for other, more germane bases of classification."[103] When the FCC seeks to use race as a proxy for some views that it believes are underrepresented on the airwaves, or a law school uses race as a proxy for educational disadvantage, crudeness vitiates the effort to be fair. The mechanical use of a suspect classification is, as Justice O'Connor puts it, "the hallmark of an unconstitutional policy."[104]

Because race cannot identify what deserves to be considered in any allocation of goods in short supply, the uses of race will include or exclude clumsily and mindlessly. When broadcast licenses are being distributed, those who receive them on grounds of race are likely to include some of the favored minority who have no intention to broadcast the views or promote the tastes the FCC happens to believe underrepresented; minority owners favored may even find those views and tastes repugnant. Similarly, contractors preferred by race may themselves have discriminated by race, and are likely never to have been discriminated against. Racial instruments in such cases are sure to be *over*inclusive. But they are also almost sure to be *under*inclusive, because persons of the disfavored majority (given lesser consideration, or no consideration) may be the very ones committed to the presentation of underrepresented views, just as professional school applicants of the disfavored majority may have been specially suited to give the medical or legal service the racial policy had been introduced to serve. And all the while, most of those who had earlier been discriminated against get no advantage from the preferences awarded now. The distribution of benefits and burdens by race can neither give nor take what is rightly deserved.

Defenders of racial preference often answer as follows: "In using racial classifications we do not achieve a perfect fit between objective and instrument, of course. But race does provide a reasonably good measure of justice, and we would be foolish to eschew a helpful instrument because it sometimes gives a rough result. If most of those who get preference because of race deserve it, and most of those who bear the burden of that preference deserve to bear it either because of their own guilt or the benefits they have received from the past discrimination of others, we are justified in using racial categories even though we know the result may prove to be unfair in some cases."

The premise of this response is simply mistaken, the real state of affairs badly misdescribed. Racial classifications are not "helpful"; they don't come close to doing justice, even rough justice. On the contrary, they are almost invariably hurtful and do injustice because the nature of the favor given is such that those who *can* take advantage of it are almost sure to be among those who do not deserve it. And those who may indeed deserve some remedy are almost sure to be among those who *cannot* benefit from the kinds of preference given. The minority business enterprises receiving preference from the City of Richmond were almost certainly not those who had suffered from racial discrimination in that city. And the nonminority firms disadvantaged by the Richmond plan are almost certainly not those who had been discriminatory (if any had been so) in times past.

Employment preferences likewise cannot achieve their aim. Black employees given preference over Brian Weber for promotion by Kaiser Aluminum[105] had not been discriminated against by Kaiser, and so far as we know had not suffered employment discrimination by anyone. Kaiser, like other firms and institutions responding to the demands of "affirmative action," went searching for blacks to fill its numerical targets; it mattered not that those advantaged had not been earlier injured by race. And those who bore the burden of the preference — Weber and other low-ranking white employees — were, so far as can be known, totally innocent of any charge that they had discriminated against black fellow workers, nor would it even have been possible for them to discriminate in ways that affected the employment opportunities of their peers.

So also in the Jackson School District,[106] as in school districts and other public bodies across the country, persons given racial preference by affirmative action using numerical targets had themselves rarely been discriminated against. And those like Wendy Wygant and her colleagues, laid off to protect the jobs of black teachers with much lower seniority, had never discriminated against anybody, and certainly not against fellow teachers given preference over them.

In the sphere of college admissions it may almost be said that the condition for receiving affirmative action favor is being not entitled to

it. That persons are in a position to accept preferential admission is normally a consequence of the fact that they come from good homes and
schools, making their university admission feasible. But those in the
racial minority who really had been discriminated against are very unlikely to be qualified for admission to any college, however extreme its
affirmative action program; the compensatory device is useless to them.
And whoever it is that may have discriminated against blacks and other
minorities in early education, it is a certainty that the guilty parties are
not the white students who are displaced by preferential affirmative action. Those displaced, it turns out, are seldom the well-prepared children of the affluent middle class who will not likely be denied, but most
often the marginal white applicants who, like their black counterparts,
had struggled to achieve the social mobility that higher education might
at last provide — only to learn that they had the misfortune to bear the
wrong skin color.

Again and yet again the pattern repeats itself. State troopers given
preference by race for promotion in Maryland;[107] highway contractors
given preference by race in Colorado;[108] applicants for admission to colleges and professional schools given preference at the University of
California and the University of Texas[109] and in almost every university
in the country — all these suffered rarely if at all from discrimination
by race. And those displaced by them were guilty of nothing. Set-asides,
admission preferences, license preferences — all are examples of the
inappropriateness and inadequacy of racial categories in the quest for
justice. The sorry history of discrimination against blacks in this country no one will deny. But now to repeat that story with a different set of
victims — once again burdened by color of skin! — is irony almost too
bitter to swallow. "Where injustice is the game," as Justice Scalia wrote
in *City of Richmond*, "turnabout is not fair play."[110]

Why is it so commonly *thought* fair? Because groups rather than
individuals are assumed to be moral agents and the bearers of rights.
Our moral reasoning is distorted by an irrational preoccupation with
ethnic groups. When our nation discriminated against people whose
skins were black or brown, it was done with the conviction that "they"
were as a class inferior, not worthy of the opportunities or respect to

which "we" were entitled. Some blacks are stupid, of course, but many more whites are stupider still; genius and talent, incompetence and indolence, are characteristics of persons, not groups, and have nothing to do with one's "race." Yet now again we seek to cope with social problems by dealing with people as members of their races first of all, counting the number who "represent" the several races, bickering inevitably over the division of the spoils by race.

The bickering is made nastier by the impossibility of determining fairly who is a member of which group, or why. Self-identification as black, or Hispanic, and so on, is perfectly satisfactory so long as the categories are informal, serving the personal or cultural interests of those who so identify themselves. But when the categories become official, with important advantages (or disadvantages) flowing from certain group memberships, the rules of membership must be made public and fair. In his dissent in *Fullilove*, Justice Stewart wrote: "Laws that operate on the basis of race require definitions of race. ...[O]ur statute books will once again have to contain laws that reflect the odious practice of delineating the qualities that make one person a Negro and make another white."[111]

The underlying mistake now is the same we made in less enlightened times: treating people as though their merits and their entitlements are a function of their group. But groups do not have skills or talents; human beings do. Groups do not exhibit industry or sloth, brilliance or determination; individual men and women do. Groups possess no rights. The right to fair treatment, the right to be considered equally under the law, cannot possibly inhere in blacks or whites "in the aggregate," but only in persons, because only persons can be the bearers of rights. The moral blunder that led to centuries of oppression against people of color is the very same moral blunder that now underlies unfairness directed at people of paleness. We are doomed to repeat all the mistakes and brutalities of a dreadful history of racial conflict if we continue to organize society, and regulate society, and seek justice within society, by apportioning goods to ethnic and racial groups. It was and is a terrible mistake from which we are now reaping a terrible harvest.

There will be no healing until we return to the ideal of honest individu-
alism.

Justice Scalia, in *City of Richmond*, condemned the uses of racial
discrimination to solve social problems as unavoidably self-destructive.
His reasoning was ineluctable:

> The benign purpose of compensating for social disadvantages,
> whether they have been acquired by reason of prior discrimina-
> tion or otherwise, can no more be pursued by the illegitimate
> means of racial discrimination than can other assertedly benign
> purposes we [the Supreme Court] have repeatedly rejected.[112]

We cannot discriminate to provide "role models" for minority students; we cannot discriminate in awarding the custody of children to
avoid social pressures; we cannot discriminate to avoid tension in pris-
ons; we must not seek to cure the disease with a remedy that insures its
perpetuation.

> The difficulty of overcoming the effects of past discrimination
> is as nothing compared with the difficulty of eradicating from
> our society the source of those effects, which is the tendency —
> fatal to a Nation such as ours — to classify and judge men and
> women on the basis of their country of origin or the color of
> their skin. A solution to the first problem that aggravates the
> second is no solution at all. I share the view expressed by Alex-
> ander Bickel that "[t]he lesson of the great decisions of the
> Supreme Court and the lesson of contemporary history have
> been the same for at least a generation: discrimination on the
> basis of race is illegal, immoral, unconstitutional, inherently
> wrong, and destructive of democratic society."[113]

It is true, Scalia notes regretfully, that in one case in 1980 (*Fullilove
v. Klutznick*) the Court did uphold the use of a discriminatory set-aside,
ostensibly as a remedy. But no single opinion in that case commanded
more than three votes of the Court, and from those assorted opinions it
is impossible to derive any satisfactory rationale for a generalized racial
preference, save only that Congress was then held to have the power to
give it. That very matter will come again before the Court,[114] but what-

ever Congress may ultimately be held authorized to do, it is certainly true that the several states and their subordinate units are absolutely forbidden by the Civil War Amendments to discriminate by race to achieve the objectives they think important. Neither Virginia nor its cities may discriminate by race; neither California nor its universities may discriminate by race; neither Michigan nor its school boards may discriminate by race. The Thirteenth, Fourteenth, and Fifteenth Amendments to our Constitution were plainly designed (as the Court has written) to be "limitations upon power of the States," designed "to take away [from the states] all possibility of oppression by law because of race or color."[115] It does not matter which racial group gets the preference, or whether the aim in giving it is invidious or altruistic. By race the business of this country may not be conducted.

Of course, as noted earlier, there are special circumstances in which racial classifications are essential to undo the known effects of identified racial discrimination by a state agency. It is the duty of the states to dismantle a state-imposed dual system of education, and to do this it may be necessary to use measures incorporating some racial classifications.[116] But if race may be used, rarely, to desegregate racially segregated students and teachers, this authorized remedial power "extends no further than the scope of the continuing constitutional violation."[117] And when the dual system has been disestablished, the authority of the states to assign students by race comes to certain end.

We are rightly determined to eradicate the effects of past discrimination. That will not be easy. But when race preference has been finally repudiated we may more vigorously attack those effects using a wide array of measures that do not involve classification by race. In the sphere of state contracting, for example, preference may be given to small businesses, or to new businesses. In college admissions we may give preference to those in financial need, or to those who have suffered unfair educational handicap. And so on. Policies of this kind may indeed have racially disproportionate impact, favoring blacks and other minorities, but they are not (and must not be) *based* on race.

And where awards were previously made on the basis of race, wrongfully discriminating in favor of white workers or white contractors, a state may remedy such wrongs using race to reallocate those jobs or contracts to others who were in fact entitled to them. Remedies of this kind do not disfavor people because of their race; they correct an injustice that was done on the basis of race, and whose correction therefore entails the use of race. Nothing stops the City of Richmond from giving preference now to contractors identified as the victims of past discrimination by that city. This policy also may benefit mainly blacks, of course — but it would not then be giving preference *because* of race.

Every preferential program that gives to some (injured or not) because of their race, takes from others (guilty or not) because of their race. The victims of such injustice are not "the majority" but individual human beings (sometimes identifiable, often not) who bear the burden of wrongs committed by others long before they had even come upon the scene. Justice Powell, in *Wygant*, pointed out that a layoff system favoring blacks imposes an intolerable burden upon a few, innocent, individual whites. In that case those victims were identifiable. But every preferential system imposes burdens borne by particular persons. An affirmative action admissions system in a medical school or a law school that gives preference to minorities entails that some whites who would otherwise have been admitted will be rejected on racial grounds. This differs from the circumstances in *Wygant* in that we may not in this case know which, among the white applicants, have been for this reason excluded. But the fact that we cannot name these victims does not eliminate the moral defect. We know those victims exist, and the unfairness to them is no less unacceptable because we do not know their names. A quarter of a century ago Justice Douglas wrote:

> A DeFunis who is white is entitled to no advantage by virtue of that fact; nor is he subject to any disability, no matter what his race or color. Whatever his race he had a constitutional right to have his application [to the University of Washington Law School] considered on its individual merits in a racially neutral manner.[118]

The anxiety to atone for the injuries so long done to blacks and others leads us to forget that it is individuals who suffer injustice, and individuals whose equal rights are guaranteed. "When we depart from this American principle," Justice Scalia wrote in *City of Richmond*, "we play with fire, and much more than an occasional DeFunis, Johnson, or Croson burns." He summed up eloquently the essential evil of preference by race:

> It is plainly true that in our society blacks have suffered discrimination immeasurably greater than any directed at other racial groups. But those who believe that racial preferences can help to "even the score" display, and reinforce, a manner of thinking by race that was the source of the injustice and that will, if it endures within our society, be the source of more injustice still. The relevant proposition is not that it was blacks, or Jews, or Irish who were discriminated against, but that it was individual men and women, "created equal," who were discriminated against. And the relevant resolve is that that should never happen again. Racial preferences appear to "even the score" (in some small degree) only if one embraces the proposition that our society is appropriately viewed as divided into races, making it right that an injustice rendered in the past to a black man should be compensated for by discriminating against a white. Nothing is worth that embrace. Since blacks have been disproportionately disadvantaged by racial discrimination, any race-neutral remedial program aimed at the disadvantaged as such will have a disproportionately beneficial impact on blacks. Only such a program, and not one that operates on the basis of race, is in accord with the letter and spirit of our Constitution.[119]

NOTES

1. 488 U.S. 469.
2. 438 U.S. 265.
3. Ibid., p. 307.
4. 467 U.S. 561.
5. 476 U.S. 267.

6. 993 F.2d 1072.

7. 448 U.S. 448.

8. 488 U.S. 469.

9. 497 U.S. 547.

10. Supreme Court Docket No. 93-1841.

11. Two cases, both rather complicated, were consolidated in this litigation: *Firefighters Local Union 1784 v. Stotts, et al.*, and *Memphis Fire Department v. Stotts, et al.* Justice Byron White was the author of the Court's opinion.

12. 110 Congressional Record 6549. Part of this passage was referred to above (see p. 126) in discussing the *Weber* case. Senator Humphrey there went on to say that the opponent's claim is not only false, but that the very opposite of it is true since, under the Civil Rights Act, "race, religion, and national origin are not to be used as the basis for hiring and firing." The sentence Senator Humphrey refers to as being in Section 707(e) was enacted, without relevant change, in Section 706(g).

13. 110 *Congressional Record* 6566.

14. Ibid.

15. Ibid., p. 7214. The same memorandum is referred to in the discussion of the *Weber* decision above. See pages 127 and 129.

16. 467 U.S. 579.

17. Ibid., p. 588 (emphasis added).

18. 476 U.S. 267 (1986). A detailed account of the issues and arguments arising in this case is given above in part D, pages 140-67.

19. 476 U.S. 274.

20. "No state shall ... deny to any person within its jurisdiction the equal protection of the laws."

21. The 'role model' defense of racial preference is discussed more fully above, on pp. 154-56.

22. Ibid., p. 276.

23. Ibid.

24. Ibid.

25. 476 U.S. 294. This failing of the school board's preferential policy is discussed more fully above on pages 154-56.

26. 476 U.S. 283.

27. These complexities are discussed more fully above, pages 162-64.

28. 993 F. 2d 1072.

29. Ibid., p. 1076.

30. Ibid., p. 1079.

31. Ibid.

32. 488 U.S. 469.

33. 822 F. 2d 1357.

34. Ibid., p. 1358. The phrase cited by the Court is from *Wygant;* the emphasis is in the original.

35. Ibid., p. 1359.

36. Ibid., p. 1360.

37. 448 U.S. 448.

38. 123 *Congressional Record* 5330 (1977).

39. 448 U.S. 463.

40. Ibid., p. 483.

41. Ibid., p. 498.

42. Ibid., p. 527.

43. 488 U.S. 490-91.

44. Ibid., pp. 512-15.

45. Ibid., p. 501. The Court is here citing *Mayor of Philadelphia v. Educational Equality League*, 415 U.S. 605, 620 (1974).

46. Ibid., p. 499.

47. Ibid.

48. Ibid., p. 507.

49. Ibid., p. 508.

50. Ibid., p. 516.

51. Ibid., p. 516-17.

52. Ibid., p. 493. This passage so often cited is from *Shelly v. Kraemer*, 334 U.S. 1, 22 (1948) (emphasis added).

53. Ibid., p. 510.

54. "Compilation and Overview of Federal Laws and Regulations Establishing Affirmative Action Goals or Other Preferences Based on Race, Gender, or Ethnicity," Congressional Research Service, The Library of Congress, Washington, 17 February 1995.

55. F.C.C. 2d 381, 411-12 (1978).

56. F.C.C. 2d 983 (1978). Other racial preferences are given by the FCC as well. Small businesses owned by ethnic minorities or women are given a twenty-five percent discount in the purchase of many wireless licences and a stretched-out period for payment. This preference was (in 1995) temporarily blocked by a federal appeals court in Washington. In addition, when television or cable television systems are sold to minority owned companies, the sellers receive a very substantial tax benefit which gives minority owners a great advantage in bidding. This preference is under legislative scrutiny.

57. 497 U.S. 552.

58. Ibid., p. 559 (emphasis added).

59. *Shurberg Broadcasting v. FCC*, 278 U.S. App. D.C. 24.

60. 497 U.S. 600.

61. Ibid., p. 565.

62. Ibid., p. 566.

63. 438 U.S. 312.

64. The racial preferences given by a federal agency are again at issue in a case quite similar to *Metro Broadcasting*, accepted for argument by the Supreme Court at the opening of its fall term of 1994. A brief account of this case, *Adarand Constructors v. Pena* (No.93-1841), is given below on p. 233.

65. 497 U.S. 602. The passage is a citation from an earlier case, *Arizona Governing Committee v. Norris*, 463 U.S. 1073, 1083 (1983).

66. 497 U.S. 604.

67. 488 U.S. 488.

68. Whether the phrase "this article" in Section 5 (referring to the Fourteenth Amendment itself) does authorize preferential policies is doubtful; but the point here is that Section 5 of the Fourteenth Amendment gives authority only to Congress and has no application whatever to minority-ownership preferences given by the FCC.

69. 497 U.S. 610.

70. 488 U.S. 493.

71. 448 U.S. 537.

72. 497 U.S. 612.

73. 476 U.S. 276.

74. 497 U.S. 612.

75. Ibid., p. 613. Justice O'Connor, dissenting here in *Metro Broadcasting*, is citing the majority opinion in *City of Richmond*, at 488 U.S. 493.

76. 497 U.S. 564.

77. 163 U.S. 537.

78. Ibid., p. 550.

79. 497 U.S. 632.

80. Ibid.

81. *South Africa and the Rule of Law*, International Commission of Jurists, Geneva (1960), p. 37.

82. Chief Justice Burger in *Fullilove v. Klutznick*, 448 U.S. 486-87 (emphasis added).

83. 497 U.S. 614.

84. *Maryland Troopers v. Evans*, 993 F.2d 1072. See above, pp. 183-84.

85. 497 U.S. 614. Justice O'Connor is here citing *City of Richmond*, 488 U.S. 507.

86. *DeFunis v. Odegaard*, 416 U.S. 312, 333. See above, p. 29.

87. 497 U.S. 615.

88. Ibid.

89. 497 U.S. 610.

90. Brief for the FCC, in *Metro Broadcasting*, at p. 17.

91. *Steele v. FCC*, 248 U.S. App. D.C. 279, 285 (1985).

92. 497 U.S. 469.

93. *Weinberger v. Wiesenfeld,* 420 U.S. 645.

94. *Los Angeles Department of Water & Power v. Manhart*, 435 U.S. 702, 708 (1978).

95. 497 U.S. 620.

96. 448 U.S. 547.

97. *Steelworkers v. Weber*, 443 U.S. 208. See also above, p. 139.

98. *Plessy v. Ferguson*, 163 U.S. 560.

99. *The Morality of Consent* (New Haven: Yale University Press, 1975), p. 133.

100. 497 U.S. 638.

101. Ibid., p. 637.

102. 448 U.S. 532.

103. *Craig v. Boren* 429 U.S. 190, 198.

104. 497 U.S. 621.

105. *Steelworkers v. Weber*, 443 U.S. 193 (1979). A full discussion of this case is given above in part C.

106. *Wygant v. Jackson Board of Education*, 476 U.S. 267 (1986). A full discussion of this case is given above in part D.

107. *Maryland Troopers v. Evans*, 993 F. 2d 1072 (1993). See above, pp. 181-84.

108. *Adarand Constructors v. Pena*, U.S. Ct. of Appeals, 10th Cir., 16 Feb. 1994. See p. 233, below.

109. An account of the racial preference given by the Texas Law School, and held unconstitutional by the Federal District Court in Austin, may be found in *Hopwood et al. v. Texas*, No. A 92 CA 563 SS, a decision handed down in August of 1994.

110. 488 U.S. 524.

111. 448 U.S. 531.

112. 488 U.S. 520.

113. Ibid., pp. 520-21, citing A. Bickel, *The Morality of Consent* (1975), p. 133.

114. In a case accepted for argument during the fall term of 1994: *Adarand Constructors v. Pena*. See below, p. 233.

115. 488 U.S. 522, citing *Ex Parte Virginia*, 100 U.S. 339, 345 (1880).

116. *Green v. New Kent County School Board*, 391 U.S. 430, 439 (1968).

117. 488 U.S. 524, citing *Columbus Board of Education v. Penick*, 443 U.S. 449 (1979), and other cases.

118. 416 U.S. 312, 337 (1974).

119. 488 U.S. 527-28 (1989).

Epilogue

The Future of Affirmative Action

Racial preference — "affirmative action" as most people now use that term — occupies a place in American society that is at once precarious and protected. Most citizens, black and white, disapprove of it; many, black and white, detest it. But the few who are in a position to impose and enforce preferential policies — administrators in the academic and business worlds, state and federal bureaucrats — must deal with political pressures that make it very costly to oppose racial preference or to criticize it, and with legal pressures that make it risky even to admit that it exists. At the same time the personal circumstances of these persons are such that their jobs or well-being are rarely threatened by racial preference given to others; they do not empathize with the Bakkes, Webers, and Wygants of the world. Widespread contempt for affirmative action does not translate into political support for its opponents sufficient to encourage forthright opposition. The vigorous critic is likely to be accused of racism, or at least of racial insensitivity. Of course the fact that one condemns racial favoritism is no sign of insensitivity to racial injustice, past or present. And charges of "racism" are often irresponsible and sometimes malicious. But *some* of the most outspoken critics of affirmative action *are* racists — and that is a company in which legislators and academic or business leaders can hardly bear to be found. The damage done by such accusations is almost impossible to undo.

In this arena, therefore, it is prudent for public figures to keep a low profile. Elected officials find it wise to express publicly their genuine concern for racial justice, while quietly going along with whatever affirmative action plans seem likely to yield the numbers (of minority employees or matriculants) that satisfy vocal demands for racial proportionality. Even Presidents Reagan and Bush, who plainly abhorred racial preference, did not use their great power to eliminate racial preference in spheres over which they had full authority. Hence the paradox: very few approve of racial preference, yet almost no one (who can be effective) is in a position to call it by its proper name and stand sharply against it.

How change all this? How can we rid ourselves of this corruption of which few are unaware, but that fewer still are prepared to condemn? Legislative reform in the near future is not probable, for reasons just given. Individual legislators have little to gain and much to lose by advocating laws that will effectively ban, and punish, racially preferential practices. Besides, federal legislation that forbids any racial preference — in employment, or in any program for which federal financial assistance is given — is *already* on the books. That prohibition is formulated plainly in the Civil Rights Act of 1964. If the unambiguous words in a law *forbidding* racial preference are converted by a court, as in the *Weber* case discussed at length above, into *permission* for such preference, what is to be accomplished by repeating those plain words?

The outspoken rejection of preference by black and Hispanic citizens could fuel legislative reform, and indeed some eminent black scholars have expressed vigorous opposition to the racial favoritism that, in their view, seriously undermines all minority members.[1] But most influential leaders of minority communities are not in a position to criticize affirmative action because of the numbers among their constituents who are professionally engaged in its management. Affirmative action has become a minor industry, and heavy investment in that industry makes effective opposition to it from within minority communities unlikely soon.

Eventually it will come. The harms that have been done to blacks, and other ethnic groups, *by* preference — stereotypes of inferiority given ugly new life — grow more evident, more widely understood. Programs that increase the numbers of minorities in some professions or employments by applying lower standards preferentially do great damage to those minorities in the long run, damage that becomes ever more apparent. All blacks, not just those given special favor, are injured when everyone (black and white) comes to believe that blacks just don't have it, can't make it on their own. An outstanding minority candidate for a demanding position is now commonly viewed not as the best person for the role, but, cruelly, as "the best black." The nasty myths will die only when the racial preferences that reinforce them have been eliminated.

Racial hostilities in the United States are exacerbated, not appeased or mitigated by giving favor. Majorities become resentful while minorities are demeaned. A different way — an old way, really — must be pursued. The coming turn away from preferential affirmative action will signal not insensitivity to historic oppression but the realization that long-term remedy cannot be achieved by shortcuts; there are no shortcuts. Affirmative action in preferential form postpones the day when all persons, of whatever race, may be judged as persons, on the content of their character. Thoughtful blacks and other minorities may long for that day, but their longing is not likely to be fully satisfied until their own opposition to racial preference is made manifest.

The tide does appear to be turning. As resentment of unfairness and stigmatization by both whites and blacks rises, the political cost of public opposition to preference falls. Affirmative action has been moving to the center of the political stage, even becoming a significant issue in presidential campaigns. Some candidates for the presidency have promised that, if elected, they would eliminate all federal racial preferences by executive order. Some congressional leaders have announced that legislation would soon be introduced that would bar the federal government from granting preferential treatment to favored groups. Reform through legislative or administrative action may be in the offing.

In the shorter term, is reform possible through judicial action? Yes, and that is more likely too. Members of the Supreme Court may be largely insulated from the influence of public opinion by their lifetime tenure, but their own antipathy toward racial preference is likely to be reinforced, emboldened, by the awareness of growing public repugnance for affirmative action, and the conviction that its favoritism is indeed corrupting. The distortions earlier imposed by *Weber* are likely to rankle those dissenting justices still on the Court, who (joined by some others) may be awaiting the opportunity to reverse that unhappy decision. Another collision of some widely practiced preferential device with the Constitution and the law is probably not long off. There is a need, moreover, to clarify and stabilize governing principles in civil rights law. The chain of cases beginning with *DeFunis* in 1974, and extending through *Bakke* (1978), *Firefighters* (1983), *Wygant* (1986), and *City of Richmond* (1988) have imposed sharp limits upon those who would award preference by race. But there remain the aberrant cases — *Weber,* approving "voluntary" racial preferences in industry, and *Metro Broadcasting,* approving racial preference given by a federal agency. The inconsistencies between these two lines of cases cry out for resolution.

In most of its forms, racial preference has been condemned by the Supreme Court and other federal courts. *Strict scrutiny* is the agreed upon standard to be applied. That is, a preference by race is tolerable only where it can be shown to serve a *compelling* governmental interest, and even then the preference must be shown *necessary* to achieve that end, and must be *narrowly tailored* to do so. There must be no other way in which that interest may be effectively served, and no other way in which it may be served with a lesser reliance upon race. This is a very high standard, designed deliberately to exclude all racial favoritism except that required to remedy racial wrongs.

Although these principles are well established, some troubling uncertainties remain. When is a racial program that does serve a compelling governmental interest "tailored narrowly" enough to pass muster? Do schools and businesses have the authority to institute "voluntary" programs of racial preference to pursue objectives they find compelling? And when an unambiguous prohibition laid down in a Supreme Court decision (e.g., *Bakke*) or in a law (e.g., the Civil Rights Act of 1964) is evaded by redescribing the program and continuing to give the racial preference earlier forbidden, what response is in order?

If the readers of this book find the contempt of courts and of the law exhibited in such continuing preference infuriating, how must the justices of the Supreme Court find it? We should not be surprised if that Court soon marks with very forceful words the narrow boundaries within which alone racial preference may be given, and identifies very specifically those alone in whom the authority to give such preference resides.

At the opening of its fall term in 1994 the first case accepted for argument by the Supreme Court was one in which, once again, the racial preferences of a federal agency were at issue: *Adarand Constructors v. Pena* (No. 93-1841). The essential facts of the case are these: Under the "minority subcontracting program" of the Small Business Administration, highway contractors who select "disadvantaged business enterprises" as their subcontractors receive substantial cash bonuses. The federal Small Business Act authorizes the presumption, absent contrary evidence, that any business owned and operated by blacks, Hispanics, Native Americans, or Asian Pacific Americans is a disadvantaged enterprise for the purpose of bonus awards. By this presumption all majority subcontractors are substantially handicapped, since all minority subcontractors enjoy a very substantial bidding advantage. Adarand Constructors, a white subcontractor who had submitted the lowest bid on a federal highway project in Colorado, lost out to a competing "disadvantaged" subcontractor, admittedly selected because of the $10,000 bonus given to the prime contractor under that preferential policy. Adarand sued, contending that the policy authorizing such bonuses for outright racial favoritism, although embedded in federal legislation, violates the constitutional guarantee of equal protection.

The similarity of this case to that of *Metro Broadcasting*, discussed in Chapter 11 above, is noteworthy. All those who had dissented in that case (but none of those in the deciding plurality) remain on the Court. The position of the dissent in that case (see pp. 200-9) may soon appear as a new Supreme Court majority in *Adarand Constructors* — one more head of the Hydra being thus cut off.

Preferential affirmative action is nearly out of control. Injustices are common, patience grows thin. Ugly anecdotes are commonly and ever more openly recounted. Ethnic resentments are on the rise, partly because some are advantaged on account of their race at the expense of others disadvantaged on account of theirs. To determine who gets and who gives under the preferential rules of affirmative action, governments must establish boards to determine who is truly black, who is Hispanic, and who may rightly claim the benefits reserved for Native Americans. Racial divisions are formally drawn, informally solidified. Public argument is pervaded by racial claims and accusations. Ethnic hostilities, aggravated by ethnic favoritism, become palpable.

Affirmative action, originally designed to counteract the evils of racism and to help eliminate the effects of racial preference, has been turned on its head. The guarantees of our Constitution are widely flouted. Racism thrives; racially preferential programs in universities and industry undermine decent human relations and fly in the face of the law. Nothing — not even the most honorable motives — can justify the damage done by racial preference, or make it right to deprive individual citizens of the equal protection of the laws.

NOTES

1. Most notable among these are Thomas Sowell [Preferential Policies: An International Perspective (New York: Morrow, 1990)] and Shelby Steele [The Content of Our Character (New York: St. Martin's Press, 1990)]. The assumption of inferiority resulting from racial preference has been the target of other pained black scholars as well, among them: Stephen L. Carter [Reflections of an Affirmative Action Baby (New York: Basic Books, 1991)] and Clarence Thomas, recently elevated to the Supreme Court.

Postscript

As this book was being readied for the printer the Supreme Court opinion in the case of *Adarand Constructors, Inc. v. Pena, Secretary of Transportation,* was handed down— and with it another of the heads of the Hydra was cut off.[1]

In that case, noted briefly in Chapter 11 and in the Epilogue as pending, the issue was racial preference as given by the *federal* government. Most federal agency contracts contain a clause that gives prime contractors financial incentives to hire subcontractors controlled by socially and economically disadvantaged individuals and that requires the presumption that "Black Americans, Hispanic Americans, Native Americans, Asian Pacific Americans, and other minorities" are disadvantaged. Adarand Constructors is a subcontractor whose low bid on a highway project for the Department of Transportation was rejected by the prime contractor in favor of a minority subcontractor because doing so yielded a cash bonus of $10,000 from the Department of Transportation to the prime contractor. Adarand Constructors sued, contending that such financial incentives to hire subcontractors by race had done them substantial injury, would probably do so again, and had deprived them of the equal treatment they are entitled to under the Constitution. The preference was undoubted; its author was an arm of the government of the United States.

Although naked preference for racial minorities had been rejected and condemned in earlier cases — in *Wygant*, and in *City of Richmond*, as we have seen— there had remained prior to June 1995 an unresolved tension between the principles clearly expressed in these cases and rulings in a small set of exceptional cases in which preference by an arm of the federal government had been found permissible. The Fourteenth Amendment to the Constitution clearly governs the several states; Virginia and its cities may not discriminate by race, nor may Michigan and its schools, and so on. The standard of *strict scrutiny*, the most rigid scrutiny of racial classifications, certainly applies to them. But the Fourteenth Amendment does not address the federal government. The due process clause of the Fifth Amendment does govern the United States, however, obliging the federal government not to deny anyone the equal protection of the laws. This much has long been clear.

The question nevertheless outstanding was this: Is the equality guaranteed by the Fifth Amendment the *same* as the equality guaranteed by the Fourteenth? Is the federal government, in its use of race-based measures, subject to the same standard, applied with the same rigor, as the states?

The answer, at long last given unambiguously in *Adarand Constructors v. Pena*, is yes. Strict scrutiny — the standard discussed at length in Chapter 8, requiring the highest level of justification — is the standard that does apply henceforth to *all* racial classifications, whether employed by state, or local, or federal actors. Justice O'Connor wrote for the Court, "[A]ny person, of whatever race, has the right to demand that any governmental actor, subject to the Constitution, justify any racial classification subjecting that person to unequal treatment under the strictest judicial scrutiny."[2]

What then of the decision in *Metro Broadcasting v. FCC*, discussed in Chapter 11 above? That case, by applying to federal agencies the standard of "intermediate scrutiny," a standard lower than that applied to the states, had permitted the continuation of preferences for racial minorities in the competition for broadcast licenses awarded by the Federal Communications Commission (FCC). *Metro Broadcasting* had held that "benign" federal racial classifications are permissible to the extent that they serve "important" governmental objectives and are "substantially" related to the achievement of those objectives. Such reasoning had now to be either accepted as precedent or overturned. But *Metro Broadcasting*, Justice O'Connor points out, rejected the proposition that *the standards applicable to federal and state racial classifications must be congruent*. And this proposition must be true because it follows from the fact that both the Fifth and the Fourteenth Amendments protect *persons*, not *groups*. So *Metro Broadcasting* must fall. She concludes,

> [W]e hold today that all racial classifications, imposed by whatever federal, state, or local governmental actor, must be analyzed by a reviewing court under strict scrutiny. In other words, such classifications are constitutional only if they are narrowly tailored measures that further compelling governmental interests. To the extent that *Metro Broadcasting* is inconsistent with that holding, it is overruled.[3]

The earlier case, *Fullilove v. Klutznick*, upon which *Metro Broadcasting* had been grounded, while not expressly overturned in the same words, is also reversed by *Adarand Constructors* to the extent that *Fullilove* was taken to authorize a lower standard for the federal government than for the states.

The preferences given by the Department of Transportation, and by the FCC, and by a myriad of other agencies of our federal and state governments, are commonly designed to achieve racial proportionality or balance or diversity. This aim of distributing benefits by race or group cannot normally satisfy the standard of strict scrutiny, because the standard requires that the interest served by the racial classification be *compelling*, and a "compelling interest" has been taken in most recent civil rights cases to require proof that the racial classification is essential to remedy earlier identifiable racial discrimination by that governmental unit. Even where that can be established, the race-based measure proposed must be shown to have been devised to address that earlier discrimination precisely, which numerical targets rarely if ever can do. The measures under review must be *narrowly tailored* to give a remedy that is justified by that earlier wrong but imposes no additional racial burdens upon innocent persons. Are there circumstances in which this very high standard can be satisfied, cases in which preference is called for and need not be naked? Yes, there are, but they are rare. The deliberate uses of race by governments ought to be rare.

Dissenting members of the Court presented two main arguments in defense of the racial favoritism given by the Department of Transportation. The first was that the majority had failed to apply the established precedents of *Metro Broadcasting* and *Fullilove*. This complaint is not very persuasive, however, since there are precedents on both sides, of course. There is nothing new in the view that Congress, like the states, must have compelling reasons to justify treating people differently because of their race. By making an "untenable distinction" between the constitutional duties of the states and the federal government, by accepting different standards for different levels of government, *Metro Broadcasting* and *Fullilove* made bad law. In *Adarand Constructors* the Supreme Court made it clear that these cases are not to be regarded as precedents henceforth.

A second, more substantive argument in defense of the preferential affirmative action program here struck down alleges that the majority opinion is morally insensitive. There is a critical *moral* difference (Justices Stevens and Ginsburg point out) between the traditional, oppressive uses of racial classifications and constructive, remedial uses of them. Stevens writes: "There is no moral or constitutional equivalence between a policy that is designed to perpetuate a caste system and one that seeks to eradicate racial subordination."[4] But, he continues, the consistency that the Court insists upon in this case mistakenly treats both alike. It would "disregard the difference between a No Trespassing sign and a welcome mat."[5] The majority, he thinks, mistakenly supposes that we are generally unable to distinguish between "invidious" and "benign" discrimination, to which very different responses are in order.

This criticism seriously misconceives the force of the decision in *Adarand Constructors*. The decision certainly does *not* fail to recognize that motivations for racial discrimination differ, that some are far more ugly than others, and that the circumstances under which race-based measures are proposed must be carefully considered in appraising them. The very point of insisting upon strict scrutiny is that there must be some general standard with which we can reliably make these appraisals, distinguishing carefully the acceptable from the unacceptable uses of race. The Court, like the rest of us, can very well distinguish between federal affirmative action officers and members of the Ku Klux Klan. But discriminating among citizens by race is so perilous, commonly so unfair and so damaging, that there must be no exception to the highest standard of judgment, no exception that may permit the use of racial measures on the ground that the motives of the actors were wholesome.

Good intentions are not all that count; we must ask what the consequences of the preferential program are, upon those disfavored and also upon those given the preference. Years before, dissenting in *Fullilove*, it was Justice Stevens himself who wrote:

> A statute of this kind [the racial set-aside approved in *Fullilove*] inevitably is perceived by many as resting on an assumption that those who are granted this special preference are less qualified in some respect that is identified purely by their race. Because that perception — especially when fostered by the Congress of the United States — can only exacerbate rather than reduce racial prejudice, it will delay the time when race will become a truly irrelevant, or at least insignificant factor.[6]

Justice Stevens was right then, in 1979; every case in which racial classifications are introduced presents the challenge to set forth the compelling need for racial measures — precisely in order to evaluate differing circumstances, consequences, and motivations. Moreover the precise *tailoring* of the remedy to the wrong is critically important when race is at issue. Justice Stevens later criticized a racial set-aside (like that rejected in *City of Richmond*) because such a law "stigmatizes the disadvantaged class with the unproven charge of past racial discrimination, [while] it actually imposes a greater stigma on its supposed beneficiaries." And just for that reason, he continued, "Racial classifications are simply too pernicious to permit any but the most exact connection between justification and classification."[7] Just so. And to achieve these objectives a reliable and rigorous standard, universally understood and consistently applied, is essential.

Justice Thomas, in a separate concurring opinion in *Adarand*, expressed his strong objections to the "racial paternalism" of preferential affirmative action. Incensed by what he takes to be the patronizing spirit of the dissent, he responds, in effect, "No, thank you; not for blacks or for anyone else may exceptions to equal protection be made." Thomas reaffirms the moral and constitutional demand for *uniform* standards in judging racial discrimination:

> That these programs may have been motivated, in part, by good intentions cannot provide refuge from the principle that under our Constitution, the government may not make distinctions on the basis of race. As far as the Constitution is concerned, it is irrelevant whether a government's racial classifications are drawn by those who wish to oppress a race or by those who have a sincere desire to help those thought to be disadvantaged. There can be no doubt that the paternalism that appears to lie at the heart of this program is at war with the principle of inherent equality that underlies and infuses our Constitution.... [R]acial paternalism can be as poisonous and pernicious as any other form of discrimination. So-called "benign" discrimination teaches many that because of chronic and apparently immutable handicaps, minorities cannot compete with them without their patronizing indulgence. Inevitably such programs engender attitudes of superiority or, alternatively, provoke resentment among those who believe that they have been wronged by the government's use of race. These programs stamp minorities with a badge of inferiority....
>
> [G]overnment-sponsored racial discrimination based on benign prejudice is just as noxious as discrimination inspired by malicious prejudice. In each instance, it is racial discrimination, plain and simple.[8]

The concurring opinion of Justice Scalia presents the sharpest and most comprehensive of all the attacks upon racially preferential programs. Individuals who have been wronged by unlawful racial discrimination should be made whole, he agrees of course. But there can be no entitlements *by race*, for any purpose. And therefore our government can never have a "compelling interest" in discriminating on the basis of race to "make up" for past racial oppression. In his view, all devices that seek to give payment by race are inconsistent with the focus of the Constitution upon individuals, not groups; he cites again the Fourteenth Amendment guarantee of equal protection *to any person*. "Under our Constitution," Scalia writes, "there can be no such thing as a creditor or a debtor race."[9] Therefore, he concludes, every pursuit of racial entitlement, even for the most admirable and benign of purposes, must "reinforce and preserve for future mischief the way of thinking that produced race slavery, race privilege and race hatred. In the eyes of government, we are just one race here. It is American."[10]

The days of naked racial preference are numbered, and by *Adarand* their number is lowered. But many heads of the Hydra remain to be cut off — by state and local governments, by our Congress, by the president, and by institutions public and private in which racially discriminatory practices have been designed to advance some special vision of how society should be organized.

Nothing stands in the way of affirmative action as it was originally conceived. No reasonable person will complain about programs devised to ensure genuinely equal opportunity for all, whatever their race or color or sex or nationality. Such programs were and are entirely lawful, fully within the letter and spirit of our Constitution, and morally right. Racially discriminatory practices ought to be unmasked and eradicated. Remedy must be given to those who have been damaged by unlawful racism. In a just society, no favor — none — may be given to anyone simply on the basis of race.

Good motives do not now make such favor right. The lesson of the last quarter of the twentieth century is clear beyond all doubting. Racism of every kind must be transcended, put forever behind us. We must uproot the habits of designing, acting, thinking in racial terms, for racial groups, on racial principles. A healthy democracy, a reasonably harmonious society, an America at peace with itself cannot tolerate naked racial preference.

NOTES

1. On 12 June 1995. The majority opinion of the Court in *Adarand* was written by Justice O'Connor, joined by Justices Kennedy, Thomas, Chief Justice Rehnquist, and by Justice Scalia in all but one respect. Dissenting opinions were submitted by Justices Stevens and Souter, and by Justice Ginsburg joined by Justice Breyer. Eventual pagination in *U.S. Reports* has not yet been determined, so references to this decision are made here by identifying the author of the opinion cited and the page number within the opinion of that justice.

2. *Adarand Constructors v. Pena*, Justice O'Connor for the Court, p. 22.

3. Ibid., pp. 25-26.

4. Ibid., Opinion of Justice Stevens, p. 2.

5. Ibid., p. 4.

6. *Fullilove v. Klutznick*, 448 U.S. 545 (1979).

7. *City of Richmond v. Croson*, 488 U.S. 516-17 (1989).

8. *Adarand Constructors v. Pena*, Opinion of Justice Thomas, pp. 2-3.

9. Ibid., Opinion of Justice Scalia, p. 1.

10. Ibid., pp. 1-2.

About the Author

Carl Cohen is professor of philosophy at the University of Michigan where he has taught ethics, logic, and political philosophy since 1955. He has served as chairman of the faculty senate at the University of Michigan, as chairman of the American Civil Liberties Union of Michigan, and for several years as a member of the national board of directors of the ACLU. He has been a visiting professor at universities in New Zeland, Peru, Hong Kong, Singapore, and Israel, and has been a consultant to the National Endowment for the Humanities, the National Institutes of Health, and the Committee on the Judiciary of the U.S. Senate. He is also a labor/management arbitrator for the American Arbitration Association.

Professor Cohen is the author of *Civil Disobedience* (Columbia University Press, 1971), *Democracy* (The Free Press, 1972), *Four Systems* (Random House, 1982), and with Irving M. Copi is coauthor of *Introduction to Logic, 9th ed.* (Macmillan/Prentice Hall, 1994). With his wife, Jan, and their two young children, Jaclyn and Noah, he lives in Ann Arbor, Michigan.